Your First Year As an Elementary School Teacher

Your First Year As an

Elementary School Teacher

Making the Transition from Total Novice to Successful Professional

LYNNE ROMINGER
KAREN HEISINGER
NATALIE ELKIN

THREE RIVERS PRESS
NEW YORK

Published by Three Rivers Press, New York, New York.
Member of the Crown Publishing Group, a division of Random House, Inc.
www.crownpublishing.com

THREE RIVERS PRESS and the Tugboat design are registered trademarks of Random House, Inc.

Originally published by Prima Publishing, Roseville, California, in 2001.

Illustrations by Tom McLelland

Printed in the United States of America

Library of Congress Cataloging-in-Publication Data
Rominger, Lynne.
 Your first year as an elementary school teacher : making the transition from total novice to successful professional / Lynne Marie Rominger, Karen Heisinger, Natalie Elkin.
  p. cm.—(Your first year series)
 Includes index.
 1. Elementary school teaching—United States. 2. First year teachers—United States. 3. Teacher orientation—United States. I. Heisinger, Karen. II. Elkin, Natalie. III. Title. IV. Series.
LB1555.R65   2001
372.11—dc21   00-065219
ISBN 0-7615-2968-3

10 9 8 7 6 5 4

First Edition

Contents

Acknowledgments —————————————————————————

Lynne's Acknowledgments

THANKS GO out to so many people. First, I'd like to thank my coauthors Karen Heisinger, who took this book "ball" and ran with it, and Natalie Elkin, my mentor, my friend, and just a cool chick who is a whole lot of fun to hang out with! Next, I'd like to thank everyone at Prima, especially Shawn Vreeland. Many teachers and administrators deserve thanks as well for nurturing me and helping me succeed in teaching; they include Patrick Godwin, Ron Severson, John Montgomery, Scott O'Connor, Jess Borjon, Kathleen Sirovy, Mike McGuire, Ramona Slack, Suzanne Laughrea, and so many others. Indeed, thanks go out to every teacher at Granite Bay and many at Roseville, too. Of course, I must thank my students. I love you all; everyday you bring joy to my life. I can't imagine another career. I know I tell you guys and girls this all the time, but I really do mean it when I say, "I never have a hard time waking up and going to work." I am blessed with the best job on the planet because of you all. Finally, a special thank you goes out to my parents, who watched my children whenever I spent long hours at the computer writing.

And—as always—thanks to my God for giving me the strength, the talent, and the perseverance to accomplish everything that I do.

Karen's Acknowledgments

I WOULD like to acknowledge all of the teachers I have worked with throughout my years of teaching—from my master teacher at Capri Elementary in Campbell to the teachers in San Jose Unified School District, Center Unified School District, and my beginning teachers, support providers, and administrators in Placer and Nevada County. Thank you for your insights as well as the validation you have given me.

I would also like to acknowledge my first teachers—the McLaughlin family (a.k.a. the "Irish Mafia" of education!). From my mother and father to my six brothers, two sisters, and twenty nephews and nieces, I have learned so much. I thank you personally *and* professionally!

My father-in-law, Dr. Brent Heisinger, also deserves a special acknowledgment. Thank you for listening to me, encouraging me, and checking up on my progress. You and mom have helped me in so many ways—thank you, thank you, and thank you!

Finally, I would like to acknowledge my number one fans—my husband, Doug, and my children, Melanie and Kevin. Thank you for putting up with my obsession with the teaching profession and for encouraging me to pursue this endeavor. I could not do this without your love and support, and I thank you with **all** of my heart.

Natalie's Acknowledgments

I WANT to first thank Lynne Rominger for giving me the opportunity to write. We have learned so much together, have helped each other, and had loads of fun together. Thank you Karen for putting so much of your time and energy into this book; it really shows. I would also like to thank our editor at Prima, Jamie Miller, and editorial assistant, DeAnne, and finally the publisher, Ben Dominitz. Shawn Vreeland, and LauraMaery Gold thank you for your patience and effort.

Thank you Mom and Dad for providing me the foundation from which I developed my writing and teaching skills. Your guidance, love, and encouragement have helped me achieve my successes and will continue to help me realize all my possibilities. David, thank you for your love.

Introduction

THE EXTRA large "Teacher" valentines; the cupcake made just for you on *their* birthday; the homemade necklaces for Christmas; the grabbing of the hand while walking in line; the hugs after a long vacation; the look on their face that says "I couldn't wait to get to school to tell you . . ."; the expectant look after you've posed an interesting question; the eyes that say "You matter to me; you're my teacher"; the "I love you" notes drawn when they should have been doing math; the look of success you see when they've mastered a difficult concept—these and a thousand other images filter through our thoughts as we recall our experiences as elementary classroom teachers.

You too will receive many blessings from your students over the years as a result of your dedication to your new profession. Your services as a teacher are desperately needed; every child needs and deserves a teacher who truly cares about them and is willing to help them grow. The compassion and caring you provide can make such a profound difference in the life of a child. And although you may not feel the direct effects on a day-to-day basis, you will feel the effects over time. It seems paradoxical that such an important person in the life of a child enters this profession with little exposure to the realities and demands of the classroom. Even though induction efforts are improving, we still have not completely figured out a way to assist teachers in entering the profession in a gradual, successful way.

This is why we wrote this book! We care very deeply about the teaching profession and about teachers themselves. It's hard to know which "fight" to pick in ensuring the success of the profession, and between all three authors, we've spent several careers up to this point trying to figure out how to make a difference in the working lives of teachers.

As coauthor Karen Heisinger recalls, "I was approached by one of the new teachers in the BTSA (Beginning Teacher Support and Assessment) project last year to write this book. This new teacher's name, of course, was Lynne Rominger. I knew I had this book inside of me, but I didn't know how to go about writing it. Lynne guided me through the process, and once I got started, the words just flowed."

This book, then, represents Karen's years of teaching (too many schools and grade levels to count!), her administrative experience, as well as her work and research relative to new teachers. It is her voice and personal experience that permeate this book, and it is meant to help you and assist you in your early years of teaching.

The book also encompasses the "in the trenches" experience of being a brand new teacher (Lynne's experience) and a relatively new teacher making it over the hurdles (Natalie's contribution). Throughout the book, we strove to not write like a thesis. Instead, we wanted a book that simulated more of a conversation with you, the new teacher, offering you suggestions and perhaps giving you some food for thought. Lynne, in particular, remembers calling Karen several times her first year with problems and concerns and appreciating the warmth and compassion with which Karen approached the situations. "She talked to me like a friend—she didn't lecture," recalls the coauthor. We hope that this book provides you with the same tone. Essentially, it is a compilation of what worked for Karen in the elementary classroom and her sound advice and nurturing that she gives to her BTSA teachers (K–12) all year.

In addition, you'll discover in these pages tons of informational text boxes. Our boxes are divided into several categories:

Teaching Terms: These boxes offer definitions of words used in the text. They serve as a rough introduction to the jargon of teaching.

Tales from the Trenches: These are anecdotes from teachers. Hey, we're all in this together. You think you had a horrible day? Check out these stories!

Making the Grade: Within these boxes, readers will find helpful statistics or excerpts from articles or information on the teaching profession in general. From helpful Web sites for lesson planning questions to the latest reports on teaching, look to these boxes for this type of information.

Teacher's Rules: The "Teacher's Rules" boxes will offer warnings as well as quick tips. Think "reminder" information as opposed to anecdotal.

From the Desk of . . . : These boxes offer anecdotal advice from other teachers and administrators on a variety of subjects related to the chapter in which you find them.

Please feel free to contact us with your own "Tales from the Trenches" and "From the Desk of . . ." advice. We'd love to include your experiences in future revisions of this book. You may write to us at 1324 Greenborough Drive, Roseville, CA 95661 or e-mail us at lynne0867@aol.com or nelkin@hotmail.com or heisinger@pacbell.net.

We all wish you much success and fulfillment in your **career** as a teacher. You have chosen a profession that allows you to give as much as you are willing to for no greater purpose—the children.

Sincerely,

Karen Heisinger, Ed.D.
Lynne Rominger
Natalie Elkin

PART ONE

WELCOME TO THE PROFESSION

Professional Expectations

CONGRATULATIONS! YOU MADE it! You survived an endless array of credential classes and landed your first teaching job.

Welcome to the thrilling and challenging world of teaching. Whether you are beginning your first year of teaching after being part of a credential program or have just been granted an emergency credential, you will soon come to find that your life changes drastically once you step into your own classroom. For some, this is your first career; for others, you've come to teaching after working in other professions. Either way, this is the first time you've been in charge of molding, developing, and empowering the minds of a classroom of young people.

> *" EDUCATION, n. That which discloses to the wise and disguises from the foolish their lack of understanding. "*
>
> AMBROSE BIERCE

The career you have selected is one of the most difficult jobs you'll ever do, but educating children is also the noblest profession, and there aren't many who can handle the workload with dignity and compassion.

Your Local Office of Education Wants You!

Registering Your Credential

So you finally jumped through all the credential hoops, right? Took that class and finished this seminar and took that test. Enough already!

But you may not be finished yet. In many cases, once the state in which you received the credential confers it upon you, you'll also need to register the credential at your local office of education. The local agency wants to make sure that your credential is truly up-to-date and you're "legal" to work at a school site.

Enter the credential analyst or the state certification specialist. You probably came across this person while in college working toward

---

Teaching Terms

◆ ◆ ◆

Credentials. When you obtain your certification, you're a credentialed teacher. The other term you'll hear all the time to describe people like yourself is not the grammatically correct "certified" but, rather, the ponderous and official-sounding "certificated."

your credential. A credential analyst certifies that the courses you took complete your credential, and you can work as a teacher in an elementary classroom.

After you register your credential, it's time to take a battery of health tests, depending on the state in which you are teaching. Again, check with the district and ask, "Are there any health tests that I need to take before I can begin teaching?" Although it's not required in all states, one test many teachers must pass is a tuberculosis test.

Wait, there's more! Fingerprinting. Chances are pretty good that the district office that hired you will send you down to the local law enforcement agency to obtain your fingerprints. In other states, fingerprinting is part of obtaining your certification.

Okay, you probably understand why you need to come in contact with a credential analyst—to make sure you really, really did take all the coursework required for a credential in the state you reside in, right? But why the tuberculosis test and the fingerprinting? TB is a communicable disease and caused quite a scare in the early 1990s when the number of TB cases in the United States suddenly began to rise (See the Centers for Disease Control's Web site at www.cdc.gov/nchstp/tb/surv/surv99/surv99pdf/table1.pdf). Many health boards regulate that a teacher—who comes in contact with hundreds of students—not carry a communicable disease.

As for the fingerprinting? Since teachers again come in contact on a daily basis with our society's most precious and vulnerable asset—kids—schools take great pains to ensure the new teacher upholds ethical standards. Criminal backgrounds are not tolerated.

Teacher's Rule

Just because you think you have met all the requirements certifying you as an instructor in the elementary classroom doesn't mean it's so! Someone in your state's regulating education office will need to verify your credentials. These people are often called credential analysts. Seek 'em out and have one sign you off!

Whoever it is that's responsible for guiding you through the certification process, it is important that these items get taken care of right away. Better to do it before the school year starts while you still have the time and energy! Believe it: Teachers have been pulled from the classroom for days, weeks, or even longer for not registering their credentials or neglecting to take the proper health tests. Moreover, during the time the teacher is out until the situation gets rectified, that teacher receives no pay. No money for missed days because you wore the dunce cap and forgot to take a TB test or register your credential. So register your credential to teach.

The County of What? The Office of Whom?

EXPLORE WHAT your county or state office of education can do to assist you as a new teacher! Offices of Education typically can lend a hand in an effort to help you stay on your career path in the teaching profession. Many offices offer a vast array of resources such as videotapes, book kits, professional libraries, instructional technology materials, and even courses for new teachers.

Just as you push your students to explore all year, you need to explore too!

Join the Club

MOM ALWAYS told you, "If so-and-so jumped off a bridge, would you?" She, of course, wanted you to forge your own way with your

Making the Grade

According to a 1996 study, each year, almost a quarter of new teachers leave the profession in their early years. The report attributes teacher attrition to a lack of support and a "sink or swim" approach to induction. Read more here:

What Matters Most: Teaching and America's Future: *www.ed.gov /comments/nationalforum97*

FROM THE DESK OF . . . Coauthor Karen Heisinger took a course her first year as a new teacher offered through the county Office of Education called "First Years without Tears." "We met one Saturday a month for six months, where we would talk about things that were happening in our classrooms, create lesson plans, and 'make and take' things to enhance our lessons," she recalls. Just like Karen, you, too, may find an invaluable course this year through your local education agency.

own ideals and not succumb to peer pressure. But sometimes joining a group of others such as yourself can make the difference between enjoying your job and muddling through the first year. And wouldn't you know it, the teaching profession offers new instructors such as yourself a tremendous number of professional organizations to join! Just a sampling include the International Association of Supervision and Curriculum Development (ASCD), the International Reading Association (IRA), and the National Council for Teachers of Mathematics (NCTM). For a look at more, flip over to the appendix; you'll probably find a group that suits you. Many of these organizations have local affiliates, publish periodicals and newsletters, and hold annual conferences. These organizations provide wonderful opportunities to keep current on what is happening in education, as well as the chance to network with other teachers in a common area of interest.

Joining Professional Organizations

Keep in mind that although many organizations may sound interesting, you will need to narrow your focus—if for no other reason than that each organization requires members to pay dues. Before joining an organization, ask other teachers on the staff and in your district which organizations they belong to. You may also want to obtain input from your principal into this decision.

Professional organizations give you the opportunity to demonstrate that you're an involved instructor who listens and wants to participate as a team player and who understands the politics of education. For example, if your district is going to convert to a year-round schedule, and it's truly something you want to learn more about, then you may be able to gain some insight into that conversion by becoming a member of the National Association of Year-Round Education and share that insight with administration.

Teacher's Rule

It's no secret—new teachers don't earn a ton of money. So plan carefully and budget during the lean years when you haven't moved over and down the pay scales. And choose wisely when joining professional institutions. Their membership dues will sock it to your pockets, and in no time flat, you'll be flat broke.

Attendance Is Mandatory: Workshops and Seminars

ATTENDING WORKSHOPS and seminars is another opportunity to learn and grow as a professional. Classes at your local office of education tend to be cheaper than you'll find at a private organization's conference.

Likewise, your district may provide workshops taught by teachers in your district; these usually do not cost anything, are very timely and specific in the content being presented, and take into consideration your unique needs as a new teacher. Attend these! In many cases, your district will either pay you for the hours you spend in the class or pay for units toward your continuing education.

In addition, your local university may provide courses to assist you. Take advantage of these as well. Not only will the content be research based; any units you earn may move you over on the pay scale.

There are also national seminars and workshops in which you may want to participate. The topics they offer tend to be interesting, important, and meaningful. So what's the problem, then? The problem centers around three areas: the content of the workshop, time, and money.

> # Teaching Terms
>
> ◆ ◆ ◆
>
> **Year-round scheduling.** Year-round schedules are taking the place of traditional summer-off schedules in districts where space is limited. Year-round schools are generally perceived as more effective in helping students retain information from one term to the next. Students on multitrack year-round schedules attend classes for about twelve weeks and then take a break of about four weeks.

Content of the Workshop

As a teacher, you will be inundated with workshop possibilities. How will you choose which one is appropriate for you? First, check to see whether the presentation is geared toward new teachers. If not, check with other staff members to see whether someone is willing to attend with you, or whether someone has attended this workshop by this presenter in the past. Second, choose a workshop in a specific area of focus, and then limit that focus—take a course supporting your district's balanced literacy program, for example.

Attending workshops and seminars is a professional growth opportunity in which you will want to participate *over the course of your career*; be selective in the first years of your career to strengthen your skills by narrowing your focus and maximizing your time and money. You'll have plenty of time to pursue professional growth seminars and conferences over time. So ease up during the first few years and devote yourself to the classroom.

Teaching Terms

◆ ◆ ◆

Balanced literacy. A teaching approach that attempts to improve literacy by providing a balance of phonics-based instruction and real-world literature.

Time

My goodness! Your days are harried enough, right? You must consider how the time away from the classroom will affect you. Ask yourself several "time" questions before making a decision:

- When are the workshops or seminars being offered?
- Is it during the school day?
- If so, will the district pay for your substitute? Make sure you ask!
- If it is after school, are you going to be able to fit it in to your schedule?
- How far away is it?

And finally, if the seminar occurs on a Saturday, keep in mind that teachers need their weekends to recharge for the upcoming week.

Money

Check the registration costs; they can be quite pricey. Are you paying for the course yourself? If so, the fees may qualify as a tax write-off. Make sure the district has agreed to pay for your substitute if one is required during the school day. Also, some courses will allow you to pay a little extra to receive units for attending. Take advantage of this opportunity! In many cases, when a teacher continues his or her education—called professional growth—units add up to increased pay. Keep track of the units and submit them to your district.

If your resources are limited, you have some options: Look on the flyer to see whether there is a book written by the presenter and order it; or see whether someone else on the staff will attend this particular workshop and swap information with you on the seminar you choose to attend.

Signed, Sealed, Delivered, Updated: Your Credential

EACH STATE issues credentials and asks its teachers to keep updated in the profession differently. This section is meant to make you aware that you will need to keep up your credentials in one way or another and that it is a task best accomplished in the beginning—not something you scramble to achieve in the end when it's almost too late.

When you receive your credential, the issuing agency should also give you some guidelines as to what documentation is required to keep your credential current and updated. If you have earned a Stage I or preliminary credential, then you may need to take courses to move to the next stage or to "clear" your credential.

That credential has to be renewed from time to time. Try to begin the process of renewal at least six months in advance of your credential expiring. You will probably need to fill out a form or two and submit a money order. By starting early, though, and being organized, you will save yourself some heartache in the end.

Teacher's Rule

Consult your district office before you attend courses or workshops for credit, as some school districts require prior approval, or they won't give you credit for the courses you attend. Usually a quick phone call to the secretary for the superintendent in charge of instruction is all it takes!

Keep It Safe: Record Keeping

SINCE PROFESSIONAL growth is such an important aspect of a teaching career, heed the following advice: Keep records of all the courses

> " *When Alexander the Great visited Diogenes and asked whether he could do anything for the famed teacher, Diogenes replied, "Only stand out of my light." Perhaps some day we shall know how to heighten creativity. Until then, one of the best things we can do for creative men and women is to stand out of their light.* "
>
> JOHN W. GARDNER

and workshops you attend, including district-sponsored seminars, in *one place*—preferably a safe deposit box. Make a copy of the flyer and agenda of the course, and request a copy of the sign-in sheet or registration that verifies you were in attendance. If you have taken a course from a university, obtain several copies of the transcripts and keep them, along with the information on how to get additional copies in the future.

I Can Prove I'm a Professional

JUST AS you are keeping records to renew your credential, start a professional portfolio to document your growth and accomplishments. The following is a list of items you'll want to include:

1. A copy of your credential
2. A copy of university transcripts
3. A copy of your resume
4. Professional letters of reference
5. Photos: take pictures of your students, your classroom, bulletin boards, etc.
6. Letters from students and parents
7. Copies of special lesson plans with student work samples
8. Positive evaluations and notes from administration
9. Documentation (flyers, receipts, certificates) from workshops you've attended
10. Copies of Back-to-School Night/Open House invitations

Many items are available to spruce up your portfolio. "Creative scrapbooking" is particularly popular right now. Don't be afraid to highlight your unique personality! Keep throwing these items in a box and compile them over winter vacation, or—better yet—add things as you go along, and you will be amazed at how much you have accumulated by the end of the year. Also, when it comes time for your annual administrative evaluation, your portfolio will be a springboard for a lively discussion. Your principal will be impressed that you have taken the time and initiative to put together such a comprehensive portfolio of your first year. And, you'll have the keepsake.

But I Just Got Out of School

You just finished advanced degree work by completing your credential, but, really, it's never too early to think about graduate work. The teaching profession offers opportunities to advance your knowledge and position in a myriad of ways. As you progress through your first years of teaching, think about what areas strike your fancy. Think about what you enjoy. Here are some examples to get you thinking more:

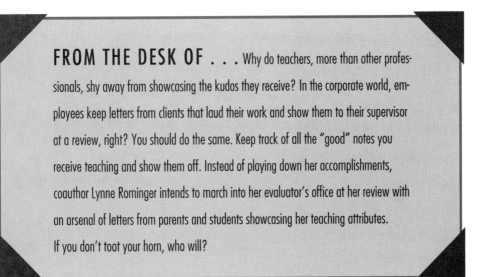

FROM THE DESK OF . . . Why do teachers, more than other professionals, shy away from showcasing the kudos they receive? In the corporate world, employees keep letters from clients that laud their work and show them to their supervisor at a review, right? You should do the same. Keep track of all the "good" notes you receive teaching and show them off. Instead of playing down her accomplishments, coauthor Lynne Rominger intends to march into her evaluator's office at her review with an arsenal of letters from parents and students showcasing her teaching attributes. If you don't toot your horn, who will?

Tales from the Trenches

"I was able to combine my involvement in a professional organization with my graduate work. Since I was involved in the California Association of Year-Round Education, I decided to focus my research on the perceptions of year-round education in California. I then researched year-round education extensively, and surveyed the superintendents on their perceptions relative to student, teacher and parent satisfaction. My research was used to help a local school make the conversion to year-round, and I spoke at two conferences: one in San Diego and one in Maui! See—combine your efforts and you just might go places!"

Coauthor Karen Heisinger, Auburn, California

◆ ◆ ◆

"Our open house was held a few weeks after school had started. Things seemed to be going smoothly until I opened the floor up to questions from the parents. It seemed like every question that came out of their mouths was something I had no control over. For instance, I was asked, 'Why are the A's in their books written fancy when they have been taught all their lives to write them another way?' I explained to the parent that I did not know why publishing companies did that, but, unfortunately, it was beyond my control. When I mentioned this incident to my colleagues, they said that in all of their years of teaching they had never heard such a ridiculous question. So here's a word of advice: Be prepared for anything at open house!"

Dawn Leighty, Harrington, Delaware

- **Administration.** You will probably come in daily contact with your site administrator. Perhaps you might enjoy broadening your level of influence from the classroom to the school site. Does the scope of the job appeal to you? Do you have the leadership characteristics to work with students, staff, parents, the district office, and the community? If so, after you've taught for a couple of years, consider taking courses in the area of administration and supervision.

- **Special education.** Many service areas fall under the heading of special education. At your school you may have a special day class, resource specialists, or full inclusion specialists, to name a few. You will encounter students within your classroom who require special education modifications as part of their individual education plans. Perhaps you enjoy working with these kids and would like to work more in the special education vein. If these positions appeal to you, then you may want to consider researching graduate possibilities under this umbrella.

- **Reading specialists.** Many schools employ reading specialists to work with designated groups of students or individual students. Reading and vocabulary can be especially challenging for non-native English speakers, so if your interest lies in that area, consider undertaking English as a second language (ESL) coursework. A special credential is required in most instances.

- **School psychologist.** Children, like adults, face serious challenges. If you find you handle the crises that occur in your classroom with special kids with special needs, you may want to pursue an advanced degree in either counseling or psychology and work within

---

Making the Grade

Report Card
A
A
A
A

Want more information about graduate school? Consider this site:

Council of Graduate Schools: *www.cgsnet.org*

Especially helpful is the category "Resources for Students."

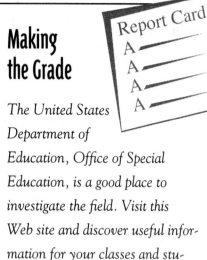

Making the Grade

The United States Department of Education, Office of Special Education, is a good place to investigate the field. Visit this Web site and discover useful information for your classes and students, as well as information about future career options.

Office of Special Education Programs:

www.ed.gov/offices/OSERS /OSEP/osep.html

the elementary school system helping those who need your support the most.

Things to Remember

Again, accept our congratulations as we welcome you to the profession! In summary, make sure you:

❑ Register your credential and get all necessary tests done

❑ Consider joining a professional organization to investigate professional growth opportunities (i.e. workshops, seminars, etc.)

❑ Keep track of your professional growth— start now

❑ Open your mind to the possibility of graduate school

Great Expectations

Voilà! You are now a teacher. What happens next? First, you learn what it means to be part of the profession, the district, and your school. This chapter discusses legal and financial issues for teachers, describes the structure of your district office, and addresses some of the expectations that your district and your school will have of you as a new teacher.

Making It Legal

In signing your first contract, you agreed to adhere to certain complex terms. In most states, you'll be on probationary status for at least your first year of teaching. During that probationary period, your district has the option of not renewing your contract, or even of terminating your employment if it appears that you and the district aren't a good match.

In some locations, your first year of teaching is a prerequisite to obtaining certification. Other locations require at least an emergency certification before you step into the classroom. You may be subject to

Teaching Terms

◆ ◆ ◆

Contractual language. The way words are used within the teaching contract. Contracts are often difficult to decipher, and legalese is only superficially like English. Because parts of the contract can be hard to understand, it is just that much more important that you know what you are doing when you agree to a district contract.

frequent reviews during your probationary period and may be matched with a mentor.

Unlike most corporate employment contracts, teaching contracts must be signed anew every year. At some point, depending on the terms of your contract, you'll go from preliminary status to probationary status to tenured status, which gives you protection from arbitrary dismissal.

It's important that you understand the terms of your contract because both your colleagues and your district office will refer to the information within it on a regular basis. In particular, you'll want to be well acquainted with sections related to items such as discretionary leave, contract renewal, and certification requirements.

Many of your colleagues have been teaching for years and so have seen many changes occur with the contract. If you have general questions about contractual items such as teacher contact days, personal leave, extracurricular duties, or adherence to curriculum, veteran teachers may be your best resource. More detailed questions about policies and procedures should be addressed to the district office. If you have very specific questions about the contract, though, it may be worth spending a few minutes with your teachers' union or even with your family attorney to get solid legal advice.

Pay Scale

As YOU begin working, you'll also want to understand your district's pay scale.

Most districts operate on a step-and-column basis: You can move down a "step" for every year you are employed as a teacher, and you move over a "column" by earning units and/or graduate degrees. Usually, you will receive a small increase in pay for every year you teach. You can then jump to a new column for approximately every thirty units you earn. You can earn units by taking college courses that have been preapproved by your district or by accumulating hours that can add up to units. For example, in some districts, fifteen hours of professional growth equals one unit.

Some districts also award *stipends* for completing graduate work. It is also worth checking into whether your school district offers

> ## Teaching Terms
>
> ◆ ◆ ◆
>
> **Stipend.** Monetary compensation for time you have invested in your job over and above your regular teaching duties. Many coaches and advisers receive stipends for the time they put into coaching practices and games or supervising meetings or after-school activities. Other districts offer stipends to teachers who complete graduate programs.

Making the Grade

How does your salary compare to that of other teachers nationwide? Statistics are tricky to come by, but one of the most reliable says that in 1997, the annual salary for K through 12 teachers four years into their careers was $25,500. Many districts are offering incentives for college graduates to go into teaching, though. Districts are offering "signing" bonuses, thus the starting salaries for new teachers are becoming quite attractive.

See this Web site for other educational statistics:

National Center for Educational Statistics: *http://nces.ed.gov*

merit pay for teaching performance or monetary rewards to schools that meet certain criteria. At any rate, being placed correctly on the pay scale is as important as knowing how to move along the columns.

If you'd taught in another school district, you'd receive credit for your years of service. Your district probably has a verification form to be completed.

In addition, if you have already taken some graduate-level courses—perhaps to complete your credential requirements—then your district will need an official transcript from the university to verify your units. Any units you earned after your undergraduate degree will count toward your advancement on the pay scale.

Benefits

As PART of your employment, you will be offered a choice of plans related to your medical, dental, and vision benefits. Your district may allow you to choose from a variety of options, and you may be required to make a quick decision. Be aware of your district's deadlines as you take the time to research the "out-of-pocket" expenses, prescription costs, local hospital options, and, most important, whether the type of coverage you are requesting covers your doctor or your family's physician or pediatrician.

Medical costs are increasing nationwide, so many school districts rely on employee contributions to cover the costs. Thus, the type of coverage you choose will impact your paycheck.

Meeting the Bigwigs

A LOT of people run a school district, and, although you may not encounter all of them the first year, you should become familiar with the role each one plays. Don't be intimidated by the people in these different positions; everyone in the district from the superintendent down to the teacher's aide is working for the same goal: an outstanding education and positive learning experience for each student enrolled in your district.

Teacher's Rule

Move along the columns of your pay scale as quickly as you can. You will find that advancing may be time-consuming, but the additional amount you earn because of those units, multiplied by the number of years you teach, will greatly exceed the price of those units. You deserve that money; make it as fast as you can!

The School Board

The district's school board is made up of members elected from the community. Some may be parents of children enrolled in the district; others may just take an interest in the education of the children in your community. They oversee the district's funding, expenditures, and curriculum development; set policy; and make important decisions for the district.

The Superintendent

The "CEO" of the school district is responsible for the day-to-day operations, reporting regularly to the school board. At times the

Making the Grade

If you've been working, you already know that money is taken out of your check each month. This may be the first opportunity you've come across for a retirement or savings plan available to teachers. It can get complicated. In some cases, the money is taken out before taxes; in other cases, it is deducted after taxes. Consult a financial planner to see what investments would be best for you in your situation. This consultation should be free, by the way, and you may want to get a couple of opinions. Beware of the person who encourages you to sign up for a tax-sheltered annuity (TSA) when that TSA might offer more of a commission for the representative instead of being the best investment for you.

superintendent visits classrooms, including Back-to-School Night and Open House. A good superintendent wants to keep an eye on things in the district, as well as keep in touch with the teachers, parents, and students. When the superintendent does check in to observe what a wonderful teaching job you are doing, introduce yourself (unless you are in the middle of a lesson), and continue doing exactly what you were doing. You're expected to conduct business as usual.

Assistant Superintendents

Assistant superintendents work with the superintendent to make sure the district is running efficiently. Whereas the superintendent oversees the entire district, the assistant superintendents have specific jobs within the district office for which they are responsible. They report back to the superintendents and can focus on one of the following areas.

- **Business.** This person is the "chief financial officer" of the district. You may not have direct dealings with this particular assistant superintendent, but he oversees many aspects of the district office, including payroll and benefits. You won't be working directly with the assistant superintendent in this area, so you will need to know who is working for him in the areas of payroll and benefits.

These are the people within the district office to whom you will take your unit transcripts for your pay increase, ask questions about medical benefits, and get assistance from regarding your pay check in general.

- **Personnel.** This person may wear a variety of hats; she was probably part of the hiring process, met with you to discuss the contract, and may be responsible for staff development in your district. After discussing your progress and teaching skills with your principal, this individual will most likely be responsible for advising the school board to renew or not renew your contract. This assistant superintendent is also responsible for monitoring the school site to which you are assigned. She may watch the condition of the site, ask about needed materials, and make sure the facilities are acceptable. In addition, this individual will also keep track of whether your credential is up-to-date. You will get to know this person very well!

> ## Teaching Terms
>
> ◆ ◆ ◆
>
> **Back-to-School Night.** An evening set aside for the parents to visit their children's classrooms. They generally follow the same schedule their child does during a regular school day and learn, from you, everything that they should know about your classroom and curriculum.

- **Curriculum and instruction/ educational services.** The person in this position is responsible for the curriculum and instruction that you use in your classrooms every day. He is typically responsible for adopting textbooks, keeping current on instructional strategies, establishing and maintaining some form of mentor-teacher program, and perhaps handling staff development. In addition, he may be responsible for the special education department in your district.

District Orientation

ABOUT A week before you start teaching, the stress of your new job sets in. You will have received the year's curriculum from your principal but probably don't yet have all the materials and aren't exactly sure where to find them. You have a completely empty classroom without any posters or decorations, and—groan—you get an invitation in your faculty box for a new teacher preschool district orientation. You think to yourself, "Oh, great. This is perfect timing. Don't they realize I have a classroom to set up and a curriculum to plan?"

In fact, they do, but there are some very important pieces of information you need at this orientation. Moreover, this is the one, and oftentimes only, time the entire district staff will be together. If you need further convincing, it's also a great way to meet other new teachers in the district and establish some adult connections.

The district office knows you're working and tries to combine district office information with time to work in the classroom. As part of the orientation, the district office may include speeches and presentations from the superintendent, a motivational speaker, mentor teachers, school board members, introductions of new staff (that's you), and any other information relevant to your first year of teach-

Teaching Terms

• • •

Open House. This is an evening late in the semester or year when parents are invited to their child's classrooms to see all the work, projects, and accomplishments that they have completed throughout the school year. Most of the children's best work is on display, and the parents can see for themselves all that their child has learned in the school year. This is a time for parents to take pride in their child, so show your students off!

ing. Administration will probably present information on subjects such as your teacher's union, changes in health benefits, and textbook information.

Participate in these meetings. You are the new kid on the block, so mingle, interact, and be an extremely active listener. You'll find sympathy for the feelings you have of being overwhelmed, and if you're visiting with other faculty members, you may well develop a connection with another new teacher in the district so that the two of you can share your concerns and questions with each other.

Take this time to relax and look around at the environment you have been hired into. Although your mind may drift back to the things you need to do in your classroom, put those thoughts away for just a little while so you can truly appreciate what your district has to offer.

Teaching Terms

• • •

Mentor-teacher program. Many districts have already adopted or are in the process of adopting a program that pairs up a new teacher with a veteran teacher. The program is intended to support new teachers, as well as provide them a valuable resource for information and advice. The veteran teacher helps the new teacher for the duration of his or her first year of teaching and often for the second as well.

• • •

Staff development. A general term that refers to periods of time allotted for teacher improvement. This time can be used for training in areas ranging from technology to lesson planning. It may be time set aside to meet with department members to discuss curriculum changes. Often, the hours spent on staff development can be applied toward professional growth hours that add up to units that will help you move across the pay scale.

Site Orientation

IT'S LIKELY you will have an additional new-teacher orientation meeting or faculty meeting before the first day of school. At this site

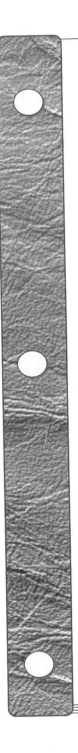

Tales from the Trenches

"Site orientations can be a blast!" states coauthor Karen Heisinger. "I worked for a new principal who asked us at our site orientation what the strangest thing was that we had done over the summer as a way to introduce ourselves. She also had us make a 't-shirt' out of paper and yarn and write words on it that described us. Even though we had a million things to do in our classroom, she made us feel connected to her and the rest of the staff in a very meaningful way. Another principal I worked for brought out plastic champagne glasses and sparkling apple cider that we could all toast to a great new year. Others had raffles, pancake breakfasts, showed funny video clips from movies, and one district even hired Harry Wong to come out and motivate us to start the new year off right."

meeting, you will learn the basic procedures and policies of the specific campus at which you are working. You may feel completely overloaded with information, so be sure you make some connections and befriend staff members to whom you can turn for help in the future.

In your site orientation meeting, you will learn the school's attendance procedures, various school-day schedules, technological capabilities, teacher expectations, copying policies, the school's tardy policy and other details that will zoom completely over your head until you need them your first day of school. Take a moment to look around the room at all the faculty members you will be working with. The human connection will be the most important connection you make.

You should now have a much better sense of what to expect from your contract and your new profession. Your district office is not there to intimidate or scare you. It is there to support you, so never be afraid to ask questions. Remember: You are a great asset to this district, and they are lucky to have you!

Making the Grade

Sometimes school districts and school sites hire people for a certain number of hours per week to help teachers grade work and papers. These "readers" or "graders" take stacks of work from your classes and—using your explicit instructions—grade the work. It's like magic: you receive the papers or assignments back all graded.

Things to Remember

You will be feeling overwhelmed at the beginning of the year, but remember to do the following:

❏ Get to know your contract
❏ Consider putting money away in a retirement fund

Teacher's Rule

At your first orientation meeting and first faculty meeting, make an effort to remember names. Write them down and include the phone extensions for these individuals.

❑ Get to know the people in your district office

❑ Relax and enjoy your district and site orientations

Back to School

Your Site's Expectations

THE FIRST TEST IN teaching is interacting with people at your school site. Different schools have different personalities, which are a reflection of everyone from the custodian to the principal. In this chapter, you'll get tips on communicating and working with them all. Let's begin with the principal.

The Big Man (or Woman) on Campus

ALTHOUGH YOUR school principal may have been part of the interview panel, she previously viewed you as a candidate; now you are an employee! She will regard you as an extension of herself from now on, as she selected you to assist in carrying out the mission of the school. For that reason, meetings and interactions with the principal are very important. This section is designed to help you develop that relationship.

"Education, then, beyond all other devices of human origin, is the great equalizer of the conditions of men; the balance wheel of the social machinery."

HORACE MANN

The school principal sets the tone and the "culture" for the school. Try to step inside his shoes. The principal responds directly to the district office. Everything from test scores to attendance fall under the jurisdiction of your fearless leader. He will want teachers who raise the standards and make the campus shine.

It may take you some time to determine "what really goes on here"—and it may differ significantly from what is written and verbalized in your school's *mission statement*—but it will happen.

Basically, the school principal will be making decisions about you and forming opinions about you *all* of the time. Yikes! Didn't you go into teaching partly because you didn't want anybody breathing down your back? Take a deep breath, because no principal worth the title breathes down her teachers' backs.

When we said the principal will be making decisions about you *all* of the time, we expected you might freak a little. But it's nothing you should worry about. In fact, it can be a great thing, especially if you take a proactive, rather than a reactive, stance toward the things over which you have control. For example, you control your time, so always be on time for everything—yard duty, staff meetings, and *school!* Let yourself shine as the perfect star of a teacher you surely are.

Similarly, when the principal requests something of you—lesson plans, goals, textbook inventory—prioritize the tasks and complete the request as soon as possible. Become known as a reliable, conscientious employee and teacher. Your principal will then "have your back."

Sometimes you are called into the principal's office for a situation that you have little control over, such as a parent who makes a phone call to the principal without calling you first. When such situ-

---

Teaching Terms

◆ ◆ ◆

Mission statement. Just as corporations write mission statements that drive their organizations, more and more elementary schools are developing their own mission statements to steer the course of the school. These statements reveal the core attitude of what's important on your campus.

ations arise—and they will—where you are required to defend your actions to the principal, be professional. Listen calmly, explain calmly, and save the venting for a spouse, a friend outside school, or your dog.

When you've got control over your emotions, take an objective look at the situation. What was useful about the conversation you had with the principal? Take what was useful from the conversation and use it, and disregard what was not useful. Go to work the next day with the knowledge that *you* determine what is useful to your teaching practice, and you *will* make changes to constantly improve your craft. You will be better for it, the profession will be stronger because of it, and the principal will be proud to have you as a member of his staff.

Teacher's Rule

Do not give your principal cause to write you a "Let's chat" note. Usually, "chat" in this context means there is a problem. If you take a proactive stance about your job and follow procedures, you'll steer clear of these notes in your box.

Behind Every Good Principal Is a Secretary

QUITE SIMPLY, the school secretary runs the shop. Without her, no child would register. No bulletins would exist. No lunch tickets could be purchased. No field trips would be scheduled. Because of her integral role in your school site, it's important to make the school secretary your advocate.

In fact, the school secretary needs to become your *best* advocate. This individual is the "first line of defense" with parents, other staff members, and the principal. You can earn his respect by behaving professionally. Be on time with requests, duties, and commitments. When the secretary issues a memo with a deadline, he often gives

FROM THE DESK OF . . . According to coauthor Karen Heisinger, "The secretary is so important! My mother-in-law, Barbara Heisinger, was the first school secretary I worked with at Almaden Elementary in San Jose. (Truth be known, I think I got my first teaching job because of her!) She was (and still is!) fantastic! Any supplies I needed, helping me get to know the staff, giving me the inside scoop on things — these are some of the things she did for me. You can imagine my disappointment when I was transferred to a different school because of low enrollment in only the second week of school."

you the closest date to his deadline. If you're late, you make *him* late and won't score any points. And you need all the points you can get!

The best way to establish a good rapport with the secretary, then, besides being prompt with requests, is to ask for advice. This is not a gimmick or technique; it is a survival tool. For example, if you are responsible for keeping track of students' absence notes (and you probably will be to some extent), ask the secretary or attendance clerk how you should do this. Some questions to consider in this scenario might be these:

- Will you be turning the notes in monthly, quarterly, annually?
- Should the notes be organized by student or by date?
- Should the notes be kept in an envelope or folder?

By asking these types of questions, you're telling the secretary or attendance clerk that you are interested in making her job easier and that you know how hard she works to fulfill her responsibilities every day. Moreover, as questions arise, it is best to ask the secretary first, not the principal. She and the principal will appreciate your respect of the chain of command.

Another area in which the secretary is invaluable involves parents. If you need to make a troubling phone call to a parent, for example, it may be helpful to ask the secretary whether he has some quick background information on the family. For example, if the child comes to school late every day, and it is the school's policy that you, as the teacher, make the first phone call home, it might be worth asking the secretary what can be expected from the phone call. Some questions in this scenario might include the following:

- Does the secretary know the family?
- Does the child have a history of chronic absences?
- Should you call the student's mom or dad at work or home?
- How does the family usually respond to "problem" calls from the school? Cooperatively? Antagonistically?

Then, after you make the call, let the secretary know the results. You will have just made an ally by showing her you respect her perspective and experience!

Beyond his knowledge of the principal and the parents, the secretary knows the "lay of the land" for your school. That's a valuable resource to new teachers.

Teacher's Rule

The office staff, in general, is the most underappreciated group at the school. So if you ever feel like doing something nice, do it for them. Bring in donuts one morning. Drop off a candy bar for each secretary on Valentine's Day and say "Thank you." Just as you enjoy hearing from a parent who appreciates your hard work in the classroom, the office staff likes to know their work means a lot to you.

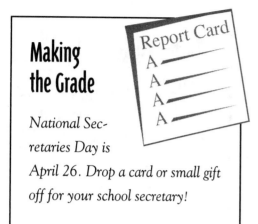

Making the Grade

National Secretaries Day is April 26. Drop a card or small gift off for your school secretary!

Finally, get to know the school secretaries for the right reasons: You value their expertise. You need their help to do your job more efficiently, and appreciate them as human beings. No tricks or gimmicks—just be your honest, earnest, friendly self. (And, again, small gifts for holidays or an occasional cup of coffee or tea doesn't hurt, either!)

Working with Custodial Staff

BESIDES THE school secretaries, the custodial staff is another population to get to know. These individuals clean your classroom, deliver your school supplies, fix things for you, and accomplish numerous other tasks at your school site.

By seeking the advice of the custodian just as you would the secretary, you develop mutual respect and help each other do a better job. As you set up your classroom, check with the custodian about the best placement for your garbage can, your rolling cupboard, and other classroom furniture. It may seem small, but it will make a big difference to the custodian whose job it is to keep track of and clean around these things.

Taking the time to get to know the custodian will also pave the way for a smoother year. In fact, we highly recommend learning the names of your custodians. When they enter your room at the end of the day to clean—and you're still there planning lessons—greet them! By doing so, you'll show the custodians that you appreciate the hard work they do to make your classroom a positive learning environment.

Working with Other Teachers

ONE OF the joys of teaching is finding colleagues who will help you. This section addresses ways to work most effectively with your fellow teachers.

Collaboration

You can learn many wonderful things from your coworkers. Although teachers have traditionally worked in isolation, the end is near for this practice. Working in collaboration is becoming the norm, and the other teachers at your school can be valuable allies.

It's most likely you'll be asked to work with others at your grade level. The beginning of the school year is often the time to make long-range planning decisions, determine who will have access to which science kits at which times, set the yard duty schedule, and make similar decisions about how you'll divide duties. Although your input may be limited at first (until you get a feel for the decision-making process), make it clear that you want to be part of the team. Take on the responsibilities with which you are comfortable, and make promises you can keep.

At the same time, you may, at times, feel put upon. Your yard duty assignments may be less than equitable, and your supplies may be limited. Bring up these facts in a problem-solving manner. For example, pose the question "I have only twenty-two social studies textbooks and thirty-two students. How do I go about getting more? Is it possible to share with you?" This is a better approach than saying, "Why do you have a complete class set and I only have a partial one?"

As the new teacher, you may be stuck with more than your share of duties from time to time. By tackling the assigned duties with style and

Tales from the Trenches

"Some lessons you only learn through experience. At our school the classrooms are built in groups of four, connected to a central 'teachers' bay,' where teachers have their desks and work areas. Three of us were working out in our bay one day while Vern, a new teacher, was in his classroom with the door open. We could hear everything going on in his classroom. He was having the kids grade one another's social studies test.

"The three of us started snickering as he grew more and more frustrated. The test had required the kids to respond in complete sentences, but Vern had way too much faith in their grading abilities; there was no way you could really get fifth graders to help grade anything but the simplest test. So you can imagine how it went. He would say something like, 'The answer to question two is "The explorers who discovered the West in the 1700s are Meriwether Lewis and William Clark." '

"Then there would be a flurry of questions. 'Can we say "were" instead of "are"? What if we said it backwards? What if he wrote "two" instead of "the"? What if he wrote "William Lewis"?' It just went on and on.

"So we started sending in 'help.' I had one of my students knock on the door, walk clear to the front of the class and ask Vern, 'Do you have any scissors?' We were planning a school-colors day for later in the week, so another of the teachers knocked on the door, walked all the way to the front of the classroom, and asked Vern, 'Are you wearing red and white on Friday?' We were in stitches outside in the bay.

"At recess he walked into the bay and announced, 'Next social studies test, you three are grading it for me!'"

Joan M., Kent, Washington

grace and following through on promises made to your team, you will find yourself enjoying the collegiality of your fellow faculty members.

Different Professional Ideals

You may find that some of the teachers you work with have a very specific way of doing things. It is important to accept this, and also nurture *your* style and *your* way of doing things. You may want to stay in at recess to provide extra assistance to students. Do it if it feels right to you. You may set up a homework club that meets after school or lunchtime sports activities. Again, do it if it is something you believe in.

In the classroom, you may want to undertake a project such as learning centers. Some teachers may see this as a chance to tell you that it's much easier to just teach all of the students in the same way at the same time. With any luck, others will pitch in to help you out! Try not to let the first group discourage you from giving a try to any other idea or innovation. And align yourself with the second group!

> ## Teaching Terms
>
> • • •
>
> **Duty assignment.** When you need to supervise an event—such as recess or an assesmbly—outside, above, and beyond your classroom duties, you are working a duty assignment. Most all districts require their teachers to take turns and lend a hand supervising various daily duties on campus.

Professional Jealousy

It's not all roses, unfortunately. Whether you are twenty-two or fifty-two, if this is your first teaching job, you are new to the profession and to the staff. You have just completed a program of teacher preparation, and your ideas are fresh and untried. Every day brings on new challenges for you, and you're always trying new strategies.

> **" *Learned Institutions ought to be favorite objects with every free people. They throw that light over the public mind which is the best security against crafty & dangerous encroachments on the public liberty.* "**
>
> JAMES MADISON

You may get your share of "been there, done it" comments from other staff members, but persevere. Take risks. Keep changing what doesn't work, and continue what is working. You have the most recent college experience and were probably exposed to the most recent and current educational theories. Apply them! Use your energy and enthusiasm to your advantage. If you come across a colleague with so much jealousy that she tries to undermine you and thwart your successes, or even attempts to cast you in a "bad light" to administration, document it. Keep a diary, and go to the principal with your concerns. Don't attack the other teacher. Seek the principal's advice. Show the principal your diary. Most important, do not act any way but professional and kind to the antagonistic teacher.

Oh, Buddy of Mine! The Mentor

You may be assigned a support teacher to act as a mentor or a buddy to you in your first year. This program can be a great opportunity for

> **FROM THE DESK OF . . .** "I really benefited from our state's mandated mentor system my first year teaching, especially in the area of discipline. I'd meet regularly with my mentor to discuss a single issue, and she'd give me fantastic ideas! I overcame several really difficult discipline issues with the sage advice of my mentor. I can't recommend mentoring highly enough. It gave me the foundation I needed to continue teaching through the rough spots."
>
> Tamara B., Michigan

you! Your mentor can be an invaluable guide to you as you wade through school policies and procedures, confrontations with parents, extracurricular activities, instructional strategies, and curriculum matters. Use this person! These teachers plan on acting as your "Rock of Gibraltar." They want to help.

Your mentor will have many different functions:

• **Colleague.** You are a fellow staff member with your mentor teacher; it is not a master teacher/student teacher relationship. In this role, then, you should expect the mentor teacher to "show you the ropes" of the school, such as how to order supplies, how attendance is taken, how rainy day schedules work, and the like.

• **Advocate.** By showing you the ropes, your mentor can also act as your advocate either by suggesting approaches for making changes or letting you know how to get necessary supplies. The mentor can also intervene on your behalf if other staff members try to take advantage of your novice status.

Teacher's Rule

Although many campuses do not adhere to strict dress codes, the unspoken dress code tends toward the conservative and more dressy. Also, often the principal prefers the staff dress more conservatively. Ask your mentor or the school principal about the "dress" culture of your campus to make sure. And remember, it's tough to overdress and easy to underdress.

- **Adviser**. In the role of adviser, your mentor may make some very directive remarks to you. Listen to those remarks! For instance, if your mentor teacher says, "Never drink coffee while on yard duty," heed the advice! If she tells you it's a good idea to participate in the winter program, do it! As your adviser, your mentor is sharing the "unwritten" rules of the school with you because she can; this is priceless information.

- **Coach.** Coaching sessions between you and your mentor will most likely be focused on your teaching practice. Expect your mentor teacher to observe you teaching and coach you through lesson plans, instructional strategies, and student assessment. These conversations will sound different from the collegial, "buddy" discussions you have been having, so be prepared for the difference.

Also, check ahead of time to see whether these observations are confidential and/or how the information will be shared with the principal.

By establishing a trusting relationship with you, your mentor will move through these various roles quite naturally. There may be times when you are uncomfortable with the different roles, though, so be up front about it with your mentor. It is okay to tell him, "I know you're supposed to be coaching me through this lesson right now, but I really need some advice on how to get enough textbooks for my students." He will probably appreciate your openness!

Besides providing support to you, the mentor teacher may be given funds for you to use for classroom resources, attend workshops, or get release time to visit other classrooms. Check into it!

Getting paired up with a mentor teacher or buddy teacher can be very helpful to you. This person should help you with the "ins and outs" at the school site—and who knows better than a fellow teacher? The support of a mentor is different from that of the principal, as your mentor teacher will most likely not be in an evaluative role, just a support role. Savor the undivided attention of this individual and learn!

"Houston, We Have Orientation"

You will probably attend an orientation at your school site before the first day of school. This one differs from the district orientation we discussed in the last chapter, as it focuses on *your* school, with *your* staff. You will hear details on the discipline plan, get a tour of the campus, discuss curriculum issues, go through the school handbook, and hopefully have time to meet with your fellow grade-level teachers.

Although the dress will be pretty casual, this does not mean shorts and a tank top for you (even though others may be dressed in this manner). Don't dress as nicely as you did for the district orientation, but do be conscious of making a good impression. You can wear the shorts and tank next summer at your second orientation!

Again, although you will be anxious to get into your classroom, enjoy the collegiality and try to get to know your fellow teachers. Before the school year, everyone tends to be more relaxed and not as stressed. Go to the back-to-school barbecue or the get-together at the principal's house. Even though you have a classroom to set up, curriculum to organize, and a thousand other things to do, the time you put into deepening your relationships early on will be well spent, even if you only stay for a little while. (Your fellow teachers know how much work you have to do!) In this informal setting, though, you may learn a *lot* about the goings on at your site, and valuable insights into teaching. Soak it up. You need to eat, anyway!

Things to Remember

To get acclimated to your school site quickly, remember to do the following:

- ❏ Establish a professional relationship with your principal, secretary and custodian by seeking their advice, and being timely with requests for information
- ❏ Enjoy the collaboration with fellow teachers, especially your mentor
- ❏ Attend your site gatherings with enthusiasm, style and grace
- ❏ Err on the side of conservative dress in your first years of teaching

School Procedures, Policies, and Schedules

I T'S TIME NOW TO understand the policies and procedures of your school site. When you signed on to be an elementary school teacher, the job description included more than just teaching school!

> " If little else, the brain is
> an educational toy. "
>
> TOM ROBBINS

Evaluations

You've worked hard to get this job; now let's discuss how to keep it! It is standard procedure for new teachers to be observed by their principal or vice principal, both formally and informally several times throughout the year. So be prepared.

Sometime around late September, your principal will arrange to come into your classroom to observe a lesson. This typically involves a preconference where she will want to go over with you what she will be observing. Be prepared to discuss some of the following topics with your evaluating administrator:

- What subject area she will be observing. This should match the overall goals of the school and the goals that were submitted to the principal at the beginning of the year

- How this lesson fits into the overall unit. In other words, are you introducing the unit, are you teaching a lesson in the middle of the unit, or are you assessing it?

- The type of student groupings being used and why

- Instructional strategies used and why

Teaching Terms

◆ ◆ ◆

Informal observation. What some administrators affectionately call a "drive-by." This means that your evaluating administrator stops by at any given time on any given day and stays for a short time to see how your classroom operates on a day-to-day basis.

◆ ◆ ◆

Preconference. This is a meeting that you will have with your evaluating administrator before he comes into your classroom to observe you formally. In this meeting, the topic of the lesson will be discussed, and a date and time are selected for the observation. The administrator will tell you what he will be looking for, and you have the opportunity to ask any questions or voice any concerns you have.

• The type of assessment strategy to be used and why

• Anything in particular you would like the principal to observe

During the lesson, the principal will take notes on what he observes. Sometimes the principal will interact with the students, participate in the lesson, and ask the students questions about what they are doing.

After the lesson, you will have a postlesson conference with the principal. You will be asked how you think the lesson went and whether you would do anything differently. Invariably, the principal will offer some suggestions to you. Take them! And take the opportunity to ask for specific assistance. For example, if the principal says that you need to work on classroom management, that is the time to say, "Is there someone here I could observe? Could you please arrange it for me?" Get the principal involved in your professional development, and get some release time, too! You'll learn more about evaluation preparation and procedures in Chapter 20.

Teaching Terms

◆ ◆ ◆

Instructional strategies. The different ways in which you teach your information. With one lesson, you may use direct instruction to help students grasp a concept while the following day, you may utilize a particular game to reinforce that knowledge. Those are both examples of teaching strategies. There are hundreds of strategies that teachers use in their classrooms daily. If you feel that you are using the same ones over and over, seek out new resources to freshen up your instruction.

School Committees and Extracurricular Assignments

AND YOU thought you were hired just to teach! Just wait until you hear about what is in store for you. Besides "just teaching" (and

Teacher's Rule

Be proactive during your preconference meeting. In other words, take responsibility for your own improvement. You can do this by asking your administrator specific questions about what you would like him to look for during the observation. If you have concerns regarding classroom management or voice projection, this is the time to ask about it. By asking questions, you are also indicating to the administrator that you are interested in improving your teaching and are happy that he is coming in to help you with that. Creating a feeling of teamwork is an advantageous approach!

teaching well), you will be expected to serve on various committees and perform extracurricular functions. There are various levels of commitment involved in certain committees. Learn about the requirements and time commitments of the following functions, and select one that is right for you:

- **PTA representative.** This duty usually entails coming to a meeting after school or in the evening once per month; you are the liaison between the teachers and the parent group at your school.

- **The sunshine or social committee.** This duty involves picking up presents and cards for faculty members, remembering birthdays, organizing baby showers, holding luncheons, or setting up holiday parties.

- **Discipline committee.** This group will seek your input into issues surrounding schoolwide discipline policies and procedures.

- **Curriculum committees.** This group researches "best practices" and is expected to stay current on issues surrounding a particular curricular area, and giving input into what curriculum materials are selected for the school.

Additional Responsibilities

Besides serving on committees, you will be expected to fulfill additional responsibilities—for example:

- **Homework Club.** This activity involves setting up an after school "club" to help students with their homework. It's comparable to a tutoring center, where students with difficulties in a particular area can get one-on-one help from a teacher.

- **Math Club/Writing Club.** This type of club can be either a tutoring center for students who need help in these specific areas or it can be a club that students join to enhance their skills and meet other students who have the same interests. This may involve a lunchtime commitment or an after-school commitment.

> ## Teaching Terms
> ♦ ♦ ♦
> **Release time.** This refers to time you take away from your classroom during school hours. Many districts allow new teachers this time to observe veteran teachers in their classrooms to get ideas and find new methods for instructional strategies, classroom procedures and policies. If your district offers this opportunity to you, take it!

- **Special events.** You may be asked to take charge of the volunteer tea, the annual field day, or the fall festival. Even if you don't want to be in charge, you could donate your time to work at these events (or at least be there to see your students).

- **Special projects.** You may be asked to take on the yearbook, the life lab, candy sales, or monitor the sixth-grade lawn to make sure the sixth graders are behaving themselves. These projects require a lot of time. You may be very interested in doing these projects. The caution to you is to budget your time wisely.

- **Student Council.** This undertaking will involve a great deal of coordination and will require you to be involved in elections, weekly meetings, schoolwide activities, and student store.

Making the Grade

Literally thousands of helpful teaching resources are available on the Web. Some of the most popular are these:

Teach Net: *www.teachnet .com—Lesson plans, tips, forums, ideas, and much, much more.*

NewTeacher.com: *www .peaklearn.com/newteach— Our favorite part of the site is the "Resources for Educators" link, which contains dozens and dozens of excellent Teaching Tips & Strategies.*

Mighty Mentors: *www.mighty-mentors.com—E-mail mentoring network for new teachers.*

What Every New Teacher Should Know about Discipline: *www.edweek .org/ew/vol-19/02keatin.h19— When the "honeymoon" ends, what to do?*

Duties

EACH TEACHER will be assigned a duty of some sort. Duties may include yard duty, bus duty, crosswalk duty, gate duty, and so forth. Hopefully these duties will be spread out equitably among all staff members, but here's a "heads up" as to what to expect:

- **Morning yard duty.** This duty will be before school, so when it's your turn to serve, you really need to have all of your copies ready, and your classroom ready to go earlier than you may be accustomed to. The difficulty of this duty is that students in all grades arrive at different times; the numbers start small and continue to grow.

- **Recess duty.** This duty involves a smaller group of students, including your own class. It's nice to be able to focus on your own students a bit. Seeing them play often gives you an additional perspective on their behavior.

- **Bus duty.** This duty requires you to watch out for the students' safety. If you serve this duty in the morning, then you are escorting the students off the bus; if it is an afternoon duty, then you are making sure the kids are in the correct bus line and are keeping their hands to themselves.

- **Crosswalk duty.** Another safety-watch duty. You may be asked to carry the stop sign, stop the cars, and signal the students to cross the street.

• **Gate duty.** For this duty, you are on the lookout for any strange behavior. Before school, you are making sure the students do not come on campus too early and go where they are supposed to go; after school, you are in charge of making sure the students are going straight home (i.e., you're on the lookout for potential fights or suspicious people hanging around the school).

> ## Teaching Terms
>
> • • •
>
> **PTA.** The abbreviation for Parent/Teacher Association. Some schools have Parent/ Teacher/Student Associations. You listen to concerns or issues brought up by the parents of the school and report these to the faculty. You also take faculty information to the parents. This keeps the lines of communication open between the school and the community.

All of these duties involve protecting the safety of the students. Even though it may seem like a good time to chat with a fellow teacher, you can't. And when a student comes up and says, "The other teachers let me bolt into the middle of the street to see if I can outrun the cars. Why won't you?" your consistent answer is "*I don't feel it's safe, so I'm not allowing it.*"

Taking Attendance

TAKING ATTENDANCE is a school function and responsibility that you *must* master. You need to get oriented on specific procedures for your site before the school year begins and stay current as to what is expected of you.

The best way to take attendance is to engage the students in the same morning activity each day while you take roll. Whether they start the day with a math review, a writing prompt, or a spelling refresher, stay consistent. Roll taking needs to be done at the beginning of the day. The office will send a student to collect the attendance, or you may be asked to send it to the office with one of your students.

Teacher's Rule

During your first year teaching, only take on a minimal amount of extra activities. You will be swamped with first-year evaluations, lesson planning, organization, and other demands that won't be as much of a concern in subsequent years. You are eager to please and to be liked, but don't jeopardize your teaching in the process.

Setting Up Field Trips

THE PROCEDURES involved in setting up a field trip can be extensive. With luck, they will be written clearly so that you can follow them step by step. Most procedures include the following:

1. Making arrangements for the field trip, such as contacting the location, selecting a date and time, and arranging a bus

2. Submitting a request to take the field trip including the rationale for the trip, along with details, such as transportation information and cost

3. If there is a cost to the trip, considering fund-raising. (Get permission from administration.)

4. Upon approval, issuing a permission slip that students need to return by a certain date that in-

cludes all of the details, a parent's signature, what students need to bring on that day, and the money that is needed

5. Requesting a check for payment from the secretary or vice principal

6. If you are using parent drivers, making sure that the proper paperwork is on file in the office

7. Making arrangements for your duties to be covered that day

8. Making arrangements for the students who cannot go on the field trip to do work in another teacher's classroom

9. Bringing a first-aid kit with you on the trip and having the students wear name tags

Field trips require an extensive amount of work, but the experience is well worth the effort. Your students will benefit greatly from getting out of their classroom and receiving hands-on kinesthetic learning. It gives them, and you, a change of scenery and gets you out of the classroom if only for a day. Most likely, they will remember it for the rest of their lives.

Teacher's Rule

You probably have heard the phrase, "You need to grow eyes in the back of your head." But you'll find that duties require that you have eyes not only in the back of your head, but on both sides as well. Coauthor Karen Heisinger remembers a vice principal she once worked for who said you need to have a swivel head when on duty. Never stand in one place too long.

Seating Chart

KEEPING AN updated seating chart is important, as you may want to change it often as you get to know the students. For this reason, the easiest way to do this is to put the students' names on a sticky note

Tales from the Trenches

"One time, we had a first-year teacher, fresh out of college, who was trying to live by the rule that you shouldn't call attention to kids or embarrass them in front of the whole class when you have an issue. He had given a child permission to go to the bathroom, and the boy was gone a long time. There was all sorts of hubbub going on in the classroom, and so when the kid finally showed up, he said quietly, 'Daniel, can you step over here for me?' They walked to a quiet corner of the classroom, where he said in a very low voice, 'Daniel, I noticed you've been gone a long time.' But instead of responding in a similarly quiet voice, Daniel shouted out, 'Well! I was goin' number 2!' Regrouping, the teacher whispered, 'Daniel, it's okay to speak quietly. Now I was just worried because you were gone so long.' Daniel replied in a voice that could be heard out in the hallway, 'Well, it takes a long time, you know!' "

Joan M., Kent, Washington

(one name on each) and place them on a sheet of construction paper in the formation of your class. This design makes it easy for you to make changes and keep up to date. Seating charts are discussed at length in chapter 6.

Referring Students to Study Team

As YOU work with your students, you will notice some patterns in their abilities. If certain students are not achieving in math or reading, or have poor written skills, they may be prime candidates for the Student Study Team.

The first person to contact is your resource specialist. Ask to talk to him informally to talk you through the referral process. In this way, you can learn about the process and get some feedback about your student. If the resource specialist advises you to go forward, you will probably go through these steps in one way or another:

Teacher's Rule

After figuring out the desk arrangement in your classroom, you will create a seating chart to assign your students to the desks. Determine your seating chart using various pieces of information such as student behavior, student achievement, or special needs of students.

1. Notify the parents of your concerns and get their approval to continue.
2. Get a date on the Student Study Team calendar.
3. Bring samples of the student's work to the meeting.
4. State positive characteristics of the student and areas of improvement.
5. Work with the team to determine whether to conduct further testing.

Computer Lab and Library

MANY SCHOOLS have a computer lab and a library. Each school operates these facilities differently, though.

Teaching Terms

• • •

Student study team. A group of people who work with students with special needs. Your district may have a different name for this group. This group monitors the progress of students and suggests modifications that can be made in their regular classrooms. Before students can be referred to the study, they need to be identified as having special needs. Once that need is determined, the study team takes over.

Computer Lab

Unless the computer lab has an assigned teacher, you need to be in the lab at all times with your students. This means you design the activities and run the show. The computer lab is a great way to reinforce skills through games, utilize the Internet for research purposes, practice typing skills, and transfer student writing to word processing or presentations.

If another teacher runs the lab, then consider it a preparation time for you! Check with the other teachers and/or principal to make sure this is acceptable, and you have some time to yourself.

Library

Library time is used to check out books for silent reading, conduct research, and listen to stories. You may either use this time as a preparation period for yourself, or you may send half your class at a time to check out books. When you are studying a particular unit, books of a certain genre, or those by a certain author, let the librarians know so they can set aside certain books for you.

Things to Remember

> *" Education is what survives when what has been learned has been forgotten. "*
>
> B. F. SKINNER

Making a good impression at your school begins with your adherence to the school's procedures, policies, and schedules. Remember to do the following:

❏ Become familiar with your school's evaluation procedure; see how often your evaluator will be observing you and when

❏ Be selective when asked to join school committees and take on extra assignments

❏ Get assistance on taking attendance, setting up field trips, and referring students who may need extra assistance from the specialists on your campus

❏ Find out how the computer lab and library work at your school so you are prepared to use this time to your students' advantage

Preparing for Absences from Your Classroom

WE KNOW—YOU'RE THE type of person who never missed class yourself. You pride yourself on never missing work, too. You're meticulous. Ethical. Hard-working. Besides that, preparing for a substitute scares you to death! Well, for a myriad of reasons, you'll probably need a substitute at some time—perhaps even several times—during the school year. In this chapter, we'll cover the situations that necessitate calling in a substitute and also help you plan activities for when you're gone.

Atchoo!

WHEN YOU spend your days in the company of young people, there'll come a morning, soon, when your bursting sinuses and upset stomach mean you can't crawl to the shower—let alone make it into school to teach twenty-eight kids about Christopher Columbus. You'll need a substitute.

You'll just have to face facts. As a teacher, you come in contact with many children a day. They'll hold your hand in the bus line and touch your phone, your stapler, your pens.

> ## Teaching Terms
>
> ◆ ◆ ◆
>
> **Substitute teachers.** Where do substitute teachers come from? If you're going to be missing for an hour or two, the substitute may hail from your own campus—a nice colleague who agrees to combine your class with hers or will supervise both your class and his outside for PE. If you're going to be MIA for a half a day or more, though, an administrator may pitch in if it's an emergency, or the substitute will come from the pool of substitute teachers who work on call for your district.

They hand in papers that have been sneezed on. You just can't escape those microscopic germs! First-year teachers get the bugs.

Before we discuss how to handle an illness-related absence from the perspective of the administration and your classroom, let's look at ways to try (notice we use the word *try*) to avoid those pesky germs. We asked teachers everywhere to describe ways they ward off illness, and here are the responses we received:

- Keep hand sanitizer gel on your desk. Use a tad between classes.
- Keep a box of tissues available, in the open, so the kids can have paper hankies whenever needed. Keep a garbage can next to the box for easy disposal.
- Take the time to wash your hands between classes as often as time permits.

FROM THE DESK OF . . . Lynne Guerne, a French teacher for ten years, recalls her first year teaching and the illnesses that besieged her. "It's the truth. I caught every cold that was on campus my first year. I was sick all the time. I lost my voice three times." Her tale is typical of first-year teachers. But by the second and third year, she'd built up an immunity to all the germs. Now, Madame Guerne rarely finds herself sniffling and sneezing—or in need of a substitute.

- Tell kids to *stay home* when infectious. As much as you want them in class—and makeups stink—it really is better not to share some sick kid's streptococcus. In the long run, it's easier on you to administer a makeup spelling test the following week.
- If a student clearly exhibits signs of an infectious illness— such as a fever or weakness—send him or her to the school nurse/office for a parent to pick up. Day care centers don't allow infectious wee ones on the premises; you shouldn't, either.
- Keep germ-killing wipes, such as Clorox Clean-up or another disinfectant wipe, in your closet. Periodically wipe down your phone, staplers, pencil sharpeners, door handles, light switches, and even desktops with these antibacterial wipes.
- Take vitamin C supplements.
- Drink water throughout the day, everyday.

- Get plenty of rest. Sleep. We know—this advice is tough during your sleep-deprived first year, but if you don't rest, you're setting yourself up for an illness. So sleep, already!
- Incorporate exercise in your day. When your body is well tuned, it's more resistant to germ warfare.
- Get a flu shot.
- Finally, when you get sick, stay home. Don't pass on the virus or bug to your colleagues and students.

I'm Not Prepared

ILLNESS ISN'T the only reason you might experience an unplanned absence. Sometimes life or natural disaster intervenes, too. Nobody plans for their pipes to burst at 2 A.M. Sometimes tragedy strikes. A family member might fall ill, or require emergency surgery.

> *An understanding heart is everything in a teacher, and cannot be esteemed highly enough. One looks back with appreciation to the brilliant teachers, but with gratitude to those who touched our human feeling. The curriculum is so much necessary raw material, but warmth is the vital element for the growing plant and for the soul of the child.*
>
> CARL JUNG

The Bat Phone

Remember those cheesy episodes of *Batman* and the infamous phone that alerted our caped hero to the evil lurking within Gotham City? Most districts maintain an equivalent phone line with as much urgency attached to it as the Bat Phone. If your district or school site has not given you procedures for procuring a substitute, ask for them now.

Hotlines are available so teachers can call in case of an absence anytime before a certain morning cutoff hour—like 6:00 A.M.—to alert the school to find a substitute for your classes. In some cases,

Teacher's Rule

Keep at hand the procedures and the phone numbers of those you must contact in the event of an unplanned absence. Actually, we recommend keeping this information in several places—your classroom, your home, and your wallet or purse. You just never know what may happen (e.g., a broken-down car at the side of the road) or where you may need to access the substitute line or coordinator.

the system operates with a computer that actually phones those on a substitute list and alerts the substitute that a job is available that day. If your district doesn't have an automated absence hotline for teachers, a live person will work as an absence coordinator or substitute coordinator for the district. This individual then scrambles to find an available substitute before classes start that morning. You, on the other hand, may now go back to bed and begin your recovery!

Typically, the hotline recorder will ask you for the following information:

- The date of the absence
- The duration of the absence
- Your name
- Your school site
- The grade you teach
- Duties you have on this day
- Any special instructions (i.e., it's "Wear Red" Day)
- A number at which you may be reached during the day

Playing Hooky: The Planned Absence

SOMETIMES YOU know when you won't make it to class. You may be called to jury duty. You may need to go to the doctor for a procedure one afternoon. You may choose to take a "personal" day when your best friend comes to town. Whatever the reason, you know in advance an absence will occur. Again, your first step is notifying administration.

Once you notify administration, you'll need to prepare your lessons for the substitute. The best thing you can do is to make it as easy as possible on the person filling your shoes during the absence.

No More Lessons, No More Books— Only the Sub's Dirty Looks

So you've called the substitute line, and you're all snuggled into your blankets. Then suddenly, you spring out of bed, a mess of antihistamine and painkillers, and think, "How in the world is the substitute going to teach eighty-five minutes of social studies?"

It'll never happen, naturally, because you are going to provide the sub a complete lesson plan. Otherwise, you've doomed that poor teacher to an eternity of spit wads and sophomoric antics. (Heck, the poor substitute will probably endure ridicule regardless, but you lessen the students' opportunity for fun and games with a well-devised plan for the victim, er, um, substitute teacher.)

No problem. Just have the substitute use your lesson plans in your lesson plan book, right? Wrong! First, most teachers we know actually take that lesson plan book home each night. Your lessons

Making the Grade

Ever doubt how loved you are as the classroom teacher? Then pick up a copy of the children's book Miss Nelson Is Missing *by Harry Allard. When confronted with the antics of the mean substitute "witch" Miss Viola Swamp, the students in the book discover how much they miss their regular teacher. You, too, will probably be a bit surprised at the warm reaction of your students when you return from your first absence; they really will miss you and they'll be happy to see you're back.*

Making the Grade

In an article "Sick Kids, Sick Teachers" found on the American Diabetes Association's Web site, the author writes "Why is it that when fall and winter arrive, cold and flu viruses descend upon us with a vengeance? In my family, I've grown to expect that I will miss some work due to illness usually about three times during the fall and winter. . . . Classroom teachers are at greater risk from all of the viruses their students bring to school. As student enrollment drops during cold and flu season, so does teacher attendance." It's true. Just another reminder that you should plan on becoming ill your first year. If you do, then you won't fret (well, as much) while you're at home nursing that cold!

may well be with you. Do you want to run on over to the school and drop it off? Probably not. Also, typically, your scribbles may make no sense whatsoever to another teacher. Or, if the substitute can read your hieroglyphics, he or she probably won't know what to do with them or where to find the activities that correspond with the lesson.

Moreover, substitutes who aren't prepared can't be expected to, say, create quizzes and handouts on the fly, explicate highlighted passages from obscure novels, locate hidden transparencies, or explain the finer points of South American geography.

Not to worry. No one is to blame in an unplanned absence. The teacher can't foresee the attack of a microscopic germ. And substitutes know the job often requires ingenuity. But you could take steps in advance to help the substitute during your absence and to lessen the chances of your lesson plans going completely to the wayside during your illness. Here are just a few suggestions.

The Pretend-I'm-Still-Here Approach

Since your lesson plans should include the lesson's objective, student activities, and assessment information, then a substitute should be able to follow your lesson plan. If you have ever substituted yourself, or remember what it was like to have a substitute as a student, though, you know that it takes longer for a substitute to accomplish things! Bear this in mind!

First, make sure your lesson plans are complete—with dates, times, and duties clearly marked. You may want to highlight recess times and lunch times, and especially yard duty times.

Second, place your teacher's editions and student worksheets or materials in the order the substitute will need them (you could even put a divider or sticky note in between the subjects with the times written down as a reminder). If possible, have the students' opening activity on their desks.

Third, take the time to update your seating chart. This will allow the substitute to walk in and know the students' names right away. This is also the time to jot down the following routines:

Teacher's Rule

In real life, playing hooky from teaching is considered a serious breech of your professional duties. If you call in sick every other Friday and arrive on Monday with raccoon eyes from skiing all weekend, you'll find yourself in the unemployment line next term.

- **Opening procedure.** This includes how and where you greet the students, the opening activity for the students, how attendance and lunch count is taken, how homework is collected, who leads the "Pledge of Allegiance," how the calendar is done, and so forth.

- **Classroom procedures.** This explains how students' signal for help; when students can use the bathroom, sharpen their pencil, get a drink; how students' line up; classroom helpers; where/how work is collected; and how discipline is handled.

- **Transitions.** Transitions include what students do after recess, lunch, and at the end of the day.

- **Special subjects.** Because different students in the class will leave and return from class at different times and for different reasons, you need to note when, where, and who goes to band, chorus; procedures for the library and the computer lab.

- **Students with special needs.** A sub will need to know where and when students go to the Resource Room or go to the office for medication; what to do if problems arise; who to call for assistance.

- **Classroom assistance.** Explain when and how parents are used; name and assignments for instructional aide.

- **Completion of work.** A sub should have a back-up assignment and know what students can do when finished.

- **Dismissal procedure.** This topic includes who takes the bus, who walks home, and who gets picked up.

Teaching Terms

◆ ◆ ◆

Personal days. Many districts offer teachers in their contracts one or more days during the school year that they may take off for "personal" reasons, such as attending a wedding, going to the doctor, or sitting on the beach to clear one's mind. Contact your personnel department to see whether you are entitled to these personal days.

Type out these procedures on your computer so that you can update them as you change them. Take a look at a sample substitute lesson plan on the following two pages.

You'll notice that the teacher interspersed other supplemental activities into the lesson that did not depend on expertise in the analysis of the literature. Instead of discussing the chapters in the novel that the kids read and covering "themes" of the novel, the kids watched a fun video to reinforce the plot. Then the teacher gave a silent reading assignment—a contemporary article on a similar theme. In each activity, the substitute did not require knowledge of the novel to lead the lesson.

SAMPLE SUBSTITUTE LESSON PLAN

Teacher: Rominger
Room: 805
Date: November 11, 2000

Hello:

Thank you for substituting for me today. This class consists of a majority of boys; it can get rowdy at times. There are no discipline problems in the class—just a large group of fun-loving, silly boys who like to laugh *all the time*. Firmly keep them in line if they chatter. I send chatterboxes to the classroom time-out area for five to ten minutes.

I've attached a seating chart after this page. The names with an X are students who typically can get boisterous. I've also highlighted the names of two students whom you can depend on for help—Jeff Wu and Holland Dickinson. Both are exceptional students who keep track of the assignments and so forth. You can depend on both students if any problems arise.

During the first ten minutes of class, a video bulletin is broadcast into each room. When you enter the classroom, the television will be on your left side in the upper corner of the room. Turn it on to channel 21. The kids like the daily bulletin and should quietly watch it.

Once the bulletin ends, turn off the television and take roll. A roll sheet is also attached. Just mark an A by any absent students.

1. Each Monday, we begin the class by going over this week's spelling. The class received at the beginning of the year an assignment sheet listing all their spelling words by week of instruction. Ask the students to take out their spelling assignment sheet. I've included a copy of it for you to peruse before class begins and to use in class. Direct the class to review their third list of words. Read aloud each word, so the kids know how to pronounce them. Remind the class that their assignment

(listed on the sheet with directions) is due tomorrow at the beginning of class, and—as usual—the test will be on Friday.

2. Over the weekend for homework, the students were to read chapter 4 of *Charlotte's Web*. On my desk, you'll find a copy of the novel for your use as well as a quiz to give the students. The quiz is copied on yellow paper. Pass out the quiz. Read the directions on the top of the page, and allow thirty minutes for completion. No books open. No talking. They must answer in complete sentences on the quiz sheet proper. No loose binder paper. Collect the quiz as they finish. After everyone is done, advise the class that we will correct the quizzes together and discuss the responses in class tomorrow.

IF THE KIDS SEEM TO BE STUGGLING TO COMPLETE THE QUIZ, GIVE THEM 25 MINUTES TOTAL—NO MORE.

3. On my desk you will find a videotape; it is the animated story of *Charlotte's Web*. It's pretty funny. This should be a fun sojourn for the kids from the seriousness of the novel. Because this activity is intended for their pleasure and just to reinforce the plot of the story in a fun way, they need not take any notes on the video. Turn the television to channel 4 and put the tape in the VCR. It should automatically begin playing. Please rewind the tape and return to my desk at its conclusion. This video should take thirty minutes.

4. On my desk, you should also find a stack of light blue copies of an article entitled "Spiders. Why We Love Them." Give students the rest of the hour to read it silently. Ask the class to consider whether they agree with the article or disagree, as they may be required to write their response tomorrow.

If students say, "I'm all finished," before recess, tell them to review chapters 4 and 5 silently for discussion tomorrow in class.

Remind the kids to do their spelling assignment tonight. No reading in *Charlotte's Web* for homework tonight—hooray!

That's it for language arts—now on to math.

Tales from the Trenches

"One thing that has helped me with classroom management is a technique I learned called 'conducting.' Conducting means getting the rapt attention of everyone in the classroom before I speak. I compare my technique to that of a conductor. Mentally, I'm standing poised, arms in the air, and when I speak, it's the downbeat, and the concert—my lesson—begins. But there's dead silence in the room just before I speak.

"I sometimes see teachers who just launch into their lesson while the class is still chattering. No wonder students don't hear. The teacher is two or three minutes into the lesson before they even recognize that she's addressing them. To me, that practice is almost rude. You wouldn't walk into a room full of adults and just start talking in a loud voice. Kids should get the same courtesy. If they're not looking at you, ready to listen, there should be no words coming out of your mouth. (OK, perhaps you need to say a name or offer a quiet nudge, but mostly, they shouldn't ever get the idea that you don't mind being talked over.)"

Maya T., Baton Rouge, Louisiana

The Recon Marine Approach

Improvise, overcome, adapt—the credo of the elite United States Marine Recon units. Let us be the first to tell you: Teachers are tougher than Marines. So you can take these warring men's advice with no fear of failure. Here's what you do. Relay to the school secretary or substitute coordinator specific instructions for each class's lesson. Detail where your overhead transparencies are, whether you need copies made, and where the original may be. Do the best you can. Hope the substitute can follow your instructions per the lessons. And be prepared to reteach the next day.

Substitute Insurance— Emergency Plans

Emergency Plans are different from substitute plans in that they are generic in nature. To literally be used in an emergency, they must contain activities that the students can do without a lot of prior preparation because you don't know when or if you'll need these plans. It may take some time to put them together, but it will provide you with some peace of mind. You can purchase blank reproducibles on grammar, reading comprehension, phonics, math, and writing for your grade level. Invest! Then, choose one or two worksheets from each book and reproduce enough copies for your class. Your students won't be overly thrilled at the worksheets, but your substitute can maintain control, and your students will get practice in areas

Making the Grade

Give your substitute a professional boost by printing out the information at these great Web sites and storing it in a folder you maintain specifically for the benefit of your subs.

Substitute Teaching:
www.peaklearn.com/newteach /substitute8.html

Tips for Substitute Teachers:
www.geocities.com/Athens /8020/subtips.html

Substitute Teaching Tricks of the Trade:
www.qnet.com/~rsturgn

FROM THE DESK OF . . . "During my first year teaching, I, of course, came down with the worst version of the flu imaginable. I was out five days," recalls coauthor Lynne Rominger. "While I was gone, the kids had a substitute one day who left me a note in my box expressing his dissatisfaction with the class in general. 'Savages' may have been the word he used," she chuckles. "He then went on to describe how one student snuck up to the board and rewrote his name from 'Mr. Jarvinian' to 'Jar Jar Binks.' I know I shouldn't have, but I couldn't help but laugh at the creative use of language my students' employed," confesses Lynne.

appropriate for their grade level. Write the lesson plan with the substitute in mind—specifically, clearly, and in as much detail as possible. Think globally here. Big skills. The basics. These lessons will reinforce the more detailed lessons you normally produce. In some cases, you may want to prepare a lesson that addresses an exercise or activity related to a certain theme in your class. For example, let's say that in social studies you're teaching U.S. history. For the first two months of school, you focus on colonial America. Perhaps you can create a lesson, group project, game or story that deals with the Salem witch trials or the Puritans. The exercises you produce will simply supplement your "big plan."

Similarly, you can select items from your textbooks that you are probably not going to get to and build these into your emergency plans. Then, you can leave school each day knowing that your class is covered in case of an emergency.

To put some fun into the substitute's day, you can set aside some construction paper or grid paper for the students to use. Leave directions, such as giving the students thirty minutes of free drawing or time to make a new name tag, make a card for someone, or draw something related to what they are studying.

You can also spice up the day by leaving a game to play, such as "Multiplication Bingo" or "Brain Quest." The game should be one that is not played too often and can be played as a whole class.

Another way to add variety is to leave a book that lends itself to specific literature response activities. Here are some good examples:

Teaching Terms

• • •

Teacher's edition. With any class set of school curriculum such as textbooks, workbooks, anthologies, or novels, a teacher's edition will accompany them. This special edition has additional information that helps you teach that particular text. For example, it has answers to all the questions in the student's version of the text, additional questions to ask for comprehension, in-depth analysis, supplemental information, and a test with the test answers.

- *Brown Bear, Brown Bear, What Do You See?*, *Fortunately, Unfortunately,* where students can create their own books afterward.

- Shel Silverstein's books are fun to read and inspire easy-to-create activities afterward.

- Having students learn a new form of poetry is educational and interesting.

Here are a few other things you need to do to help your substitute:

- Provide the substitute with a seating chart. Mark on the chart those students who may prove disobedient or a challenge. Likewise, list the names of helpful students on which the substitute can depend.

- Provide the substitute with the names and extensions of the teachers in the room surrounding your room. In the case of an emergency, the substitute will know where to go and who can help.

• Provide the substitute with a detailed schedule. Break down the routine into the approximate number of minutes each activity will take. Include unusual items. For example, if the morning bulletin must be read during the first ten minutes of class, list that fact and give the sub a copy of the bulletin or instructions on where to procure the bulletin.

• Plan activities that do not require extensive knowledge or expertise in the discipline.

• Provide the substitute with teacher copies of all handouts and texts.

• Ask the substitute to provide you with a short note detailing how each class behaved and worked.

• Tell the substitute where to put any work accomplished in class (i.e., on your desk, in your in box).

Showtime

By far the easiest program for a sub to follow—the movie! When you find yourself sick in bed, scratch your planned lesson and supplement the unit with an appropriate video. As in the example given, if you're studying *Charlotte's Web* and happen to possess a copy of the animated film of the novel, ask the substitute to pop it in and let the kids relax and enjoy the literature on screen for a day.

The key to using a video successfully during your absence, however, is *not* using videos in your

Teacher's Rule

If a substitute shows a video to the class, advise the sub to have the kids take notes on the program. Tell the substitute you'll have students take a quiz the following day on the content of the tape. You need to hold students accountable during any film or video, so that they don't nod off and to reinforce the purpose for showing a videotape in the first place.

own instruction very often. In the circumstances of a substitute, a video can serve a greater purpose, reinforce your lesson, and give a break to the sub and kids.

On a final note, don't beat yourself up if you need to miss school a few days. During your first year, expect it. Administrators and your colleagues all know the deal.

Things to Remember

Are you convinced that you'll need a substitute by now? Our intention is not to scare you, but rather to make the process of preparing for a substitute less intimidating. Remember to do these things right away:

- ❏ Try to prevent illness as much as possible by taking a few, simple precautions
- ❏ Learn the logistics of calling in for a substitute
- ❏ In the case of a planned absence, set up for a substitute by writing in detail the procedures and routines you have established in your classroom, as well as specifics in each content area
- ❏ Write out Emergency Plans for the unplanned absence that not only include your procedures and routines, but also enough copies of generic activities for your class to do in case you are not able to be there

PART TWO

SETTING UP YOUR CLASSROOM

Your Home Away from Home— Your Classroom

THIS IS IT! You are now the king or queen of your own castle—your classroom! You walk in and see . . . nothing. Yep. Nothing. Your room—until you put your mark on it—is still *tabula rasa*. There are so many things to consider—everything from decorations to adding individuality to the seating arrangement of the class. Getting your room ready can take quite some time. Plan on spending the week before school opens to prepare your room. Right now, we'll walk you through some of the more important facets of preparing your room. Consider this chapter a "checklist" for setting up your classroom.

> *" His lack of education is more than compensated for by his keenly developed moral bankruptcy. "*
>
> WOODY ALLEN

Sit Your Backside Down!

YOU FINALLY made it into your classroom. Now what? The first area on which to focus is how you are going to arrange your students' desks. Your seating arrangement will depend on whether you have desks or tables and what grade you are teaching. Also, the suggestions given here are for the initial arrangement;

Teacher's Rule

Oh, sure! You'll provide your students with a seating arrangement, right? But then, a few weeks into the school year, you'll notice how noisy and boisterous some sets of those sitting near each other can be. Be thankful— you've now determined who you don't want sitting next to whom under any circumstances. Move them. Move them away from each other now and forever!

you will make many adjustments throughout the year as you get to know your students better.

Primary Seating Arrangements

If you have tables, then you will want to arrange them within easy accessibility to you and each other. No student should have a back to you when you are giving instructions.

Students will also need to have access to the *carpet area*. Not only will you assign students specific seats at the tables by having a name card on their desk on the first day of school; you should also put their names on pieces of tape and put it on the carpet where they will be sitting. Take control! As you get to know the students, you need to move them to the best spot for learning, maintaining equity among groups between boys and girls and also between students from various ethnic groups. You will know the names of your students from your class roster, which administration should provide you the week prior to class beginning. Though you may find you can tell the diversity of ethnicities from the names, you may not. You will probably want to consult with the school secretary or pull the *cuum files* on each child.

Once you arrange the tables, you will need to consider how to arrange your supplies for the kids. Since the students—in a table setting—don't have desks, they do not have a place to put their own supplies. You probably will ask parents to provide supplies for each child and then distribute the supplies between all the children as needed. If you are fortunate, your district and school site may provide enough supplies for your class. Regardless, you need an organizational system—and this system should be in place for textbooks, too.

With table seating, medium-sized containers placed on the tables for the kids to use together work really well. Place all the supplies the kids will use in your class—pencils, crayons, markers, glue, scissors, etc.—in each of the containers. Each container will then be placed on the table for the kids. Put this container in the middle of the table, and hold the students responsible for having all the crayons back in the box, no pencils on the floor, and all of the scissors back in the container. Whatever supplies you provide, the children need to understand how to take care of everything.

> # Teaching Terms
> ◆ ◆ ◆
>
> **Carpet area.** In elementary school classrooms, the teacher often gathers the students together and seats them in a circle or in front of her for instruction on a rug or carpet area. Especially in the lower grades, a carpet will be the center of instruction.
>
> ◆ ◆ ◆
>
> **Cuum file.** A cuum short for "cumulative) file or folder holds all the records and documentation for each child from the moment that child enrolls in school until the end of that child's school career. A teacher can find valuable information about a child from the cuum folder, which can greatly help the teacher plan lessons and seating arrangements — anything — that will better serve the child in the classroom.

Desk Arrangements

If you are teaching grades 3 through 6, your students probably will sit in individual desks. The best arrangement for your students at the beginning of the year is either in rows or in a horseshoe/double-horseshoe arrangement. (See appendices 1 and 2 for examples of these arrangements.) You want to know what's going on with your students at all times and you want them facing you. Less chance of spit wad production this way! In a few weeks, you'll know your students well enough to put them into groups.

When you do put them into groups, you need to decide whether they will be in groups at all times or work in groups at specific times only. If they are only in groups for certain portions of the school day, then have them in rows for the rest of the day. In this way, you can seat group members near each other, and then train them to move easily into their groups; it should take them less than a minute to get into formation. In fact, the kids will rise to the challenge if you time them as part of their training.

Relative to supplies, this may be a challenge for some of your students. Keeping their desk clean may be a struggle. If you give students their own pencils, crayons, rulers, scissors, calculators, textbooks, and folders, they are going to need help organizing their desks. Surprise desk checks can help, where you announce that 100 percent of neat desks will earn the class ten extra minutes at PE or art or listening to a favorite story—whatever incentive works! If a particular student's desk continues to be messy, the child can haul it out to the hall and clean it out at recess!

Making the Grade

Looking for more ideas for classroom organization and seating arrangements? You'll find research and tips galore at this Web site:

Classroom Arrangement: *www.peaklearn.com/newteach /arrangement.html*

Safe Haven: The Teacher's Desk

As IMPORTANT as the kids' space is your space. After all, you run the show each day, necessitating a nook and cranny to put things and organize your materials. Amazingly enough, as you diligently arrange the kids' seats, you may forget about your own desk. You need to factor in a place for your desk in the overall arrangement of your classroom. In actuality, you truly won't be spending much time at your desk during the teaching day (in fact, when you do sit at your desk, the students will act up, so you will be walking around and monitoring them a *lot*!). But you will spend time before and after school at your desk taking care of administrative paperwork and lesson planning.

So place your desk in an area that is not obtrusive to the students. Many teachers have their desks at the side of the classroom as opposed to the front of the class.

Besides choosing a location for your desk, you will need to have specific essential items in and on your desk. The following are "must-have" items:

In your desk:

- Scissors
- A ruler
- A set of markers for your use only
- Special art items: yarn, glitter, special glue
- Pens and pencils
- Sticky notes
- Note pad
- An eraser
- A container of liquid paper or white-out
- A hole punch
- Paper clips
- Bandages
- Change for the soda machine
- A drawer for file folders with a folder for each student (to use for student work, parent notes, etc.)
- Highlighter pens

FROM THE DESK OF . . . "The most fun part of teaching is simply listening to the things kids say. On the first day of school I was introducing the subject matter we'd be covering in American history. I asked the kids to think of how a knowledge of history could help people to get along better in life. One of the tough kids in class wasn't volunteering any answers, so I called on him to respond. As he sat up straight in his seat, some of his buddies began guffawing behind him. I ignored them and repeated the question. 'How do you use history to get along?' He turned around to his friends and said, without missing a beat, 'Knock off the laughing, or you're history.' "

Becka R., Mesa, Arizona

- Thumb tacks
- Tape: double-sided, masking, rolls of transparent tape for the dispenser
- Staples
- Thank-you notes
- A drawer for your personal items: purse/wallet, car keys, pocket mirror, snacks, and breath mints

On your desk:
- A stapler
- A tape dispenser
- Pens and pencils
- Paper clips
- Sticky notes
- Note pad
- A file box of 3-by-5 or 4-by-6 cards with students' names and parents' phone numbers

- A stacking letter tray to put things that need to be copied
- A stacking letter tray of things that need to go to and from the office
- A small container where students can put absent notes, notes from parents
- A box of tissues
- A specific spot for your keys, yard duty whistle, and sunglasses

Extra! Extra! Hey, Look at the Headlines

OKAY, so you have both your desk and your students' desks situated. Now, it's time to look around you, survey the classroom, and begin decorating. An integral part of the elementary school class is, of course, the bulletin board. Don't you remember those teachers whose rooms always contained the best bulletin boards—all themed for the seasons, colorful, and interesting? Those great boards did not miraculously appear. Preparation went into all of them.

As you figure out what to include on your bulletin board, you can begin the process toward super-duper boards with the basics of set up. First, you'll need some butcher paper to cover the background. You may want to cover the area with different layers: one color for each grading period, for example. Then, you can just take the butcher paper off layer by layer; in other words, you do all the work up front and save time later.

Making the Grade

Need ideas for a classroom bulletin board? Here are some winners:

Bulletin Board Ideas:
www.perpetualpreschool.com /bboardideas.html—You'll find many cool ideas for bulletin boards—everything from holiday themes to class specific ideas. Check it out if you need some creative fuel to get you started.

Next, select a border to staple around the bulletin board. Your school probably has many different colors to choose from; if you want to spend some of your PTA money, the local teacher's supply store or on-line supply site will have many different (and cute!) borders to choose from as well.

Now it's time to decide what *type* of bulletin boards you want. Bulletin boards can serve different functions: (1) to provide information, (2) to display student work, or (3) to provide interaction with the class and its lessons. It is best to include a combination of all of these ideas in your classroom. Generally speaking, try to maintain a bulletin board for language arts, math, history, and science, thereby covering the major curriculum areas. Your other boards may serve as focal points for everything from seasons to pictures of the children. You decide.

Once you have decided which type of bulletin board to design, think of a title for it. Let the creative juices flow. Imagine yourself an editor of a newspaper and let the headlines happen. Get creative! If you have access to an Ellison lettering machine, cut out the title letters and staple or pin them up. If you don't have access to a lettering machine, write the title of the bulletin board on a sentence strip or a strip of construction paper.

Good material for informational bulletin boards? The multiplication tables, rules of division, the stages of the writing process, types of poetry, vocabulary words, and science facts. You will want students to be able to refer to this important information during the course of a unit.

Student work is also a great way to use a bulletin board. Let's look at an example of how you might integrate student work into a lesson-oriented bulletin board. If you are reading a particular literature book, for example, you can display an art project that relates to the book. Have students draw scenes from the book and write a description of the scene. Have students create a jacket for the book.

> ## Teacher's Rule
>
> *Don't get overly fond of your creation. Destructive children will pull apart your boards when you are occupied. To counteract this, assign a student to help you keep bulletin boards looking sharp.*

In math, if you have done a cooperative math project, you can post visual displays of numbers or art that relates to math such as tessalations. In history, you could display art projects for a particular period of study—written descriptions of events, map renderings of the area of study, or drawings of period clothing. Finally, in science, try displaying drawings of the subject being studied, synopses of experiments, or definitions of facts with student-drawn pictures.

Beyond subject area and student art boards, you may consider making interactive bulletin boards in your classroom. These boards are meant for students to use to reinforce skills in the areas being studied. They incorporate information that the student can use as an activity. For example, if you are studying homophones, you might post several pairs on one side, and the student must choose the corresponding homophone and place it on the bulletin board. Students can then check an answer key to see whether they answered correctly.

All of these bulletin boards provide the students with additional opportunities to learn or to receive necessary information. Bulletin boards should be changed regularly but don't change them all at the same time. They'll naturally stagger if you time them to correspond with the end of various units.

Finally, another bulletin board to consider is a "Best Work" bulletin board. The background and lettering stays the same all year, but the work changes as often as the student wants it to. To save some time, let the students choose the background color of a 9-by-12 piece of construction paper, and put it up so that work can be mounted on top of the construction paper.

Wide Open Spaces for Art and More

Although you may display student work on bulletin boards, you won't want to limit the display only to bulletin boards. As part of your room preparation, you'll want to devote space for future work. This may mean that you have little up and around your room the first few weeks. But slowly, consistently, you'll find you need more space to post student projects. Art projects, for example, may proliferate all around the room. You may choose to post spelling tests and quizzes in a ladder fashion on the backs of doors or on the sides of cabinets. Another great idea and wall space saver? A laundry line strewn from end to end with student work hung from it by clothespins. Not even the ceiling is immune from the ingenuity of elementary school teachers. Try using bent paperclips and yarn to hang student work from the ceiling. These are just some of the ways to enliven and enrich your classroom!

Code Red Information

Not necessarily a bulletin board, but a space does need to be devoted for important information. Here, you should post the monthly lunch

Tales from the Trenches

"I have discovered over the years that there is no technique that always works. What was magic last week is boring this week. To that end, I frequently change the environment by rearranging furniture, updating the materials I place on my walls, and completely changing the look and feel of my classroom. Sometimes I arrange desks in concentric circles. Another week, I might create seating groups. Another week, we might have rows. Another week, it's a horseshoe. Sometimes we push the desks against the walls, and I have all the kids on the floor or in chairs without desks. And of course, I change my teaching to fit the arrangement. In traditional rows, I'm sitting on the edge of my desk with a book. In a circular arrangement, I'm teaching 'in the round,' and it's a high-drama week. When the kids are seated in work groups, we do lots of small-group activities. Sometimes we simply stand up and do class SRO (standing room only). Ever since I gave up the 'nailed-to-the-floor' mindset, teaching—and learning—has been exciting for all of us."

Genna R., Phoenix, Arizona

Teacher's Rule

When hanging posters or prints in your room that pertain to your personal likes, practice caution. Avoid any pictures with an overtly sexual or violent connotation. Don't post that Carmen Electra poster, for example, in the fifth-grade classroom—or any room, for that matter. Keep the Dennis-Rodman-in-drag print out of the classroom. No matter how much you love the adult world, you don't work in it. You work with sensitive children whose parents don't want Johnny or Janie exposed to certain things.

calendar, the daily or weekly school bulletin, the daily class schedule, due dates for major assignments, major events that are coming up, nightly or weekly homework, copies of your class newsletter, and copies of the school newsletter.

Getting to Know Me, Getting to Know All about Me!

Part of decorating your room includes putting your personality into it and making your classroom your home away from home. Bring a plant from your house and place it on your desk. Pick out some pictures of your family and either frame them for your desk or post them on a bulletin board. Situate items relating to you—such as an inexpensive decorative box or a miniature sculpture related to a hobby—on your desk. If you have some space behind your desk on the wall, put up a print you like—something related to your hobbies. If you dance, find a cool picture of dancers. If you rock climb, get a rock-climbing poster. Tack them up and show them off. The kids will appreciate knowing a little bit more about you than your last name. You'll help them connect to you better if you share a small part of yourself.

File This

As YOU begin your career as a teacher, you will be inundated with ideas, copies of lesson plans, bulletin board ideas, and samples of art projects—to name just a few things. You may even have some items in storage from your student teaching days.

To maximize your time and efficiency, we recommend setting up your files by

- month
- school information
- district information
- curriculum areas
- classroom management ideas
- instructional strategies
- assessment ideas

Monthly Files

Label file folders by month, starting with the first month of the school year. As you progress month to month, keep copies of the activities you did in the corresponding folder. You'll pat yourself on the back the next year when you need only pull a file to begin all your planning! Likewise, when you find suggestions on activities or lesson plans relating to holidays or themes, such as starting or finishing the school year, you can put them in the monthly folder that corresponds to the theme. The next year, when you pull the February file, for example, you may find a really cool bulletin-board idea that you didn't have time to use the year prior!

School Information

A general file for school information will be useful to file information that comes from the principal. Any information that involves dates should go into your lesson plan book, and then the back-up information could go into this general file.

District Information

As with "School Information," memos or directives from the district office with dates on them should go into your lesson plan book. Additional information, though, should go in this file. This file might include information on benefits, staff development offerings, or testing as well as copies of everything you send to the district office.

Curriculum Areas

Start file folders with the following headings:

- Math
- Problem solving
- Reading comprehension
- Vocabulary
- Literature book by title
- Spelling
- Writing
- Speaking
- Listening
- Handwriting
- Art
- Music
- PE
- Social studies by topic
- Geography
- Science by topic

Then as you create handouts and project ideas, you can file them away neatly for use over and over again.

Classroom Management Ideas

Start a general file folder for classroom management. You may read an article with suggestions on how to use students as helpers in the classroom, or you might take notes on how another teacher distributes and collects assignments. Put these in your file and refer to them when you are ready to make a change in your own classroom.

Instructional Strategies

" Education is a progressive discovery of our own ignorance. "

WILL DURANT

As with classroom management, you will come across a variety of ideas for instructional strategies. Put them in one file so you can access them when you are searching for a particular strategy or want to try something new. This will include cooperative learning strategies, use of computers, grouping strategies, and brain-based learning to name a few. Often, your district or school site will provide seminars or workshops on instructional strategies. You will already have a handy file to put the useful information safely away and accessible.

Assessment Ideas

At times, you will expand your repertoire to include a range of assessment strategies besides tests and quizzes. You may observe a particular assessment being utilized, such as a rubric or a portfolio, or come across different types of assessments in journal articles. Keep them together in one place!

Feels Like Home

Now, YOUR classroom is ready. You've organized your desks, gathered your supplies, planned your boards, decorated your walls, implemented a file system, and integrated a little bit of your own personality. Get ready to welcome your class to their new home for the year!

Things to Remember

You will spend a lot of time in your classroom the first year, so making it organized, efficient, stimulating and homey are practical suggestions. Remember to do the following:

❑ Arrange your seats in rows or a double horseshoe at first until you know the students well enough to group them and consider how the students will keep track of their supplies

❑ Put your desk in an accessible area with essential supplies for quick and easy use

❑ Create bulletin boards for each major curriculum area, as well as one for "Best Work"

❑ Set up files now so that you can add to them as the year progresses

Gathering Materials

BEG, BORROW, AND STEAL

IMAGINE, IF YOU WILL, the following scenario: The supply room at your school is set up on a first-come, first-served basis. Four times a year, the shelves are stocked with everything that makes up a teacher's fantasy: bundles of construction paper, stacks of transparent tape rolls, reams of binder paper, boxes of scissors, dry erase pens in every color of the rainbow, new erasers, endless boxes of number two pencils, glue sticks, and even some boxes of colored pens and pencils. You have the arrival dates marked on your calendar, and you even know the approximate time of delivery. On the blessed day, you recruit two of you strongest students, dress in fatigues, and prepare to enter the gold mine. You sneak in the back door with students in tow. You're in luck! No other teachers have beaten you to the fortune. You begin flinging cabinet doors open, grabbing handfuls of supplies, emptying them into boxes that your students are holding, and work your way around the room like Dr. Seuss's Grinch, leaving "a crumb much too small for the little Who mouse." When the boxes are full to the brim and your students are sweating under their weight, you usher them out of the office and back to the classroom where you revel in your success. Quickly you store your boxes away under lock and key. After all, you never know when someone might come searching through your cupboards!

Sometimes you may feel that this is the only way to get supplies. Actually, there is a better way. Although you will probably spend some of your own money on supplies, consider the sections of this chapter to maximize your spending.

Budgets

BEFORE YOU start gathering materials, do some investigating as to the budget you have available. Check with your principal to see how much money you are allocated for supplies from the school and the district. Also ask the principal whether or not the Parent-Teacher Association allocates money for teaching supplies and, if so, how you go about accessing it. If your state has a lottery and some of that money goes to education, you need to find out how much, if any, you receive. Sometimes that money is divided equally among teachers; other times, the administration determines how best to use the money. Either way, it can't hurt to ask.

When searching for monies from which to purchase supplies, you will become very resourceful. There is often quite a bit; you just need to know where to go and who to ask. Whatever you do, don't automatically shrug your shoulders and say, "Oh, well, if there's no money I guess I'll have to buy this out of my own pocket." That is a last resort, so exhaust all other possibilities first.

> " *Next in importance to freedom and justice is popular education, without which neither freedom nor justice can be permanently maintained.* "
>
> JAMES A. GARFIELD

Teaching Supplies

YOU WILL need certain items to run an effective classroom. These will most likely be found in a central supply room, and you'll need to find out from your principal how these items are accessed. Some schools have an "open supply room," meaning that you can get items as you need them, while those operating with a "closed supply room" mean that you must check out the supplies when you take them. Still other schools require you to order supplies from a person at the site (either a secretary or a custodian) or from a location at the district office. Find out how you go about getting teaching supplies, and use the following guidelines as a starting point.

Sit down and think about your needs. This will help you save time and gather what you need without leaving anything behind. As you make your wish list, think about these points:

• The ways in which you will pass on information to your students. You will probably use the chalkboard or whiteboard and the overhead projector frequently, so make sure you stock up on supplies for that.

• The materials your students will need to complete the activities you assign

• Supplies for your personal use. You need to have everything that teachers need for their desks, for correcting, or for instructing.

• Educational texts and supplements

So, once you have brainstormed all the materials you will need for these four classroom categories, you can begin collecting and gathering.

Supply List

First, depending on whether you have dry erase boards or chalkboards, you will need markers or

---

Making the Grade

Report Card
A
A
A
A

Want free stuff for your classroom? RHL School has what you're looking for. At this site you'll find links to more than thirty resources for free teaching materials.

RHL School: *www.rhlschool .com/free/freelinks.htm*

Teacher's Rule

Put your name in indelible ink in every book you bring to school. Most teachers do purchase their own reference materials and keep them in the classroom. Unfortunately, any number of well-meaning people may borrow your books. You'll stand a better chance of recovering a lost book, video, or other high-demand item if you take the time to mark it up with your John Hancock, as well as setting up a notebook denoting who borrowed any of your supplies and when.

chalk. In addition, you will need corresponding erasers or board cleaners. One set of supplies that is not necessary but is very helpful is different-colored markers or colored chalk.

The overhead projector is a teaching tool that will become your best friend. Be sure you have plenty of different-colored overhead projector pens on hand, and devote a used washcloth to use for quick cleaning. Bring in a spray bottle filled with water to keep on the overhead projector stand. You can also use transparencies for something that you have prepared ahead of time and want to print out and put up on the overhead. Various types of transparencies are available, so be sure you are getting what you need. Some can be used in printers attached to your personal computer so your document will print straight onto the transparency instead of paper. Other types go through copy machines because they can withstand the heat without melting.

You will need many different kinds of paper. The furniture in your room will determine where you store the paper, but here are the types of paper you will need:

Construction paper. Get colors of all type in both 9 by 12 and 12 by 18; get extra sets of white as you'll use it most often for drawing.

Writing paper. Get appropriate writing paper for the age of your students (i.e., binder paper for fourth through sixth graders).

Newsprint. This paper has a special feel to it and is much less expensive than binder paper. It is often in abundance in supply rooms! Use it for spelling tests, scratch paper, drawings, and work that will be ungraded.

Miscellaneous paper. Tag board and chart paper are nice to have on hand, but they are expensive. You may need to get these as you need them from the supply room.

You will need many different kinds of containers in your classroom. Put that school budget and/or PTA budget to good use! You will need:

- **plastic boxes** with lids for student supplies
- **letter trays** to collect homework and assignments

Teacher's Rule

Stay organized! Make sure that you have designated areas for each of your supplies. If you don't, you will find that they disappear very quickly, and you are unlikely to get new ones. Being organized also helps your students and reduces transition time because they know exactly where to go to get what they need and where it all should be put back. This rule also allows you to quickly check to see that everything's been returned, so you can move on with the next lesson.

- **small jars** to hold pencils, pens, markers, overhead pens
- **file boxes** or plastic tubs to hold teacher's editions and instructional materials
- **a large tub** for PE equipment
- **a basket** for lunch boxes
- **a tape recorder** or a CD player. Some schools provide each classroom with one, but you may need to bring one from home (especially if you do not have an adopted music program)

Teaching Terms

◆ ◆ ◆

Textbook adoption. When companies come up with new educational materials, they need schools to try it out to determine whether it is useful material. When a school or district tries something new, it is called piloting a product. When that product has proven to be beneficial and the school or district has decided to keep using that product in all classrooms, the product has been adopted. Adoption also depends on the funding cycle of your district.

Teacher's Editions and Textbooks

Now THAT you have gathered everything you need for your students to work comfortably and enjoyably, it is time for you to gather together what *you* need to be a successful teacher and to make your days at work as problem-free as possible.

Districts go through cycles of *textbook adoptions*. When districts adopt a particular program, they have options as to the components they purchase. Use the following as a checklist to make sure all of the subjects are covered and that you ask about the additional resources mentioned:

Mathematics. A teacher's edition and resource books that may include *blackline masters* for remediation, enrichment, homework, and practice.

Language arts. A teacher's edition and resources that may include extra writing, handwriting, listening, and speaking practice for remediation and enrichment.

Reading. If your district uses a *basal reader*, then you will have a teacher's edition, resources to use for homework, extra practice, enrichment, a master skills book, and literature enhancement activities.

Spelling. You will have a teacher's edition, and perhaps a binder with additional resources.

Social studies. Not only will you have a teacher's edition, but you should have a resource book for extended map and writing activities, chapter reviews for students, and tests to copy.

Science. Depending on the program your school has adopted, you will probably have a teacher's edition and some type of student-response journals, or you may have kits with necessary resource materials.

Teaching Terms

◆ ◆ ◆

Blackline masters. Pages of teacher resources that are reproducible. This means that they are on white paper with black ink only so copies made from it are the highest quality possible. These masters are also called originals.

◆ ◆ ◆

Remediation. A teaching strategy. If a student is having great difficulty learning a particular subject, the teacher may be forced to remediate—in other words, to break down the parts of the lesson even further, reteach them, model them, and review them until the student understands.

All of these subject areas will most likely have student textbooks of some sort. You just need to get your hands on them! As with supplies, check with the principal or vice principal on how to order textbooks and other resources. Unfortunately, you may be told to "deal with" not having enough textbooks; if that is the case, you will need to adjust your instructional strategies. You could use partners for most subject areas and incorporate cooperative learning and centers with other subjects. You will have to be creative; here are some ideas to help you:

> ## Teaching Terms
>
> ◆ ◆ ◆
>
> **Basal reader.** A textbook that's developed as part of a reading program. Contains stories, readings, quizzes, explanations, and assignments chosen to teach different aspects of literature. The teachers' guide has the same pages reproduced in smaller size, with supplements and suggestions for ways to teach the material.
>
> ◆ ◆ ◆
>
> **Student response journals.** Often, the best way to assess learning is to find out what the students observed and what they thought or how they felt about a particular piece of knowledge. The journals allow students to give their own unstructured feedback about a particular lesson. You may supply the facts or information that you would like them to respond to; then they express, in an informal writing style, their questions, concerns, thoughts, or feelings about what they learned.

Share. If you don't have enough texts for every student, use one text for every two students. They can share by sitting side by side and both reading the same page. You could also have them share by assigning a particular part to read. Have one read while the other listens and then switch.

Rotate. If you have a limited number of history books and reading books, you can split up the class and have half working on history while the other half uses the reading books. This is difficult because you can't be in two places at once. If you have a teacher's aide or parent involved in your classroom, you could certainly use the second pair of eyes.

Copy. Depending on your access to copies, you could make enough copies of the portion of the book or text that you needed to complete the class set. You may not be allowed to do this; however, look into it. It could save you some grief.

Do a lesson/practice trade-off. Half the class can be using the texts while the other half practices what they learned. They could trade after the lesson and practice are done.

Student Supplies

BESIDES TEXTBOOKS, your students will need some basic supplies. Schools in most areas of the country require parents to purchase certain supplies for their children. Your school may set an upper limit—say, $25—on the amount of money you can expect parents to pay toward their children's school supplies.

Some districts require parents to purchase generic supply packets that include items as diverse as pencils and PE uniforms. Children whose families qualify for free or reduced-price lunches may receive financial assistance from community organizations or from the school itself to purchase required items.

Or you may be in a very affluent—or a very poor—district that simply provides students with necessary school supplies, *gratis*. In any event, you must consider a few management aspects.

Sharp as a Tack

When will the students sharpen their pencils? Some teachers allow them to sharpen their pencils at certain times, such as right before and after recess, or before and after school. Other teachers keep a container of sharpened pencils that they sharpen

> ## Teaching Terms
> • • •
>
> **Surprise desk inspection.** Because students need to learn to organize their schoolwork, you will want to require them to keep their desks in an orderly manner. You may even give a separate grade for organization. To ensure that they keep organized, you will inspect their desks without forewarning. This is a surprise desk inspection.

themselves—students put their dull pencil in a separate container and take a sharpened pencil. How will you handle this when it comes up?

Lost and Found

You may choose simply to keep a container for "found" supplies. Ask willing parents to *donate* a plastic milk jug full of spare stationery supplies—crayons, pencils, rulers, erasers, glue sticks, calculators, or anything else they find lying about the house—at the beginning of each term. Add in supplies found when desks are cleaned out at the end of each teaching term, and simply whenever you stumble across dropped pencils or rulers. After your *surprise desk inspections*, you will have a lot of supplies in these containers!

Name That Bag

Ask parents to mark their children's personal supplies, book bags, boxes, and binders with a permanent marker. This practice will eliminate some confusion and avoid some potential arguments.

Teacher Supply Stores

YOU WILL need to take a trip to the teacher supply store if, for example, you discover that there are gaps in the district's curriculum that you are seeking to fill. But beware: Going into a teacher supply store can be a dangerous endeavor! You'll feel like a child in a candy store. You see cute stickers to the left, colorful posters to the right, wonderfully creative workbooks ahead, and interesting story time books behind the cash register. Every aisle holds something you know your students would love or you would love to give them or use in your classroom. If you're not careful, you could end up spending a couple hundred dollars on fantastic educational tools, supplies, and decorations that you really don't need. Have a list of what you intend to buy before you go in, if you are easily sidetracked.

If you need to supplement your supplies in the areas of art, music, and PE—the areas in which you will be most tempted to supplement out of your own pocket—you should look for these kinds of materials:

Art. Either choose "how-to" books surrounding the holidays or books that relate to the social studies topics you are studying. Make sure the materials that are suggested are either readily available or cheap and easy to find.

Music. If your district does not have a specialized music program, choose a tape or CD that has patriotic songs and the words to go with them. Write the words out on transparencies that you can put up every day until the students have memorized them. Play a song a day and stop the tape or CD when finished (and keep the transparencies in order—this is an easy way to be ready for the next day). If your district requires that you assign a grade for music participation, keep a class roster on a clipboard and write a "+," "/," or "−" depending on whether the students sing or do not sing.

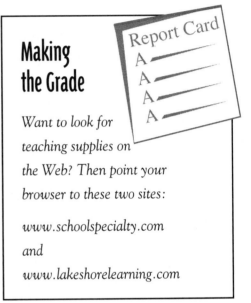

Making the Grade

Want to look for teaching supplies on the Web? Then point your browser to these two sites:

www.schoolspecialty.com and www.lakeshorelearning.com

PE. As with music, if you do not have resources, then you are going to need to get creative. Before purchasing any materials, check the Internet for rules of games you want to play. At the teacher's supply store, you may want to purchase books that have rainy-day games or any special PE activities.

The teacher supply store has much more to offer. Visit one for ideas and materials for decorating your classroom, too. You can purchase posters with the rules of the scientific method, the words to the Pledge of Allegiance, the days of the week, or just about anything! Be selective. Take a notepad and write down the ideas you see. It basically comes down to money versus time. You could probably make all of the posters yourself, but it might be worth it to spend $2.95 on a poster of the Declaration of Independence. Purchasing a manuscript or cursive alphabet train is also a worthwhile purchase.

In addition to decorations, you may also want to supplement your lessons. Teacher supply stores have plenty of ideas. Along with posters, the teacher supply store has instructional materials such as games and kits relating to various content areas, as well as resource books on specific subjects. Examples of kits include Egyptian stamping and scientific inquiry kits. Examples of especially useful resource books are writing prompts from ancient China, Egypt, or medieval times; books that teach types of poetry; books that integrate curriculum areas; and blackline masters of designs your students can use on rainy days.

Gathering your materials can be a very time-consuming task, so give yourself enough time to collect student supplies, teacher supplies, decorations, organizers and educational materials. Do what it takes to find the money or resources to purchase all the items you need. Then relax. Buying everything is the fun part!

Teacher's Rule

Art, music, and PE are often troublesome spots for elementary teachers. These are great subject areas for teaming up with your fellow teachers, if your principal allows this. You can each take one subject, combine two classes, and the third teacher gets a prep period.

Things to Remember

To maximize your time and energy, remember the following things:

❏ Check out the procedures for accessing supplies from your central supply room and/or your PTA before you purchase things on your own

❏ Make sure you have the necessary teacher's editions, student texts and additional resources for each curriculum area

❏ Obtain basic supplies for your students and establish a routine for keeping track of them

❏ Enter the teacher supply store with caution

PART THREE

EFFECTIVE LESSON PLANNING

Organizing the Curriculum

Curriculum—wondering where to start? It can be overwhelming. Some schools outline the skills and concepts you're expected to cover and to deliver to the students, but they leave it up to you to decide how you'll make it happen. Some schools deliver the curriculum in a set package, with lots of information and support. In these schools, all teachers in a given grade level follow the same program—same topics at the same time.

Either way, you will still need to plan your lessons and have a firm understanding of the dictates of your curriculum. Help is on the way!

> *" Books are the quietest and most constant of friends; they are the most accessible and wisest of counselors, and the most patient of teachers."*
>
> Charles W. Eliot

Consider This First: The Calendar

When you sit down at your orientation, your school administrators will provide you with a calendar of the entire year. Depending on the school, the calendar may follow any of several schemes: traditional calendar, single-track calendar, or multitrack calendar. The first

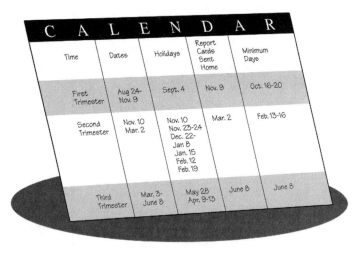

				Report Cards Sent Home	Minimum Days
Time	**Dates**	**Holidays**			
First Trimester	Aug 24– Nov. 9	Sept. 4	Nov. 9	Oct. 16–20	
Second Trimester	Nov. 10 Mar. 2	Nov. 10 Nov. 23–24 Dec. 22– Jan 8 Jan. 15 Feb. 12 Feb. 19	Mar. 2	Feb. 13–16	
Third Trimester	Mar. 3– June 8	May 28 Apr. 9–13	June 8	June 8	

thing to consider then, as you organize the curriculum, is your school calendar.

Your calendar and reporting periods will determine how you organize the curriculum for your students. You need to think about the breaks and how they affect the learning in your classroom. You don't, for example, want to start a thematic unit on photosynthesis a day before the kids go on a break for four weeks! Everything they learn in that one day will be lost over the vacation, forcing you to completely reteach the material.

Teaching Terms

◆ ◆ ◆

Curriculum. A specified course of study. In your situation, the curriculum is what your district, state, and school require you to teach the kids in your classroom, modified by your own creativity and approach to teaching.

Traditional

If you are on a traditional calendar, you typically begin in late August or, even more traditionally, after Labor Day. Your students will be in session full-time until Thanksgiving vacation—now almost a week in many districts. Back in school a few more weeks and the kids are off again for winter break—about two weeks in December. The next big break occurs in the spring. Finally, in June, the students are released for a long summer vacation. These significant breaks influence the way you teach, particularly at the beginning of the year, when you may need to review concepts and teach procedures and routines that will have been forgotten over long summer days languishing by the pool or playing at camp.

Single-Track Year-Round

The single-track year-round calendar means that the entire school is on the same schedule, as with the traditional calendar, but the vacations are arranged differently. Typically, this calendar will start in late July or early August, and instead of having two weeks in December, you may get three weeks of vacation or more. Similarly, instead of having a week off in the spring, you will have two or three. Then, instead of a twelve-week summer vacation, you will have perhaps eight weeks. In addition, students may be offered an intersession for either *remediation* or enrichment. Thus, you still teach the same number of days, and you still have the same number of days off, but the periods of teaching and vacation are different.

Multitrack Year-Round

This schedule allows a school to house more students than it can actually hold, without having the fire chief banging down the door. How? The teachers and students rotate—each operating on a

> ## Teacher's Rule
>
> *In the olden days, schools took their "Christmas break" during December. But today, in a culturally diverse society that observes Hanukkah, Solstice, and Kwanzaa during the same month, the more politically correct term "winter break" has replaced the old terminology.*

Teaching Terms

◆ ◆ ◆

Intersession. Sometimes schools offer remediation classes to students during times of the year when the session is on a break. These sessions are called intersessions. In the summer, you may know intersession by the name "summer school."

track-specific calendar. Students and teachers still attend school for the specified number of days, but each "track" has its own calendar. If you find yourself "tracking" as a first year teacher, you'll need to understand when the engine, if you will, gets on and off the track—and whether you need to change classrooms every twelve weeks.

A multitrack year will affect the way you organize your curriculum, as well as the way you organize your classroom. With this system, you will work in constant flux—almost like a professor who never knows where the university classes will land! But take heart: The kids who move in a multitrack school grow accustomed to the changes. You'll just need to be keenly aware of the big breaks and possibly reteach upon students' return.

ABC . . . and D and F, Too

YES, EVEN in elementary school grades do count. In many places, parental requirements for accountability have lead to the elimination of S for satisfactory and U for unsatisfactory. More and more, elementary classes use standard grading—A, B, C, D, and F—to report students' progress.

Grading periods—sometimes called *marking periods*—are the single most significant factor in determining how you'll organize your curriculum. If, for example, your school operates on twelve-week grading periods—or trimesters, as they are called—then you might organize your curriculum into corresponding twelve-week blocks. Make sure that your units finish prior to the end of a grading period—and usually within days so you have time to finish grading everything and calculating the grades for the report card.

Oh, No! The Report Card Is in the Mail

BESIDES THE calendar and the report periods, it is also important to consider the actual report card that you will be using to evaluate your students. Some report cards are very detailed; they include not only a space for a letter grade in reading, for example, but also places for progress to be indicated in areas such as "reading comprehension," "vocabulary," or "ability to read aloud." It is essential to look at the report card early on, so you can organize the curriculum to match the report card and start assessing the students in these specific areas of the subject matter. This way, you won't be surprised several weeks into the school year when it comes time to fill out your first set of report cards.

Teacher's Rule

If you hear nothing about curriculum, ask. Don't take it for granted that you can just soar through the year doing what you want, when you want. Remind someone that you need the curriculum.

District or State-Mandated Curriculum

SOME DISTRICTS are very clear about the curriculum for each grade level; some districts are not. If your district has clearly outlined what you need to teach and when, then ask for these materials and follow the plan. Ask for items entitled "content standards," "educational standards," "district curriculum expectations," or "grade-level expectations."

Because curriculum changes from year to year, consider making overhead transparencies so that you can briefly explain the updates to parents at Back-to-School Night.

Exit Skills

If your state, district or school is focused on prescriptive *exit skills*, rather than curriculum expectations, you may find that you'll need to "check off" which students have mastered the skills in certain grading periods. These skills may seem basic, but they do, at least, provide you with a starting point.

> ## Teaching Terms
>
> ◆ ◆ ◆
>
> **Exit skills.** The list of skills or specific learning objectives a student is required to master before moving on to the next grade level.

Brain Drain

CURRENT BRAIN research indicates that humans learn better when information is integrated and patterns can be formed. It is for this reason that "integrated thematic units" were created. Integration of curriculum makes sense for a variety of reasons:

1. There is too much curriculum to cover.
2. You have your students for large blocks of time and so are able to correlate lessons.
3. It aligns with the way the brain processes information.

Unit studies involve organizing the curriculum around certain themes. The best way to approach a thematic unit is to work around your social studies curriculum. Organize the social studies curriculum into three or four sections, depending on the number of reporting periods in your district. Then, choose the major concept to be studied within that grading period. Once you've decided on a theme—South America, for example, or the Civil War—you can then organize the other content areas around this concept: literature books, writing prompts, certain science activities, art projects, and music and games of the period can all be chosen to amplify the same theme. Even field trips can be arranged to support the topic. Thus, by choosing a theme, you can tie concepts together and make learning more cohesive and meaningful to the students. Believe it! Their brains will actually process the information better because every subject creates a bridge to and from the other subjects.

We Gotta Get Out of This Place

Do you remember the joy of field trips? Ah, yes you do! Coauthor Lynne Rominger still remembers the excursion her son's first grade class took to a wetland and all the cool birds and plant life the scientist showed off. He pulled cool things out of jars and pointed out interesting birds in the sky. What a day! For many reasons—including to relieve the drudgery of the classroom for you and your students—field trips need to be part of your curriculum. Field trips are a great way to wrap up and reinforce key ideas within a thematic unit.

Making the Grade

Need a quick copy of your state's curriculum standards? It's all on-line, for free, at this Web site:

Developing Educational Standards:
www.PutnamValleySchools.org /Standards.html

As with district expectations, some districts have outlined which grade levels go to which locations during a field trip. Your district may send all sixth graders to environmental camp for a week, for example. Mandated field trips can be very specific and leave little room for teacher creativity. At other times, though, you'll be allowed to decide where you want to go, when you want to go—so long as the funds for the event are available and it relates to an instructional goal. Here are some suggestions for successful field trips:

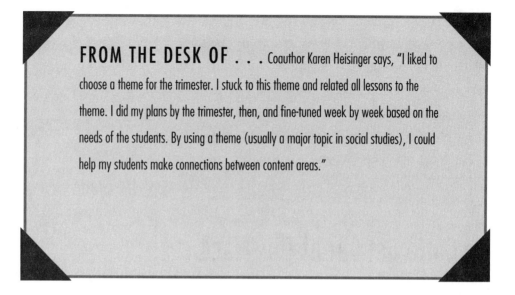

FROM THE DESK OF . . . Coauthor Karen Heisinger says, "I liked to choose a theme for the trimester. I stuck to this theme and related all lessons to the theme. I did my plans by the trimester, then, and fine-tuned week by week based on the needs of the students. By using a theme (usually a major topic in social studies), I could help my students make connections between content areas."

Join up. Since so much work goes in to a field trip, go as a grade-level team or at least with another teacher, so you can split up the duties and responsibilities. Joining up lets both classes enjoy the outing, without leaving one class feeling "ripped off." It's awful when you sit in a desk practicing spelling and your best friend—whose teacher Ms. Action makes field trips happen—spends the day at a nature center and gets to hold something totally cool like a skunk!

Match up. Use the historical sites in your area to align with your social studies curriculum. If you teach fourth grade in the gold country, then you had better take your students to Coloma, the site where the California Gold Rush began. If you teach in Boston, well, then get those kids over to the harbor where our forefathers tossed their tea!

Go local. Check out the local museums, which can be great places to illustrate the period you are studying. Let's say you are studying the 1950s and find out that the local history museum is featuring a history of baseball in your town from 1950 to the present. Moreover, a special dis-

Tales from the Trenches

"Last year our grade level decided to use Chinese New Year as a thematic unit for winter marking period. My sister was living in Asia and somewhere along the line had picked up period costumes from a Hong Kong television studio that films costume dramas. So I agreed to come to school one day dressed to illustrate how Chinese women had dressed in medieval times. The one thing I should have arranged was a sedan chair, because—you guessed it—I got a flat tire on the way to school. There I was on a busy residential street, at 7 A.M., with my hair all extravagantly wound up on top of my head, wearing multiple layers of brightly colored robes and bad makeup. I think next time I'll just bring photos!"

M. Lee, Cherry Hill, New Jersey

FROM THE DESK OF . . . "I live in an urban area, but the place where I teach is very rural. It's amazing to me that the kids in my part of town, and the kids where I teach, can have such different values. My students worry about farm prices; the neighbor kids worry about the cut of their jeans. This experience of teaching in the hinterlands is changing my life in ways I never expected. My students are hard-working, salt of the earth. Everyone should have the experience of teaching outside their 'comfort zone.' It's eye-opening!"

Linda A., St. Louis, Missouri

play showcases the physics of the bat hitting the ball. Voilà! You've just found a way to merge science, social studies, and physical education!

Get outside. Local fish hatcheries, nature preserves, wetlands, and even zoos can be a source to visit if it relates to your science curriculum. What if, for example, you're studying the concept of extinction, and your local zoo is trying desperately to keep a species from going extinct—and the species has digs right there at the zoo, too? Go, go, go to the zoo and show the kids the animal that may not live on forever. The kids will engage with the concept better if they see something concrete—the animal—struggling to survive.

Get a library pass. Going to the public library can be a way to spark interest in reading and involve the community. Many city-run library programs offer puppet shows, dramatic readings, professional storytellers, and other cultural events for eager little literary minds. More often than not, these events are free, too!

Amuse yourself. Local amusement parks can be informational and fun, especially if they involve animals, aquatic centers, or special displays with an educational slant. In fact, try contacting the amusement parks in your area to find out whether they have a special "educational division" within the company. Many do. And the more kids walking through the turnstile, the better the rate for these places.

Make it all business. Factories and businesses can provide kids with numerous lessons—and a goodie bag at the end of the festivities, too. Students are often amazed at the inner workings of a bread factory or doll manufacturer. Oftentimes, you can integrate a math lesson into a business visit.

Party Time

BESIDES THEMATIC units, holidays and events seem to permeate the elementary curriculum. The students' energy will be different on the days of holidays (yep—it'll be crazy!), parents may expect certain things to happen on holidays (such as a party or play), and the school may have its own traditions surrounding holidays (such as a Columbus Day rally where everyone watches a cartoon detailing the discovery of the New World).

For these reasons, holidays and events need to factor into the organization of the curriculum. Here are some holidays and events to consider:

Columbus Day

If you are teaching second, third, fourth, or fifth grade, then Columbus Day will probably factor into your lesson plans. You won't need the whole day, but during social studies, this may be a day of debate for the older students on the activities of Columbus; in science, you may have a regatta of ships to re-create the journey; for the younger students, you may have them draw the ships and map where Columbus started and finished.

Halloween

Check to see what the school's tradition is with regard to parties and costumes for staff and students. If you show up dressed as Raggedy Ann or Andy when no one—we repeat: no one—dresses up on your campus, you'll feel like a fool. Just talk with a few other teachers and find out the score—to dress or not to dress up?

" In later life, as in earlier, only a few persons influence the formation of our character; the multitude pass us by like a distant army. One friend, one teacher, one beloved, one club, one dining table, one work table are the means by which one's nation and the spirit of one's nation affect the individual. "

JEAN PAUL RICHTER

Thanksgiving

Depending on your grade level and the subjects being studied, Thanksgiving is an opportunity to either re-create the "First Feast" or to hold a "Friendship Feast." This will take some organization on your part, but you can also use those parents in your classroom that would love to be involved in an activity such as this.

December

This month is both exciting and tiring. You may be asked to be a part of a schoolwide performance—which will take a huge amount of your time and preparation. As with Halloween, you may be expected to have a class party—but this time you may be expected to include a gift exchange; you may also be expected to have the students make something for their parents. Again, check with the principal and your fellow teachers for guidelines and ideas.

Martin Luther King, Jr., and President's Days

As with Columbus Day, this may be a time to recognize the contributions of these men. The students will be excited because of the days off, and because of the four-day school weeks, your normal schedule will be thrown off a bit. To counteract the imbalance and build on the excitement, you can have your students do some research and/or projects related to the contributions of these famous men.

St. Patrick's Day

The traditional "wearing of the green" will probably be a part of your school day. As with the other holidays, find out whether a party is de rigueur. At any rate, have green stickers or cutouts of shamrocks and pins available to the students who come to school without wearing green. Some primary teachers use this time to stage elaborate "leprechaun activities." If it is approved by the principal, go as far as you want and have fun!

Teacher's Rule

If your school site includes a gift exchange for students, try your best to make sure every student receives something from their "Secret Santa"—even if that means getting the kid a "token" just to show you care. Also, put a limit on the price of the gift. With so many "dollar" stores around, even $1.50 is a reasonable cap for a gift.

Easter

As with December, this is an exciting time for most of your students, if for no other reason than spring break is coming. As with other holidays, check school policies, and exercise sensitivity for the diversity of your class when determining whether to schedule an Easter party.

There you have it. Once you've accounted for the calendar, your reporting periods, report cards, district curriculum expectations, thematic units, field trips, and holidays, you've done your long-term planning. Congratulations!

Things to Remember

To make this long-range planning meaningful, make sure you do the following:

❑ Find out what calendar your school is on: traditional, single-track or multitrack year-round

❑ Get a copy of your school's report card to determine grading periods and grading expectations

❑ Use your district curriculum guides and integrate topics into major themes to teach throughout the year

❑ Organize field trips and class parties to enhance the curriculum

Content Areas

THE ELEMENTARY SCHOOL TEACHER is usually expected to teach all content areas: mathematics, language arts, reading, science, and social studies. Although you may even be required to teach computers and technology, music, art, and physical education, the emphasis in education today is on mathematics and language arts instruction. Teaching the 3 R's is alive and well in today's classrooms, but you are still supposed to be the jack- or jill-of-all-trades! Use this chapter to help you think through the various requirements of each content area.

You may find that the subjects you disliked growing up are still subjects that you are not fond of teaching today. This is natural. You have strengths in some areas that will help you excel as a teacher, but it's important that you become aware of your weaknesses, those subjects you tend to push aside. Make an effort to be a strong teacher in all areas. The subjects you aren't fond of may be the very ones that really turn on some of your students.

Always be on the lookout for new and creative ways to teach all subjects, and keep in mind that all of your students learn in different ways and enjoy a variety of subjects. If you organize and transition

Making the Grade

Elementary school teachers are expected to cover so many areas it's overwhelming. Here's help:

Kathy Schrock's Guide for Educators: *http://school .discovery.com/schrockguide— Links to hundreds and hundreds of resources for educators, categorized by subject area. You'll find everything there is to know about literature, language arts, math, science, history, social studies, and much, much more.*

correctly, your shifts from one subject to another throughout the day will be smooth and natural.

Mathematics

Mathematics is a complex discipline. As you progress through the grades, you can expect to teach problem solving; basic computations in addition, subtraction, multiplication, and division; fractions, decimals, and percentages; measurement, including time and money; statistics and probability; even algebra and geometry.

Teaching this content area well involves, first, a commitment to teach it every day and, second, skill in balancing hands-on experiences with paper-and-pencil tasks. Because of the way math curriculum is currently organized in American public education, you've got a lot to fit in. It is especially important to focus the curriculum, then, in mathematics.

One common error of new teachers is that they will teach a concept and then go on to the next concept without providing a practice or review. Using math as a *transition activity*, both to provide daily practice and to shift gears with your students, will resolve this problem. It is imperative that you have the students do some review work in mathematics every single day!

As a transition activity you could, for example, start the day with a daily math exercise that asks the students to compute the answers to four questions: one on addition, one on subtraction, one on multiplication, and one on division. You might also ask them to solve a word problem or engage in a problem-solving strategy. These activities can be done daily as the students enter and can be corrected by having students switch papers with one another. This daily review will provide your students the opportunity to practice computation skills before and after you study them in depth.

> # Teaching Terms
>
> ◆ ◆ ◆
>
> **Transition activity.** When shifting from one activity to another or one subject to the next, you want that transition to take as little time as possible. A transition activity requires the students to stay focused on an assignment that may only take them five minutes to complete but gives you time to prepare for the next lesson and accommodates the various lengths of time it takes students to get adjusted to a new task and complete it.

Another common error is to teach to the whole group the same material. It's much better, as skills are introduced, to hone in on the students who need individual instruction. Most math series provide pretests for you to use with your students to determine who needs help in certain areas. If you present the pretests as opportunities for *you* to learn something about your students and don't let wrong answers cause students to feel bad about their abilities, then the tests can provide valuable information.

Use pretest results to isolate the group of students that need individual instruction to master the skill. This small-group instruction may lend itself to more hands-on experiences with block, cubes, and other *manipulatives*.

All students should still have the same homework, so that even though some students have already demonstrated knowledge of a certain skill, they are still practicing it so as not to lose the skill. Thus, all students are still working on the same skill, but some are being enriched, and others remediated. *Posttests* will indicate who still needs work in certain areas and will assist you in generating grades in math.

Areas such as geometry and measurement lend themselves to whole-group instruction more readily than computation skills do and so do not necessarily need to involve a pretest.

Teaching Terms

◆ ◆ ◆

Pretest. Elementary textbooks often include pretests that can help teachers determine what basic skills need to be reviewed, what parts can be skipped, and how students can be grouped by skill level. Students who "pass" a skill on their pretest can work on an enrichment activity related to the skill area, as provided by the textbook series. The other students can then work with you on the area of need.

◆ ◆ ◆

Manipulatives. Items and their corresponding activities that require students to use their hands. They may be working with blocks, objects, or puzzles that require them to pick parts up and move them around to solve the problem. For students who are kinesthetic learners, this will be the best learning tool you use.

These are also good areas to use at the beginning and end of grading periods, as they often lead naturally to projects, group work, and hands-on experiences.

Language Arts

Language arts is an absolutely critical subject in elementary school. This is not to say that other subjects are not important. But it requires a mastery of language arts skills to learn and acquire all the other skills that will help them succeed in middle school, high school, and life. Be sure that none of your students are falling through the cracks at this level. If they are left behind here, it's likely they'll never catch up.

Language arts covers the following areas: spelling, the mechanics of writing, the forms of writing, handwriting, listening, and speaking. All of these areas deserve attention.

Teaching Terms

◆ ◆ ◆

Posttest. Students may be required to earn a 70 percent on the posttest to have mastered a particular skill set. Many teachers use the same questions for their posttest as they did for their pretest.

Teacher's Rule

Repetition is the key to mastery. This is a valuable rule to remember because skills that are easily learned are just as easily forgotten. These skills need to become second nature to your students. They should do problems so many times they are able to teach others how to solve the problems. When your students can do this, you know that your repetition has worked and your students have retained the information.

As with math, some of these areas can be used as a transition activity and provide a daily review. If students enter the class after recess with sentences on the board that they need to edit, they are getting practice in the mechanics of writing and perhaps spelling, every day.

Spelling

Many opinions are floating around about spelling. Some experts believe that kids will automatically pick it up from reading and seeing the word. Others believe that you should teach a word in context; this means that spelling words are drawn from passages and texts they are reading. Still others think that lists of spelling words totally unrelated to readings is a perfect way to teach students to spell.

If you haven't already, you will probably hear a great deal about how spelling should be taught. In the past, there has been rather large controversy between two opposing approaches: *whole language* and *phonetic* methods. You will read, discuss, and develop your own opinions regarding spelling over the years. As you begin teaching this subject for the first time, though, keep it simple.

Another area of spelling to address is the integration of words in the students' actual writing. Every time you grade a writing assignment, you should include a grade for spelling. The way to do this is to count up the number of words the students have written overall and the number of words they have spelled correctly. This generates a percentage: the number of words they have spelled correctly divided by the number of words they spelled overall. This grade should also go in the grade book.

Week at a Glance. When teaching spelling, use the cyclic nature of teaching to your advantage. Have your students fold their paper in three columns, and give a pretest of words on Monday (from whichever publishing company your district has adopted). Students write the word that you have written on the over-head projector in the first column, and then they write the word correctly, touching each letter as they write it, in the second. In the third column, they write the word again for practice. Make sure you throw in some challenge words for your high-achieving students—draw from the topics you are covering in science and social studies for ideas.

> ## Teaching Terms
>
> ♦ ♦ ♦
>
> **Whole-language learning.** An approach to teaching reading and spelling that requires students to memorize each word as it appears in context.
>
> ♦ ♦ ♦
>
> **Phonetic learning.** A method that teaches the sounds of letters and combinations of letters so the student can sound out words and attach sounds to letters and words.

For homework, students write the words in sentences or create a story using the words. On Tuesday and Wednesday, the students can either work out of their spelling workbooks, or you can create activities for them such as using the spelling words in sentences that define the word, making a word search, or creating a crossword puzzle.

On Thursday, you can give the students a practice test that they use for homework on Thursday night to check themselves. Have a parent sign their paper.

The final test is on Friday, and that is the grade that goes in the grade book.

Teacher's Rule

Want to make some kids really happy? Instead of inventing your own sentences to administer a spelling test, use the sentences they created during their midweek homework assignments. You'll hear lots of giggles and encourage creativity.

The Mechanics of Writing

Many students manage to get all the way to high school without knowing what a noun is. In the same way math requires repetition for comprehension and mastery, writing requires practice. All students should have a strong background in the parts of speech and the understanding of basic sentence structure. Once those are developed, paragraphs and essay composition make up the next natural step.

Grammar and punctuation are boring if done in isolation. Generate interest in the topic by using some of the students' own writing to demonstrate the need for practice in certain areas. For example, at the beginning of the year ask your students to write a paragraph on a specific topic. Consider it a pretest. Look for grammatical errors in the paragraphs, cross out names, and copy them onto an overhead transparency. Let their own errors become the topic for a lesson! You can then use follow-up materials from your textbooks for practice.

The stages of writing are another important area of focus. Most students want to complete the assignment and never see it again! But it is important to get them to prewrite, write, edit their work, revise, and publish their work. Again, the cyclic nature of teaching can work to your advantage by allowing your students to go through all of the stages within the week.

Week at a Glance.   On Monday, have the students prewrite by using word webs, collaborative groups, or other brainstorming techniques. For homework, students can outline their ideas into the conventions you are teaching: sentence, paragraph, essay, short story, or research paper.

Tales from the Trenches

"My favorite essay ever? When I was a new teacher, I was teaching a fourth-grade social studies unit on the settlement of the West and the Northwest Territories. At the conclusion of the unit, we asked each child to write a report on the Northwest Territories. Trisha turned in her report. It went like this:

"'A long time ago in the Northwest Territories there was a mom, a dad, and their dotter. One day the mom said to the dad I want a baby rot now. He said you caint. Don't you re-meber? You had your toobs tide. The mom sad oh thats rot. Then pretty soon the dotter said to the mom I want you to have a baby rot now. She said I cain't. Dont you remeber? I had my toobs tide. The End.'

"We considered having Trisha read her Northwest Territories report in front of her parents for Open House Night, but after much discussion, decided against it!"

Jenna L., Seattle, Washington

On Tuesday, they can share their homework with their collaborative groups or partners. This way, the students can edit one another's work, give each other suggestions, and get involved in a minilesson if you notice some common errors they are making. They can also share their writing with the whole class in a group-sharing situation, incorporating the suggestions from their peers into their first rewrite to be done on Wednesday. This is the first time you see it, and you need to correct it on Wednesday or Thursday.

On Thursday, while you are correcting their writing, the students can be drawing illustrations for their writing. Usually a picture of the content of the writing will be sufficient; some students may want to create a cover for their writing or use other art supplies as an illustration. Thursday's homework, then, is to rewrite their assignment and get a signature from a parent.

On Friday, the students need to publish. They combine their final draft (from homework) and their illustration (from Thursday) to become a final draft. The students need to attach their prewriting, outline, and rough drafts, but the final draft is what you grade and enter in the grade book.

Forms of Writing.   Writing comes in many forms. Using different types of writing will keep the spice in your writing program. De-

---

Teaching Terms

• • •

Prewrite. The organizational part of writing. Before students even begin a paragraph, they must decide what the first paragraph is going to be about, the subject of the second paragraph, and so on. Prewriting helps the students determine the topic of their paper, the subtopics (body paragraphs), and what they want to include in each subtopic. This portion of the writing process only requires organizing thoughts and jotting down words or phrases. You should also consider teaching them how to outline their ideas.

pending on your grade level, give your students the opportunity to write in these different forms.

Creative writing. Use the holidays, daily *writing prompts,* and critical-thinking exercises as vehicles for creative writing. Students need to know that they can write without fear of being corrected, which may stifle creativity. Give them a notebook at the beginning of the year to respond to writing prompts. Then, give them prompts every week.

The prompt can be related to social studies or science (critical thinking questions are often built into the end of the chapter questions). Grade them on fluency (how much they write) and content (what they write), but leave out the corrections of grammar and spelling. You can highlight or underline one or two key points on which to comment. You can usually find prompts with holiday themes at teacher supply stores. These also make excellent bulletin-board ideas.

> ## Teaching Terms
> ♦ ♦ ♦
>
> **Writing prompts.** The various writing topics you give to your class. This gives them a focus for their writing instead of having them write about whatever they want to.

Conventional writing. Choose a form conducive to your grade level and stick with it! Younger students need to master the conventions of a good, expanded sentence, building up to a combination of sentences relating to a theme. Older students need to master a solid paragraph and build up to an essay.

Story writing. Teaching your students to write a story requires time and energy, but it is a wonderful creative outlet. Teach them the difference between paragraphs and stories, so that they know that a story includes a beginning (the setting, a description of characters), a middle, (a conflict or a problem to be solved), and an ending (the resolution of the conflict or solution to the problem).

Quickwrites. When introducing a new lesson or unit, it's good practice to connect the information you are about to teach with the lives of your students. One way of doing that is to give them a quickwrite. You give the students a specific prompt just to get them thinking about the topic. They write for five to ten minutes, without worrying about organization or structure. You can then have them share their thoughts with the class.

Journals. Journal writing is a very versatile learning tool. For starters, it's a good way to get students writing regularly. It also makes for a great transition activity or a consistent way to begin class every day. You can provide students with a journal, have them buy one (a simple ring binder or theme notebook will do), or make one out of white paper. The prompts you give for the journals should be relatively personal so the students can write about their own thoughts and feelings. You can collect the journals every week or two and check for completion. You can also include grammar practice, spelling, or quickwrites in the journals.

Letters. Letters are easy forms of writing, and they can be used with virtually any subject. Students can write letters to businesses, parents, celebrities, or scientists. You can have them make up fictional letters to famous historical figures. It is important for them to learn the proper heading for personal and business letters and the various ways of closing a letter. One thoughtful letter assignment is having the students write a letter to themselves in five years. They can explain what their class and lives are like now and make predictions about the future. Then, if you had a method of either mailing

FROM THE DESK OF . . . "I know handwriting is going the way of the eight-track tape, but I think it's still a critical skill," says Miranda C., a sixth-grade teacher in Tacoma, Washington. "I know kids prefer to keyboard. From my perspective, though, I've seen that learning to hand write helps them learn how words are formed, memorize the spelling, and literally 'get a feel' for language. One thing I have found successful, once they've mastered a standard script form such as D'Nealian, is to encourage them to get creative — develop their own 'fonts' and writing styles. In this way, penmanship is more like an art form, and less like punishment."

them in five years or passing them on with teachers, your students would really enjoy reading them in the future.

Handwriting

This is an area that generally does not receive a lot of attention, but it's still important. Handwriting can produce some quiet time in your classroom and give the students time to practice their lettering. You can purchase books to duplicate pages for your students on which to practice. Then, set the timer to give your students a chance to practice handwriting. When the timer "dings," then the students can underline or circle what they feel to be is their best example of handwriting. You can then analyze their choices and give them a grade. As with spelling, do not just grade this assignment but also assign them a grade for handwriting when they turn in a formal written assignment.

Making the Grade

Handwriting help is available on the Web, for free. These resources all have excellent material and suggestions for teaching the subject.

Handwriting: http://ericir.syr .edu/Virtual/Lessons/Lang_arts /Handwriting—*A well-written lesson plans from the AskERIC project. Explains how to help children improve bad handwriting.*

Kids Fonts:

http://kidsfonts.mivox.com— *Download fonts that teach handwriting (D'Nealian, tracing, and coloring fonts), and use them to create your own worksheets.*

Handwriting:

http://thegateway.syr.edu/index2 /languageartshandwriting.html— *A small number of lesson plans, sorted by age, are provided by the U.S. Department of Education's Gateway to Educational Materials project.*

Listening

You may be expected to assign your students a listening grade as part of their language arts grade. "Grading" listening can be done in a couple of ways: (1) you can use a workbook of listening exercises with your students and assign them a grade; and (2) you can assign your students a grade when they are listening to others' oral reports. A combination of these two would be appropriate and can be done in alternate weeks.

Teaching listening should focus on active listening: looking at the speaker, nodding to show understanding, paraphrasing, clarifying, and interacting with the speaker.

Speaking

A grade for speaking can be generated when you have your students do oral reports. Teach them the skills of effective speaking: making eye contact with the audience, speaking clearly and loudly, and giving an interesting presentation.

Reading

The current emphasis on reading is at an all-time high for very good reason. Research has demonstrated that the ability to read is the key to success in many areas of life beyond school. Districts allocate a great deal of fiscal and personnel resources to ensure achievement in this area. The reading program that your district utilizes can range from basal readers or literature programs to a very prescriptive "Teach this on this day at this time in this way." The report card you use will determine how you organize your reading curriculum. Regardless of how your reading program is set up, you must ensure not only that your students can *decode* but also that they *comprehend* what they read.

The following, then, are suggestions to use when you are responsible for teaching reading without much structure or guidance:

Balance. Balancing literature with a basal reader (if you have one) is probably the most straightforward way to approach teaching reading. Both approaches should address reading comprehension, vocabulary, opportunities to read aloud, and extension activities.

Making the Grade

The following Web sites suggest innovative ways to teach students critical listening skills:

Listening Skills:
www.kidsource.com/kidsource/ content2/How_Can_Parents_ Model.htmlKidSource OnLine provides lots of suggestions to improve listening skills.

Listening Comprehension:
http://thegateway.syr.edu/index2 /languageartslistening comprehension.html. Young kids learn to rhyme; older kids describe an image while their partner draws what he hears. A very large collection of lesson plans from the U.S. Department of Education's Gateway to Educational Materials projects is also here.

StoryArts:
www.storyarts.org/classroom/use stories—How to assess children's listening skills through storytelling.

Basal reader. You may be provided with a teacher's edition, workbooks, and student reading books. This may be your reading program. Basal readers do not often mean high motivation for students! If this is the case, then take a look at the stories you will be teaching and the skills involved. For the most part, you do not need to teach all of the stories in sequence, so be selective. Look at your social studies topics, and see whether any of the stories align with what you are covering. Nothing's wrong with going through the basal reader as outlined; if you can make connections, though, it might make it more interesting for your students.

Week at a Glance.   A typical week using a basal reader would include the following cycle:

- **Monday.** Do a prereading activity related to the story. The activity could be a writing prompt or a "tell us about a time when you. . . ." Introduce vocabulary words. There may be a workbook page that includes a vocabulary activity.

- **Tuesday.** Review the vocabulary, read the comprehension questions the students will be answering, and assign the students to read the story independently.

- **Wednesday.** Review the vocabulary and comprehension questions, and have the students read the story out loud together, taking turns (make notes of reading ability). Discuss the story as you proceed. The students can then answer the comprehension questions independently.

- **Thursday.** Assign workbook pages, and have the students review their comprehension answers in partners, rereading the story together. Students turn in their reading comprehension questions for you to grade and do an extension activity, which could be an art project or a creative writing activity.

- **Friday.** Have students share their extension activities.

Literature

In elementary school students learn to either love or hate literature. You need to introduce them to literature they can connect to. It's critical that you get everyone's noses in books. Helping your students connect to literature means you must know your students. What kind of a community is your school in? At what levels are your students reading? What types of books or subjects are they interested in? When you have answered these questions, select books that match their experiences or backgrounds in some way. Wouldn't it be wonderful if the worst thing you ever had to deal with as a teacher was barking at kids to put their books away?

Integrating literature into the reading program may be something you need to do yourself. Again, look to social studies for inspiration. Sometimes the textbook publisher will suggest titles of books that relate to the topics being studied.

This is also the time to consult the local office of education for a book kit, so you can get your hands on multiple copies of the books

Teaching Terms

◆ ◆ ◆

Decoding. If students are able to decode a word or sentence, it means that they have sounded out the word and identified it. This does not necessarily mean that they understand the word or the sentence, but they have been able to recognize all the characters.

◆ ◆ ◆

Reading comprehension. This means that a student understands what he or she has read. The skill requires both decoding and processing skills. The best way to check for understanding is to have the students answer questions about a passage or tell you or another student about it. Reading comprehension and inference comprise a large portion of the score on most standardized tests.

Teacher's Rule

Look for students who are struggling. If they are having a seriously difficult time keeping up or learning, take action. Get them tested for a learning disability, find outside help such as a tutor, or tutor them yourself. The sooner you get them help, the more successful they will become.

without purchasing them yourself. If the textbook publisher does not offer suggestions, you can ask a colleague or look up the theme at the teacher supply store.

A balanced program will include multiple reading resources. The basal reader may be used as the foundation, and literature drawn from social studies topics can be added to the curriculum. This will not only keep your students' motivation high; it will also provide a variety of reading experiences.

Science

Your science curriculum will be determined by the series your district has adopted. Choose one main topic per grading period and focus lessons around the topic. Allow students to go deep into the inquiry of the topic, giving them time to do the reading associated with the topic and opportunities to do research and hands-on activities to apply their new knowledge. Incorporate the scientific method into your lessons so that your students become familiar with the terminology.

You probably won't teach science every day, so consider this as part of your week.

Week at a glance

On Tuesday you may do some reading together on a particular subtopic related to the overall focus for the grading period. You may formulate hypotheses that students want to do further research on, as well as have them answer comprehension questions from the reading you have just done together.

Then, on Thursday, you may involve the class in an experiment on the topic studied on Tuesday. This might be a cooperative group activity designed so that every student has a role in the experiment so that they can test their hypotheses and get results.

Week in and out, then, you will have grades for your students in their mastery of science content knowledge, as well as a grade for them in conducting an experiment through the use of the scientific method.

Social Studies

When you first look at the curriculum, you might be surprised how much you are supposed to cover in a year. Rest assured that you do not have to cover it all! Pick one major topic per grading period, and, as with science, go deep into that topic. Besides exploring the content, engage your students in geography, journal writing, and critical thinking activities related to the topic. Even though you may only be able to devote two days a week to social studies, consider planning your week this way.

> # Teaching Terms
>
> ◆ ◆ ◆
>
> **Scientific method.** The systematic pursuit of knowledge. Involves recognizing and formulating a question, collecting data through observation and experimentation, formulating and testing hypotheses, and coming up with conclusions.

Week at a glance

On Monday, introduce the topic for the week by generating interest through a journal activity, a map activity or perhaps a group discussion on the topic. Do whatever it takes to get your students excited about the topic. Then, because the text is so complex, you may need to read it together. This puts you all on the same page so that you can discuss, enrich and connect the topic to their lives. You should also consider taking notes on the overhead for two reasons: 1) to teach note-taking skills; and 2) so you can easily copy them for students who are absent or out of the room at this time. Generating interest may be easier said than done when you are teaching about ancient India, but your effort and enthusiasm on the first day of instruction will make all the difference. Before the period ends on Monday, make sure you have looked at the comprehension questions at the end of the section. Tell them you will be focusing on these on Wednesday, so they had better be prepared.

On Wednesday, allocate some time for the students to review the section and perhaps answer some of the questions in a small group. You might have already used some of the critical questions for writing prompts as part of language arts, so the questions for your groups or partners to focus on should be to check for their comprehension of the topic. Homework may include an extension activity suggested by the textbook publisher.

In this way, you will have connected the students to history, and generated a grade by using the quickwrite, the map activity, group participation, and their answers to the comprehension questions.

Art

Your art curriculum can be organized taking the following things into consideration: (1) topics or periods being studied in social studies, (2) holiday art, and (3) art as a form of creative expression. Devote a specific time for art every week, and do one of the previously mentioned types of activities. Your students will look forward to it, you can teach them art and art history, and your classroom will look great!

Using the suggestions from this chapter, art will most likely be done on Friday afternoons or on Thursdays during the illustration part of their weekly writing. Occasionally, you could use an art project to spark the students' interest in social studies.

Music

The way you teach music will depend on your level of comfort in this area. As with art, you can relate music to social studies, the holidays, and pure musical expression. Singing patriotic songs every day is a beginning, and teaching songs relating to holidays is fun and easy. Learning songs or the type of music relating to social studies may take some research on your part, but it will enhance your social studies program as well as provide a format for music education.

Switch off between art and "formal" music on Friday afternoons if you are comfortable teaching music. If not, then relax in the knowledge that your students are at least singing everyday.

Physical Education

Physical education is not a subject that many teachers feel comfortable with. When setting up your PE program, think about what sports *you* enjoy playing. Choose one or two to focus on during a grading period, and then analyze what skills are needed to play that sport. Teach the skills to lead up to a series of games. Be sure to include time for your students to warm up, teaching them stretching exercises, physical fitness activities, and running.

You should make time to do PE at least three times a week. This does not mean that you're playing a game with your students three times a week, but rather using the following guidelines.

Week at a glance

Say you're teaching basketball. On Monday, after warming up the students with calisthenics for 5 minutes, you lead them in a couple of dribbling and passing drills with small groups. You then end the period with a dribbling relay with one half of the class against the other.

On Wednesday, again after calisthenics, you lead the class in some shooting drills. Then, each group of students plays "Around the World" on his own basketball court.

On Friday, after calisthenics and a lap around the field, the students line up in two teams to play a basketball relay against each other.

You see, PE is so much more than a game or fierce competition; it is also much more than a glorified version of recess. Again, find sports that you like to play and center your curriculum and instruction around that.

If you're still not sold on teaching PE, then try finding another teacher who will teach it for you, and trade. Maybe you could teach art and music to their class while they teach your class PE!

Now that you have an idea about the content areas you will be teaching, gather up all the curriculum materials your school has to give you. Look through it all to help you organize your units and lessons. Whatever you do, don't be afraid to include your own activities that add creativity and bring about enthusiasm in learning. Repetition is necessary for mastery, but variety will keep students interested!

Making the Grade

If you're on your own for teaching physical education, take heart. So much good material is available on the Internet that you might actually be able to fool your students into believing you're a gym rat! Here's one of the best:

PE Central: *http://pe.central .vt.edu—The ultimate Web site for health and physical education teachers, parents, and students. Lesson plans, adaptations for disabilities, top Web sites, and ideas for teaching preschoolers are all here.*

Things to Remember

Even though it seems like there is so much content to cover, you can and must do it! Remember to do these things so that you do so much more than "cover" the curriculum.

- ❏ Choose one major topic of study per grading period for social studies and science; 2-3 areas in mathematics; and 2-3 stories in reading

- ❏ Use the school week to your advantage in language arts by doing pretests in spelling and writing on Mondays; practice and drafts during the week; and final tests and drafts on Fridays

- ❏ Make the limited time you have to teach social studies and science count by connecting content knowledge to the students' lives and interests

- ❏ Use the social studies curriculum as a springboard for art and music instruction

" The good man is the teacher of the bad,
And the bad is the material from which the good may learn.
He who does not value the teacher,
Or greatly care for the material,
Is greatly deluded although he may be learned.
Such is the essential mystery. "

Lao-Tzu (fl. 600 b.c.)

10 Long- and Short-Range Plans

PERHAPS THE MOST time-consuming part of teaching is lesson planning. New teachers, in particular, have a heavy workload because they don't have the benefit of last year's lesson plans to draw on.

But the old gag about how you eat an elephant—one bite at a time—doesn't apply here. Rather than plan each day as it comes, take some time to look at your long- and short-term plans. Even if the process seems like a pain at first—and an organizational nightmare!—the benefits will outweigh the lost time. In this chapter, we look first at long-range planning for the entire school year.

"Education is the best provision for old age."

ARISTOTLE

Lesson Plan Book

AN ADMINISTRATOR or substitute teacher walking into your classroom will need to see your lesson plan book. The best place for it, then, is in the middle of your desk!

Year Long Planning in a Snap

To include all of the different aspects of the curriculum, think about your plans for the year in this manner:

• **Math.** Focus on one main topic per month. Plan your instruction around the information you glean from the pretest you give. In addition incorporate geometry and measurement into math groups/stations.

• **Spelling.** Create weekly lessons that include a pretest, practice, tests, and a monthly review of previously studied words.

• **Reading.** Do daily basal reader activities, read-alouds, and sustained silent reading (SSR). Ask for book reports once a grading period. Study one or two literature books each trimester.

• **Writing.** Teach structured process writing every week. Have the students submit a final draft of the process writing once a week and an assigned writing project, such as a story or a poem, once a month.

• **Social studies.** Choose one focus per grading period with weekly lessons, map activities, chapter tests, and a research report.

• **Science.** One focus per grading period. Weekly labs, quizzes and tests. Third-trimester science fair project.

• **Art.** Work on weekly projects.

• **Music.** Incorporate daily singing using music related to social studies. Participate in scheduled school performances.

Making the Grade

Does formal lesson planning feel like too much work? The cavalry is here.

How to Write a Lesson Plan—10 Steps: *www.LessonPlansPage .com/WriteLessonPlan.htm—Ten steps to developing a quality lesson plan. And when you get to the end, click the link to the lesson plans pages, where you'll find hundreds of lesson plans contributed by working teachers. Lesson plans are organized by subject matter and grade level—a dream come true for a first-year teacher!*

PE. Lead exercise, skills, and games, changing the focus per grading period.

What to Expect the First Trimester

AFTER YOU look at all of the areas and topics you need to cover in a year, break your plans down by grading period. Plan for the trimester by subject area, and remember to correlate your plan with your report card to make sure you are covering all of the appropriate areas.

In the last chapter, we suggested using social studies as the foundation of your curriculum themes. This is how you incorporate that advice into lesson planning: Typically, you would choose one major theme per trimester and plan from there. Literature and reading will lend themselves to integration with social studies, as will art and science. PE will probably be completely separate, but you can get creative! Use language arts, then, to guide the processes for teaching and learning the content.

Let's look at an example of how this process might be integrated in a fifth-grade classroom. Your three broad topics in social studies for the year might be Exploration, Colonization, and Becoming a Nation. We'll focus the discussion on the trimester plan on the Exploration theme, covering all subjects as follows:

• **Math.** Exploring numbers (since this is at the beginning of the year, you'll need to review addition, subtraction, multiplication and division anyway); distances traveled by explorers; how much money each explorer was given; the time it took to travel to different countries

- **Literature.** *Pedro's Journal*, the *Discovery of the Americas*, *Paddle to the Sea*, and the *Usborne Book of Explorers* (these can be read aloud to the class or used as the basis for small-group discussion. If you can obtain a class set, they can be used as the basis of your reading program.)

- **Writing.** Persuasive paragraphs on whether Christopher Columbus was a hero; comparison paragraphs on explorers' motivations to explore

- **Research report.** Explorer report

- **Oral report.** Share Explorer report

- **Science.** Sink-or-float activities; shipbuilding; effects of wind; oceans; navigation

- **Social studies.** Follow textbook guidelines on Explorers Unit; mapping activities

- **Art.** Self-portraits; design ships; portraits of explorers; flags

- **Music.** Music of the fifteenth century; music from the native countries of the explorers

- **PE.** Children's games of the fifteenth century

Teaching Terms

♦ ♦ ♦

Trimester. In elementary school, grading or marking periods are typically one third of the year — a trimester. Also popular is the quarterly reporting period, which has the advantage of more frequent reporting, but it requires more frequent input from teachers.

Your Monthly "Plan"

LET'S SEE what the Exploration unit might look like over a month by weeks and content areas by looking at figure 10.1. Remember that your district goals, academic content standards, curriculum programs, and school schedules will also impact your plans.

Everybody's Working for the Weekend

ONCE YOU get through the monthly planning, you can break your lessons down to a weekly format. Figure 10.2 on the following page demonstrates how a typical week might look.

Weeks	Math	Writing	Reading	Social Studies	Science	Art/Music/PE
Week 1	Multiplication review facts	Paragraph (why you like to explore)	*Pedro's Journal*	Lesson 1	Sink or float?	Fall art
Week 2	Multiplication 1 digit × 10s	Creative Story on Exploration	*Pedro's Journal/ Log of Christopher Columbus*	Lesson 2	Compasses	Native American music Use compasses to race
Week 3	Multiplication 1 digit × 100s	Comparison paragraph of *Pedro's Journal* and the *Log of Christopher Columbus*	*Usborne Book of Explorers*	Lesson 3	Ship building	Designs for ships Holiday art
Week 4	Multiplication Double digit	Research Report introduction	*Individual books on explorers*	Lesson 4	Ship building	Regatta

FIGURE 10.1 Sample monthly plan

Content Areas	Monday	Tuesday	Wednesday	Thursday	Friday
Math	Multiplication groups: practice, enrichment Computers Geometry/ measurement	Multiplication groups: practice, enrichment Computers Geometry/ measurement	Quiz/games	Multiplication groups: practice, enrichment Computers Geometry/ measurement	Multiplication groups: practice, enrichment Computers Geometry/ measurement
Spelling	Pretest	Practice	Practice	Practice test	Test
Language arts/reading	Prewriting centers: grammar, computers Guided reading Groups: vocabulary, intro to story	Rough draft centers: grammar, computers Guided reading Groups: read-aloud, questions	Final copy centers: grammar, computers Guided reading Groups: read individually, questions	Illustrate centers: grammar, computers Guided reading Groups: extension activities	Share Writing Literature extension activities
Social studies/ science/ art	Prereading of social studies lesson: outline or use graphic organizer	Science reading	Group reading in Social Studies, discussion, notes	Science lab	Art

FIGURE 10.2 Sample weekly format

Day by Day

Now that you have a plan to address what you are teaching by the week, how do you organize it into a cohesive day? There are several factors to take into account. For instance, if you have a group of students who leave your room for a period of time for band or chorus, then you probably want to arrange your day taking this time block into consideration.

FROM THE DESK OF . . . *"It's odd, but there's no best way to teach. Some great teachers are tough disciplinarians; others are relaxed. Some lecture; some facilitate. Some have quiet, orderly classrooms, while others are casual and easygoing. The best way to teach is whatever way works for you! Go ahead and experiment with other styles, but if they're not working, go back to your roots."*

Vivian Widdell, St. Louis, Missouri

Also, if you have a group of students who leave the class for special education, try to coordinate with their program by teaching the same subject at the same time. This way, those students won't receive double instruction in, say, spelling, and miss out on reading.

Another consideration is teaching materials. If you have access only to certain materials at certain times, then arrange your day according to when materials are available. You are not going to be able to accommodate everyone's schedule, but if you plan around the large obstacles, it will make it easier for you. Except for extracurricular subjects or activities, you cannot hold students accountable for something they missed while they were out of the classroom (this is why using transparencies is helpful).

Try the following format to see whether it works for your day:

- Opening: Math review activity, attendance, music
- Math
- Spelling

- Recess
- Language arts
- Reading groups
- Read aloud to students. (Students can draw or do origami or clay while they listen.)
- Lunch
- SSR
- Social studies/science/art
- Recess
- Writing: writing prompt related to social studies or science
- Study hall or PE

Teacher's Rule

Before integrating your subject areas, check with your grade-level coordinator or administrator. Every school does things a little differently. You don't want to step on anyone's toes your first year by blazing a trail with your grand plans when the program has been laid out in a manner that prevents this type of integration.

For Whom the Bell Tolls

ANOTHER CONSIDERATION for planning your day is bells—recess bells, lunch bells, late-bird and early-bird reader bells. Here a bell, there a bell, everywhere a bell, bell! You may, for example, know that you need to spend sixty minutes on a new math lesson. But perhaps today an assembly will interfere with the schedule, and your lesson

Teacher's Rule

Yes, you do have to be a know-it-all. Your students will spot a phony and will be sorely disappointed if they discover they know the material better than you do. If you want the respect of your kids—and believe us, you do—come to class prepared! Better prepared, in fact, than you expect any of your students to be.

will be interrupted by a recess break that typically occurs later.

The best way to accomplish planning with time in mind is to "guesstimate" the time it will take for each portion of the lesson. Then fit the lesson components—the subject-matter instruction—into the daily lesson plan as you would a puzzle, where the subject best fits without interruption. You want to make sure the kids receive continuity in their instruction, so use the suggestions on timing provided in your teacher's editions.

Educational Trends

JUST AS pop culture has its fads, and the stock market rises and falls, education has its own peculiar trends. Current educational trends involve "curriculum mapping" (see the work of Heidi Hayes Jacobs) and "backward planning" (see the work of Grant Wiggins and Jay McTighe). Search these authors out at professional conferences, or pick up their books and build your professional library. Here is a *very* simplistic explanation of these important ideas.

Curriculum Mapping

The advocates of this type of planning encourage teachers to map out the curriculum for the year in an integrated way so that assessment guides instruction. You could start your planning, for example, by looking at what is covered on the annual standardized test. Then, you could look for matches in the textbook your district has adopted to see what instructional strategies you have available to assist your students in learning this material.

If your school district has adopted student standards, then the standards need to be addressed and reflected in your plans. Ideally, the standards relate to the instructional materials your district has adopted, and then the assessments match both the standards and instruction.

Backward Planning

In this approach, you determine which assessments you will use and then develop key questions to shape your overall planning. You plan activities and exercises on a daily basis that will answer those questions. At the same time, you're leading students toward the assessments that are based on the fundamental points behind the unit of study.

The foundation of this planning is to ensure the students understand the material in a meaningful manner. Planning with the "end in mind" links assessment and instruction. And don't forget: Your preparation and planning will make learning that much more enjoyable for you and your students!

Making the Grade

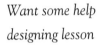

Want some help designing lesson plans and thematic units? Need some ideas for activities? Here's a site that provides a breakdown of various subject matter and levels with helpful lesson planning ideas.

The Teachers' Corner: *www.theteacherscorner.net*

Things to Remember

I know all of this planning will seem overwhelming at times, but it is absolutely essential. Remember the following to assist you in this process:

Tales from the Trenches

"I'm starting to think the only way to teach effectively is to be the same age as your kids. One day one of my students gave a great response during a class discussion, and I held up a hand to high-five him. Almost in unison, a dozen kids in my class started singing the chorus to a Britney Spears song—'Hit me baby, one more time!' We all broke up laughing. You just never know what to expect!"

Amanda J., Olympia, Washington

* * *

"Be prepared for escape from boredom. There will be days when your lesson doesn't meet the highest standards of art or entertainment. There are times when the ho-hum of a long day will lead students to jump at the slightest diversion—a funny sounding name, a mispronounced word, a dropped pencil. Be prepared. Expect these small releases of pressure, allow a bit of appropriate silliness, yet don't veer far off course. Maintain control."

Leanne G., Pleasant Hill, California

❑ Examine your teacher's editions first so that you are using your district's curriculum before you seek out additional resources

❑ Try to plan for the entire grading period in a very general way, hitting on key topics in the major content areas

❑ Break down trimester plans into monthly increments

❑ Work up a daily schedule that hits all of the content areas and make your day flow as smoothly as possible

Instructional Strategies

LET'S LOOK BACK over all that you have accomplished so far. You've familiarized yourself with all the content areas you must cover daily with your students. Your back is aching from lugging around all of the materials you need for each content area. You've talked with some veteran teachers to get some ideas, pointers, materials, and general wisdom. In other words, you know the *what to teach,* so now you are ready to begin organizing your curriculum and deciding *how* to teach it. This is the part of teaching that translates those hours you've spent planning directly into the hearts and minds of your students.

This chapter will give you some strategies for teaching the curriculum. Although you may start with "Direct Instruction," try adding a few grouping strategies to your repertoire. Not every student is the "A" student you were, so make sure your day is packed with different strategies. We cannot afford to leave any student behind, and it is up to you to make learning happen for each and every student! This may sound like an intimidating task, but don't worry, help is on the way.

Direct Instruction: The First Weapon in the Arsenal

Noted and respected educator, Madeline Hunter, has perfected the lesson plan for direct instruction. Her system has very specific steps. She believes in first using an "attention grabber," then stating the objective; transferring previous learning; input and modeling; checking for understanding; offering guided practice; providing for independent practice; and, finally, having closure. We'll use her model to demonstrate direct instruction here:

> ## Teacher's Rule
>
> *Never be afraid to try something new in your classroom! You may discover a wonderful and effective strategy for teaching a particular subject. If your new idea flops, throw it by the wayside. No harm done. Forge ahead until you find a strategy that suits your style.*

1. **Use an "attention getter."** Do you want to know the secrets of being an awesome teacher? (Do I have your attention?) You can't teach when you don't have your students' attention. You shouldn't yell at them and (sorry) you can't threaten them with bodily harm for not paying attention, so you need to come up with an alternative. Figure out a way to intrigue them and get them interested in the lesson! Getting the attention of the older students is sometimes half the battle, so grab their attention by proposing a provocative question: "Imagine a world with no green plants. What would we do to survive? What do green plants need to survive? Does it matter?"

2. **State the objective.** This book will help you become an awesome teacher. That's our objective! Surprisingly enough, we sometimes forget to tell the students what it is they are going to be

learning and why! Students know in general they are supposed to go to school to learn, but they often don't understand how what they are learning is useful in life and the "real world." They also don't know how some information is a necessary building block for other information to come, or how it relates to information they have already learned. Tell the students what they are going to learn and the relevancy of it: "Today we are going to start an experiment to see *why* plants need sunlight and water to grow."

3. **Transfer previous learning.** Now that you have their attention and clearly stated what they are going to be learning, you want to remind them what they have already learned on that topic. You want to make connections between past learning and present learning. For example, "Last week we compared different types of soil to determine what kind of soil is necessary for plant growth. Today we will use that knowledge to experiment with the amount of sunlight and water needed to grow plants.

4. **Allow time for input and modeling.** In this book, we've given you input, input, and more input! We've told you "First do this, and then do this and then do that." In this part of the lesson with your students, you'll need to do this, too. If the students are sitting on the edge of their seats (because you have captured their attention), they know what they are going to do and why (because you have clearly stated the objective and built upon prior knowledge), then you can demand that for the next 30 minutes or so, they can't breathe until you tell them to. This time, then, is devoted to giving specific instructions on how to meet the objective of the lesson. In this part of the lesson, use the overhead, read the directions out loud to them, lecture, write instructions on the board, model the procedure, show examples from past students, teach from a PowerPoint

presentation—anything to get your point across in the best way possible. This is your teaching time! To set up the experiment, say "I am going to give you three instructions to follow to set up this experiment. First, . . . Second, . . . Third, . . ."

5. **Check for understanding.** An example of checking for understanding to you, the reader, would be to pose the question, "What have you learned from this book so far?" It's at this point in the lesson that you want to make sure that your students understand what it is they are doing. Ask questions to determine if they are ready to move on to the practice stage. One question never to ask, though, is "Are there any questions?" You'll know the answer to that one if you have 20 students with their hands raised after you've given the command to begin the lesson! Instead, try something like "Who can raise their hand and tell me the first thing you are going to do when you get your plant?" and have other students repeat what that student said. Reteach as necessary, or move on to the next stage.

6. **Offer guided practice.** To help everyone in the class be successful, proceed with the active portion of the lesson at a slow enough pace so every student has the opportunity to follow along and learn. You will need to monitor their progress while they are working to ensure this. "The distributor is going to give each person a plant, a ruler, and a worksheet. Make your first measurement, and I'm going to walk around to see if you are ready to go on to step 2."

7. **Provide for independent practice.** After you have guided your students and observed their progress, you can let them do some of the work on their own. This gives them the opportunity to work at their own pace so you can assess their learning when they are finished. "In just a moment you are going to complete steps 2 and 3 in this experiment on your own."

8. **Have closure.** Review what you have taught the class and what the students discovered on their own. In other words, restate the objective. This wraps up the lesson, and the students know the activity is over and it is time to move on. "We know that plants need sunlight and water to grow. This experiment will tell us how much water and sunlight a plant needs to grow as we check our plants over the next few weeks."

This is a very useful guide for you to follow when designing your lessons. However, don't think that every element must be present with every lesson. Many times a step or two doesn't fit, or a couple steps need to be combined. All elements should be present whenever you are using direct instruction, though, to make the most of this strategy.

Cooperative Learning: United We Stand

ANOTHER EFFECTIVE teaching strategy is group work, otherwise known as cooperative learning. This can be a very powerful model to employ, and it teaches the students to work together so that they are

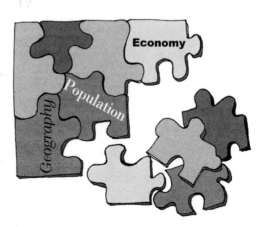

not learning in isolation. When you get comfortable with your students and know their personalities, you are ready to put them into cooperative learning groups.

Use Jigsaws

Jigsaws—not the puzzles but parts of a great cooperative learning strategy—are a wonderful way of having students help you teach. There's a switch! The students really learn to take in and process information and are then required to synthesize it and teach it to others. It's an effective way of getting students involved in the material while exposing them to group dynamics and getting comfortable with working together. The jigsaw method can be used when you have a topic to cover with large pieces that can be easily divided. It works this way:

1. Divide your students into groups.
2. Give each group a different piece of information. They are required to learn about that piece of information and figure out how to teach it to the other groups.
3. Once the groups are ready, have the groups split up. One member of each group joins a new group so each group now has students representing each piece of information.
4. In these groups, each student takes turns teaching his or her particular piece of information to the rest of the group.
5. Conclude with a culminating exercise to check for understanding by all.

If you were teaching the counties or regions of your state, for example, you could give each group a region to study in detail. Then the groups can share information about their region with the whole class so everyone can benefit from the entire topic. Cooperative learning not only teaches content, but those oh-so-necessary social skills.

Do I Have a Job For You!

Use cooperative learning groups for doing art, problem-solving, science projects, social studies projects, and literature projects. With this method, each student needs to have an individual job, and that job needs to be interdependent with the other students, meaning that each individual student is integral to the learning of the whole group. Here are some typical jobs:

- **The supplies manager.** This student is responsible for getting the supplies for the group (e.g., worksheets, books, paper, and anything else the group needs to perform the task or activity) as well as for putting all the materials away at the end of the lesson. In this way, you can have all of the supplies in one place, and only 5 or 6 students are out of their seats at one time instead of 25 or 30.

- **The checker.** This student checks the other students' understanding of the assignment and is the only person who may ask the teacher for assistance if the group has a question. This is also the person who keeps track of the time during a timed assignment, trying to keep everyone on task. Again, only 5 or 6 students are out of their seats at one time.

- **The recorder.** Instead of each member of the group having to write down the answers, findings, or questions, only one—the recorder—is responsible for the writing for the entire group. This student should be thorough and have relatively legible handwriting!

- **The encourager.** This student compliments the other students' contributions and suggestions and makes sure all of the students are responding. The encourager should also thank everyone for doing their duties efficiently and effectively. Wouldn't we all like to have someone encouraging us while we are completing our tasks?

All group members are required to contribute, stay on task, and sign the paper that is turned in to the teacher. Hey, only five or six papers to grade instead of thirty! You can also judge the students' level of participation during the lesson by observing body language (i.e., are they hunched together or is one student sitting back in his chair) and by recording students' comments on a transparency. Debrief the lesson by reviewing the comments you overheard; the students love to be praised publicly for their encouraging words, and will subsequently really ham it up. There's no such thing as *too much* encouragement!

Grouping Students: Divide and Conquer

FOR COOPERATIVE learning, you probably grouped your students *heterogeneously* (with students of mixed ability in each group). In heterogeneous groups, you can use the skills and talents of the more advanced students to assist the students with lesser ability; each student has a role to play, though, so everyone feels like part of a team.

To maximize instructional time to best meet the needs of each and every student in math and reading, you'll want to group your students in a different manner. Remember that pretest you gave on multiplication? Use the results to group students *homogeneously* (with students who have similar needs) so you are teaching this smaller group what they need to know. The smaller you can make your groups, the better chance you have of individualizing their instruction for success. In this case, less is more!

Teaching Time: Tick, Tock, Tick, Tock

GROUPS ARE effective ways to individualize instruction. They are a great instructional strategy because students are constantly stimulated with something new and are practicing a variety of skills at the same time. To set this approach up, you need to teach students how to move from station to station and to work independently while you are working with another group. It may feel as though you're running a three-ring circus at times, but you are really maximizing the students' learning time by tailoring the group work to meet their needs.

For example, your math period may look like this: in twenty-minute intervals, one group will work with you on the main objective of the lesson, say double-digit multiplication, whether you are re-teaching this information, enriching and extending what they already know, or just monitoring their progress; one group will work on word problems using multiplication; one group will work with manipulatives related to multiplication, such as blocks, flash cards or graph paper; and one group will play a math game, you guessed it, on multiplication—on the computer.

The first time you do rotating groups, it will seem confusing for both you and the students. Minimize the confusion by doing a little practice exercise with something relatively easy so the students are able to walk through it and understand what is expected of them. It's well worth the effort.

> " *If you think education is expensive, try ignorance!* "
>
> ANDY MCINTYRE

Learning Centers: Group Work with a Twist

LEARNING CENTERS are a variation of the instructional strategies we've just discussed. Instead of using homogeneous groups, though, like you might in math and reading, learning centers allow you to use heterogeneous groups to access more of the curriculum.

Although you could have learning centers for all subjects, you may want to employ this strategy in a limited way. Just as you wouldn't want to rely on *direct instruction* all day—boring!—you don't want to over-stimulate them, either. With this in mind, language arts especially lends itself to learning centers. As in math, you will be covering a lot of ground in this subject. Language arts learning centers offer a chance for you to mix up your groups and have some fun with the English language. Think about the major components of language arts when you think about creating your centers. It just might look like this. One center might include a hands-on grammar activity or a practice worksheet. Another might focus on a short-term creative writing project. Another center might be used to practice listening

Tales from the Trenches

"What did I learn my first year of school? Get organized!

"You see, my student teaching experience had gone very well. Too well, as it turns out. I think I went into teaching with an unbelievable level of arrogance. I assumed I could just sort of 'wing it,' and the kids would be so dazzled by my brilliant teaching that school would practically teach itself.

"My theory worked great for the first three days. After that, I ran out of ideas, and my magic bag of tricks was empty. Students expected me to keep up the same quality of handouts and lessons, but there I was fumbling around for pieces of paper, sending students to the office to make copies, and hemming and hawing as I was trying to figure out what the day's lesson would be on the fly. By the end of day four, my class was utter chaos. Kids were passing notes, talking over me, and actually standing up walking around the classroom while I was juggling lost papers.

"I earned the disrespect. Believe me when I tell you I spent a long weekend getting things back under control. Every single night for the next several weeks, I spent hours catching up on the preparation I should have done over the summer. Now I know: Even two minutes of disorganization results in complete chaos for the rest of the hour. Get organized."

Robert T., Galveston, Texas

skills, and the computers—can't live without 'em—will be used for yet another. The difference here is that they may only do one center a period, thereby hitting all centers within the week instead of within one period like math.

The Language Arts period, then, can be further broken down as follows. See if this works for you! After you make the spelling transition, give the day's lesson on process writing, whether you are teaching the paragraph, the essay, or how to write sentences. After twenty minutes or so, the learning centers begin. Each group will be doing a different center, but it's different than the procedure described in the prior section, because this time the activities come to them (except for computers), and they don't rotate during the period. For the next twenty to thirty minutes, each group will work on a grammar lesson, creative writing, listening, *or* computers. You have four different activities so that each group works on one activity each day. Fridays can be used to catch groups up or give the students free choice.

You do not need to make up these activities; they should be part of your district's language arts program. Listed here are some suggestions for the different centers:

- **Grammar.** Take this directly from the book your district uses for language arts, or purchase a grade-level book on grammar exercises.
- **Computers.** Use the computers for the students to practice grammar or typing, type their written work, or do research via the Internet on an upcoming topic in social studies or science.
- **Creative writing.** A variety of books have prompts for you to draw upon. Students can write letters, for example. Holiday writing can be done during this time as well.
- **Listening.** Your students can listen to books on tape, listen to each other read, or even practice listening exercises.

If you don't have computers in your classroom, substitute that center for another one that develops a skill such as etymology, vocabulary, critical thinking, or appreciation of literature. Learning centers are applicable to virtually any content area, and you can get creative and develop them into anything you want. Have fun with it!

Factoring in Students' Interests = Success

YOUR MOST successful lessons will be the ones in which you consider the backgrounds and interests of your students. That said, put the subjects you are teaching into *their* context—that is the life of your students—as much as possible. How might this be done, you ask? You can create an "interest inventory" before you begin a unit to determine which aspect of the upcoming subject is most appealing to your students or you can discuss what the students already know about a topic and generate questions of interest. This could be done through a quickwrite, such as "For the next 30 seconds, write down everything you know about spiders."

Some potentially boring lessons will come alive the minute you give your students choices. For example, if you are studying ancient Egypt, some students may be interested in the pyramids, while others are more interested in the mummifying process. As long as they have a choice, you have a better chance of keeping them engaged in the unit.

Effective Transitions: Every Minute Counts

IMAGINE THIRTY students entering your classroom after a wild game of kickball at recess. They are wound up with energy and bubbling over. They are sweating and, in some cases, muddy. They are talking over one another as they argue about who won the game, and the bell rings. Everyone should be in their seats ready to learn, but half are still up and around because they have to wash their hands or go to the bathroom. The seconds go ticking by, and you are getting frustrated waiting for them to calm down and get focused on the next lesson. Without intervention, it could easily be ten minutes before everyone is settled in and listening intently to you.

This transition time from recess to the next lesson in unacceptable. You need to figure out a way to get them in their seats and ready to learn in less than two minutes. Here are some tips for making your transitions smooth and seamless so that no learning time is lost:

1. **Have a routine.** Always have something for the students to do when they walk into the room so they can immediately get to work. Because this is done every day, they know exactly what to expect and what you expect of them.

2. **Give crystal-clear instructions.** When you make the transition from one subject to the other, be very explicit about what you expect students to do. Tell them it is time to put away their math books, put their work in their math folder, and get out their spelling workbook.

3. **On your mark, get set, go!** Time students to see how quickly they can make the transition. Some teachers keep track of the transitions made under a minute and reward the students with extra time at the end of the week. Classroom Management expert Fred Jones recommends keeping track of all of the time in seconds on the board to count toward "preferred activity time." Either way, if you are prepared, then you can monitor this transition time very closely.

Study Hall aka Time to Catch Your Breath

CARVE OUT some time for your class to catch up on their assignments. Remember those names you've put on the board to track missing assignments? Here's why: those students can use this "study hall" time to catch up. The students whose names are not on the board need to have something to do that is not disruptive to the others, such as extra computer time, word puzzles or extra library time. Make sure you set firm boundaries for this time and try to hold a study hall two or three times a week.

Organizing the Day: So Much to Do, So Little Time

ONE OF the most important things you need to do is to decide how to organize your day so you reach the maximum number of students. You must take several factors into consideration. Many of these factors may seem virtually impossible to work around, and you will probably not be able to accommodate everyone, but you certainly need to try.

" It is only the ignorant who despise education. "

PUBLILIUS SYRUS

Cocurricular Activities

Often, classes that include your students are held simultaneously in different classrooms, which means that some of your students disappear for a time and reappear later in the day. Band and chorus are notorious student consumers; so are the school play, student government, and the yearbook. If your students are involved in these activities, try to accommodate them by assigning work that would be easy to make up or an activity that you could excuse them from. The former is easier than the latter; fortunately, kids who are involved in co-curricular activities tend to be the best and brightest anyway, so the makeup work won't break them.

Special Education Students

Before you organize your day, you need to know which students in your class are a part of the special education department. Some of these students will leave your class at different times during the day, or they may just require an aide in the classroom to help them with the assignments you give. It'll take some work on your part to coordinate your teaching topics with their schedules, so you'll have to find out from the special education teachers what they teach and when.

Teaching Materials

Another consideration is teaching materials. If you have access to certain materials only at certain times, then arrange your day according to when materials are available. For example, your school may have only purchased one class set of a science text , but two classrooms are sharing it. Get organized so you can coordinate transfers without undue interruption. Another great opportunity to collaborate with other staff members!

Except for extracurricular subjects or activities, you cannot hold students accountable for something they missed while they are out of the classroom Let kids who are out of the classroom during your teaching period have copies of your transparencies so they can read

Making the Grade

To capture the student's attention, and vary your day, here's a site with a trick for staying on top of things.

Learning Calendar: *www .educationworld.com/learning—This on-line lesson calendar describes every event on the calendar and provides lesson-planning suggestions to match. April, for example, is National Hospice Month, and it's also International Creative Child and Adult Month.*

whatever they missed. That way, you don't have to reteach the lesson to every single student who missed it. There's no way you would be able to do that anyway!

Let's see how your day is shaping up now in terms of the instructional strategies you will experiment with:

Teacher's Rule

You're not going to be able to accommodate everyone's schedule. Life will be a little easier if you plan around the large obstacles, and figure everything else out as you go along. Don't try to set up the perfect schedule because that is impossible. Simply do the best you can.

- Opening: Math review activity, attendance, music
- Math (homogeneous groupings)
- Spelling (direct instruction)
- Recess
- Language arts (centers)
- Reading (homogeneous groups)
- Read aloud to students. (Students can draw or do origami or clay while they listen.)
- Lunch
- SSR
- Social studies/science/art (cooperative learning)
- Recess
- Writing: writing prompt related to social studies or science (direct instruction)
- Study hall or PE

Well, now you should feel better prepared to teach the content areas because you've got a handle on a variety of teaching strategies to engage your students and make your instruction efficient and effective. The beauty of these teaching strategies is that they can be adapted to fit just about every content area and can be changed around to fit any lesson exactly.

Things to Remember

Remember to do the following to spice up your teaching day and maximize learning for all students:

❏ Use direct instruction to convey information in a specific format

❏ Group your students according to need for subjects such as math and reading

❏ Try a cooperative learning activity for social studies and science

❏ Use groups of mixed ability to circulate through your language arts centers

Incorporating Multimedia

OES THE CONCEPT of multimedia seem too difficult or time-consuming? Take too much time to learn? Your students are growing up in an environment filled with technology, news sound bites, and MTV. They have shorter attention spans than people who grew up thinking *Lassie* was entertaining. They are technologically more advanced and are accustomed to being entertained.

Using a variety of multimedia equipment in your lessons will not only help you become a more effective teacher and improve your lessons; it will also help your students learn better, because you are using their environment as a teaching tool.

On the plus side, it cuts both ways. You should use multimedia equipment as part of your lessons, of course, but at the same time, you can require students to use multimedia as a part of their assignment or projects.

The Pros and Cons

USING MULTIMEDIA in your lessons has many advantages. It allows students to take ownership of their learning by creating and producing their assignments using the latest technology. This involvement is essential for those students who are not already active learners. It also adds an exciting new dimension to your reservoir of teaching strategies.

On the other hand, there are some down sides to using video cameras—and all technology, for that matter. Electronics can be time-consuming. The video camera or video machine might not always work, and you'll waste valuable time trying to figure out how to fix it. (Avoid this pitfall by checking out all the equipment ahead of time.) Another drawback to using multimedia equipment is the problem of availability. You cannot assign a project that requires students to use video cameras at home if their families don't own the equipment.

That said, welcome to the twenty-first century, where you're expected to find ways to incorporate media, even if it's a struggle.

A Star Is Born!

THE VIDEO camera is a piece of multimedia equipment that is rarely used in classrooms but can add a new dimension to a lesson or unit. Although using a video camera requires taking some time to learn how to use it, it is well worth the time you put into it!

Teacher Use

If you decide to incorporate video cameras into your lessons, you'll find that they are a very useful tool for evaluation and assessment.

Teacher's Rule

In a school district where you have to beg for extra chalk, you're not going to have an easy time laying your hands on high-grade electronics equipment.

If you want to take advantage of technology, you're going to have to work out the problem. Approach the PTA. Talk with parents individually. Join a committee to meet with local businesses and large corporations. You may find individuals who are willing, if not to make an outright donation, to at least loan *equipment for a school term or longer.*

FROM THE DESK OF . . . "Too many teachers end up isolated from the rest of the faculty. They actually get competitive! They guard their worksheets, their notes, their videos as though they're state secrets. That's crazy! We're all in this together, and anyone who genuinely cares about kids ought to care about every kid, not just the ones in their own classes. Building good relationships with your fellow teachers ought to be one of your main preoccupations during your first years teaching. Be willing to share. Offer your videos; copy interesting articles for teachers who teach a related subject; recommend Web sites; do anything you can to let people know you're a team player!"

Laurel H., Sparks, Nevada

You will probably not use them often unless you have a personal penchant for drama, but it is a resource you should have available. Here are some ideas for their use in the classroom:

• **Student assessment.** Whenever you ask students to prepare or present in front of the class, use a video camera to record the project or performance. For example, you might ask students to perform a scene from an assigned book or to reenact a skirmish from the Revolutionary War. If your students are learning a second language, you might ask them to write and perform a thirty-second skit in that language. Using a video camera allows you time to enjoy their performances and to go back later and critique each part of the presentation to determine grades.

• **Student self-assessment.** After recording students' performances, you may want them to evaluate themselves on the quality and accuracy of the assignment. In this case, you would prepare a *rubric* for the performance or presentation based on the elements you are grading them on, pass the rubric out to each student, and play the video of their performance for the class. During the video, students assess their own work.

- **Self-assessment.** Sometimes, new teachers (and old, as well) have trouble in their classes. For example, they find that they lose their students' interest halfway through a lecture or there is constant talking and disruption coming from one area of the classroom. In dealing with these diffi-

> ## Teaching Terms
>
> ◆ ◆ ◆
>
> **Rubric.** A type of assessment that uses specific criteria to compare with a student's work.

culties, it might help you see yourself at work. Videotape yourself teaching your classes to get a whole new perspective on your teaching style and strategies. Don't be afraid to do this. You're the only one who has to see it! Set up the video recorder at the back of the room or in a part of the classroom where it would be unlikely to be noticed, and let it record a class period.

Student Use

Students love to use technology and will jump at the chance to use a video camera, especially if it means avoiding a live performance in front of their peers! Let them express their creative side by adding film to your teaching strategies as an additional method of learning. Here are some possibilities:

- **Performance assignments.** Instead of having your students perform in front of the class, you might require that they prepare for, perform, and record the assignment outside of class time and just play the video for the class. You may also offer video recording as an alternative to a live performance.

- **Research resource.** Video cameras can also be used to document a primary source of research such as an interview. Perhaps as part of a family history lesson you want your students to interview elderly family members about their childhood. You might decide to require students to record their interview as part of the assignment.

Coming Soon to a Classroom Near You!

LET'S FACE it, we all love movies. We go to theaters to see them, we rent them, we catch them on cable, we talk about them, and we follow the lives of the actors in the movies. Your students are the same way. Incorporating movies into lessons can boost the entertainment factor of your class as well as help your students learn.

Teacher Use

Not only do movies help students make connections between your lessons and their world of entertainment, but you are also teaching

them to think critically while they are watching. There are many times when showing a movie or a movie clip is appropriate for your lesson, but be sure that movies do not drive your curriculum. Show only what is necessary for improving understanding. Here are some tips to wise movie viewing in the classroom:

- **Start off with a bang!** Movies are often a good way to start off a unit or lesson. You might start off a basketball unit by showing a movie clip of Michael Jordan demonstrating how to shoot a lay-up and discussing the strategy of the game. If you're reading a historical novel, you could show a biography about the subject of the novel before you start. A social studies unit on the Great Depression might start with the opening sequence of *The Wizard of Oz*.

> *" I have learnt silence from the talkative, toleration from the intolerant, and kindness from the unkind; yet strange, I am ungrateful to these teachers. "*
>
> KAHLIL GIBRAN

- **Keep 'em interested.** Varying your teaching strategies and lessons periodically helps keep students engaged in the lesson and learning. In addition to using a movie at the beginning of the unit to get the students' interest, you can also use movies and movie clips periodically throughout the unit to enhance their comprehension and entertain them. Oftentimes, teachers will show the movie version of a novel throughout the unit while the students are reading along. As part of an art project that focused on contrast, you might select a black-and-white movie that demonstrates strong examples of light and shadow.

- **Winding down.** Movies are often used to wrap up a unit, which is particularly helpful if students are working outside class to finish up a project or report on the unit. By showing a movie here, you are creating lessons that are still relevant to the unit without giving them any more information, and without moving prematurely to the next unit before you have finished the assessment of the first.

FROM THE DESK OF . . . *"I was surprised my first year of teaching at how difficult it was to obtain the materials I needed to teach effectively. Cost cutting is always painful for public education because it means every modern tool we have for teaching — videos, computers, educational programming such as the History Channel, A/V equipment, scanners, printers — it's all nearly impossible to come by without spending your own money. And heaven knows, it isn't as though teachers are overpaid!"*

Paul Healey, Boston, Massachusetts

Choose Wisely, Young Jedi

Be very selective when choosing your movies and movie clips. You do not want parents or administrators calling to question your choice of movies. Remembering three important rules will ensure a success-ful movie-viewing experience:

• **Make it relevant!** Do not use a movie unless you can directly connect it with the material you are teaching in your unit. You want your students to get some educational value from everything you show.

• **Follow policies.** Know your district's policy on movies and their ratings. Some districts allow teachers to show only those movies that appear on that district's approved movie list. Some allow all G movies at the elementary level but discourage PG and forbid PG-13 and R-rated movies. Others allow relevant PG movies to be shown as long as the teacher has acquired *permission slips* from all the parents or guardians of the students in the class. It's imperative that you become familiar with your district's and school's policies on movie viewing in the classroom.

- **Keep it clean.** Even if you *are* teaching a unit on the 1960s British youth movement, *Austin Powers, the Spy Who Shagged Me* doesn't belong in the classroom. Loose ratings don't give carte blanche when content is inappropriate, so be sure you are familiar with the content of each movie you intend to show. You do *not* want to risk offending students or their parents with scenes of graphic violence, explicit or implied sex, or the glorification of alcohol, tobacco, or illegal substance abuse. Domestic violence is out. Implications of nonmarital sex are out. In short, anything you wouldn't want students doing in your classroom is *out*. If you don't want to see it, don't encourage it.

- **Cut away.** Use only the parts of the movie that you actually need to help the students learn. Oftentimes, teachers show the class the entire movie and waste an hour and half when they only needed to show a ten-minute clip in order for the students to grasp the point. By keeping your video short and concise, you help keep your students focused on the lesson. If they are allowed to watch the entire movie, the relevance may be lost. If you show a clip from the middle of the movie, play Letterman and give no more than a one-sentence outline of the plot line up to that point.

The Overhead Projector: A Teacher's Dream, But a Student's Nightmare

THE OVERHEAD projector can be a student's worst nightmare because it means that, while the teacher is comfortably perched on a

Teaching Terms

* * *

Movie permission slip. When you find a movie that you feel is relevant to your unit or lesson and think it would be a valuable and educational addition, you need to first check the rating and get approval from your principal. Upon approval, you may need to get permission slips from each parent. If this is the case, create a letter to the parents that explains the importance of the movie to the class and what content makes it rated PG. Have the students return the signed permission slip before showing the movie.

stool with the overhead pen poised meaningfully in hand, the student is scrambling for a pencil and paper to take notes. This piece of equipment does not have to be the bearer of such bad news; it has many other uses.

Teacher Use

Overhead projectors are a great way to project a single image or page of information onto a screen for the whole class to see and diligently record. You can also use them to do the following tasks:

- **Give directions.** If you are giving a set of complicated directions to your students and want transition times to be as short as possible, it is helpful to your students to be able to quickly refer to your directions. If you have these directions displayed on your overhead projector, they can give the screen a quick glance and know exactly what to do next.

- **Model the work.** The overhead projector is an excellent place to give examples or do problems for your students. This method is sometimes better than using the blackboard because, when you're using the overhead projector, you can face the class, allowing you to make eye contact, check for understanding, and respond to questions.

- **Reward excellence.** Reward students who have excelled or shown progress or creativity. Make an overhead copy of their exceptional work and display it for the others to see. Explain why this work is getting rewarded so the class recognizes it as a positive part of your lesson. Give the student whose work you rewarded a thumbs up, a high five, a homework pass or a special certificate. Students will be quickly drawn to the overhead whenever you get ready to use it.

• **Simplify note taking.** And last but not least, the overhead use all students dread: the projection of information that is intended to be copied by the cramped-up hands of students everywhere. When you want students to retain certain information and they have not yet learned to take notes from your lectures, your only other option is writing it down for them to copy. With the overhead projector, you can either write out the notes as you lecture or conclude your lecture with a preprepared transparency sheet with the information already on it. Either way, you have made it easier to pass on information and explain as you go, while also retaining a copy to use with the students who were out of the room at the time.

Pros and Cons

The benefits to using an overhead projector are many. The equipment itself is easy to use and the preparation for its use requires little time and effort. It is also an efficient way to give students critical information. The machine is convenient for you because you can stay in one place, face the class, and give your lecture and demonstration without losing eye contact with your students.

However, an overhead projector limits your movement around the room and is an easy piece of equipment to rely on. Be very careful that the overhead projector does not become a constant presence during your daily lessons; students will begin to tune you out. Also, if you actually stand by the overhead and write down the examples or notes, you are not able to circulate throughout the room to check on your students' progress and comprehension. This problem may be compounded by the necessity of dimming classroom lights to view the screen. When the lights are out, students may feel anonymous and use the anonymity to write notes, fiddle with toys, whisper, sleep, or daydream.

Teacher's Rule

Use a homework pass as an incentive. When students do something worth rewarding, they receive slips of paper (about the size of a coupon) good for one homework freebee. When students decide they are going to cash in their homework passes, they simply turn in their coupons instead of the homework and receive full credit. These can only be used only on daily homework assignments and are void with projects, essays, or long-term assignments.

Student Use

Teachers often assign projects that require a presentation to the class. Whether students are working on their own or with a group, the overhead projector is a great way to present what they have learned.

If you have assigned a presentation and have given your students the option of using the overhead projector, the following are some guidelines you should share.

- **Enlarge.** Any information that is typed and copied onto a transparency for use on the overhead projector should be in an eighteen- to twenty-point font. The entire class, even those at the very back of the room, should be able to see every word on the screen.

- **Set the timer.** Students may have only a limited time on the overhead within their overall presentation. Otherwise, their classmates lose interest and focus. Students need to practice their public speaking by being up in front of their classmates instead of behind the overhead projector.

• **Grade it!** Let your students know that you will be grading their overhead information for spelling, grammar, and content. Students often don't bother to spell-check or edit their typed information before making a transparency. Once the damage is done, the errors are flashed up on the screen for all to see. This is unacceptable and should be reflected in the overall presentation grade.

> ## Teaching Terms
> ◆ ◆ ◆
>
> **Transparency sheet.** These are thick pieces of plastic onto which you can copy any information that you want to project onto a screen using an overhead projector. Some transparencies can be used in copy machines, while other types of transparencies can be used in printers.

Cave of Computers

SOME TEACHERS avoid their school's computer lab completely because they view technology as more of a hassle than a benefit to education. Don't be that way. The computer lab at your school is a wonderful resource, and you help your students learn valuable skills

Making the Grade

How important is it that students use technology in schools? They are growing up in a world where unfamiliarity with the tools of technology may consign them to failure in college and the workplace. Want to know more? What better place to look than the Web?

Technology: *http://oeri3 .ed.gov:8000/Teachers /nonmembers/index.cgi?do= listmsgs&conf=Teach.Techn— An excellent discussion of how and why teachers use technology in the classroom, by Anne Jolly, an eighth-grade science teacher at Cranford Burns Middle School in Mobile, Alabama*

when you expose them to computers. Make lab use part of your lesson plans when possible.

Venture Inside

Before you take your class to the computer lab, you need to find out about it. Introduce yourself to the people who run the lab and who maintain and repair the machines. Examine the facilities to determine whether you can successfully use the lab in conjunction with one of your assignments. Here are some of the questions you should ask:

• **What about sheer numbers?** Can the lab accommodate your entire class? Count the numbers of computers that are up and running.

• **It can save, but can it print?** Find out how many printers are available and whether they're accessible to everyone over a network or can be used only from specific machines. Are they all working?

• **What?! No Word 2000?** Identify the software available in the lab. Is it right for your needs? What policies are in place if you want to install additional software? (Hint: The larger and more complex the lab, the less likely you are to have any privileges there. Your district may be so large that it hires technology managers to keep the computers up and running. If so, consider yourself locked out. Technicians and administrators often run the show when it comes to *networked* labs.)

- **Can you check e-mail?** Is there Internet access through the computers? If so, does the district assign you an e-mail address? Do your students get e-mail addresses? What policies are in place regarding personal email? Are the machines filtered to prevent access to pornography or other inappropriate information? Can you get a record of what sites your students visit when they're on-line?

- **Where do I sign up?** Do you need to sign up for the lab? What hours are available? What do your students need to do to get before- or after-school access?

> *" The real object of education is to have a man in the condition of continually asking questions. "*
>
> Bishop Creighton

You need to gather all of this information before you take your class to the lab.

Stand Guard

It can be frustrating monitoring students in the computer lab because they work at different paces and are at different stages of their assignment. The smart ones know how to flick off the game screen in the background whenever you walk past. These factors make it difficult to monitor progress and ensure that everyone is being productive and using the computer lab time wisely.

So before you take your class to the lab, lay down the ground rules. Let them know that you have certain expectations to be fulfilled by the end of their time in the computer lab and that they will be receiving a grade for the quality of their time spent.

- **Monitor.** Throughout the period, continuously walk around the lab, keeping an eye on your students and answering any questions that might pop up. This is the best way to ensure that your students stay on task and use the time wisely. If you have any say in how the lab is arranged, encourage a formation that allows you to monitor every screen at once. Nobody smuggles in a game of *Lode Runner* when the teacher is actually watching.

Teaching Terms

◆ ◆ ◆

Networking. If your computer lab has fewer than fifteen stand-alone computers or is operated by the nice librarian who isn't really sure where the "on" switch is located, you probably don't have a network. If your district is well funded, though, and has staff members who do nothing but take care of computers, you are very likely to be part of a network. Networks allow file and software sharing between computers — a big advantage on collaborative projects — but have a tendency to cause severe disruptions when the entire network comes crashing earthward, and you find yourself making finger shadows to entertain your students.

• **Get the evidence.** Hold your students accountable for their time in the computer lab! Require that each student turn in something to you at the end of the period that reflects the work accomplished in the computer lab. This can simply be a printout of their work in progress. If you take your class to the computer lab weekly, you can compare their evidence from week-to-week. This will be the most accurate way to determine progress. Some labs are even set up to track computer usage, so read reports if they're available.

• **Make 'em earn the grade.** Tell the students ahead of time that you will be giving them points for their ability to stay on task in the lab. Then follow through. When students goof off or use the computer for something other than your assignment, tell them you are deducting a point. At the end of each session, give students their lab grades.

• **Troubleshoot.** Have a backup plan. Take a few blank disks with you, and if a printer goes down, have the students save their documents to disk. Make sure that the lab can accommodate a few more students than you have in your class so that if one of the monitors, keyboards, or mice doesn't work, students can move to another machine.

Program It In

THOUSANDS OF educational software titles are on the market. Many are designed to help teachers be more efficient. The majority help students develop their academic skills.

Teaching Programs

There is some software no teacher should be without! Here are the most critical applications for teachers:

- **Grades.** It is essential that you have some sort of grading program that allows you to enter scores and automatically calculates overall grades and percentages, prints reports, and weighs scores the way you prefer them.

- **Word processing.** As a teacher, you will be creating, changing, or retyping tests, assignments, quizzes, and other handouts. You need a word processor. If you're using Microsoft Windows, you already have a rudimentary package (WordPad and/or NotePad), which might be sufficient for your requirements. Owners of Apple Computers are also supplied with a basic word processor as part of their original software. If you do complex documents with footnotes, endnotes, graphics, or other formatting, you'll require a more robust package.

- **Presentation creator.** This software would replace the overhead projector. A program such as Microsoft PowerPoint or Lotus

FreeLance allows you to create slides with text, artwork, photographs, Web pages, charts, and graphs that can be used during lectures and for note taking. You can print out your presentation on paper or overhead transparencies or create a live show with the assistance of a screen projector or adapted video equipment.

• **Specialization.** If you teach an elective or class that deals with specific skills, you will need a very specific program that helps you accomplish your job. For example, some specialized software packages are practically required for creative and technical subjects such as photography, publishing, business, drafting, and graphic arts.

• **Internet access.** At a minimum, you'll require dial-up software (it's free), a browser such as Netscape Navigator or Microsoft's Internet Explorer (they're both free), and a mail reader such as Microsoft Outlook or Qualcomm Eudora (also free). If you intend to build Web pages, you'll need FTP software (it's free), graphics software, and a Web authoring package such as Front Page, Macromedia's Dream Weaver, or any of several dozen less expensive, even free, Web authoring packages.

If you find that your school has not purchased and installed a particular piece of software on your school or classroom machines, talk with your grade-level chairperson or the principal to find out how to go about obtaining a copy.

Externals

If your school or district has a large budget for technological equipment, you may be able to get your hands on some of the peripheral devices that can accompany a computer. The following equipment will make your teaching experience easier:

- **High-capacity storage.** Back up files with a CD-RW drive, which writes to compact discs; a tape backup; a second hard drive; or a high-capacity zip drive. Most of these devices will fit inside a standard desktop or tower computer case, and all of them can be attached to a laptop using either the parallel or USB port. These devices help you store backups of all your units and lessons in one location.

- **Printer.** A central network printer is nice, if you have access to one, but it's also useful to have an inexpensive color inkjet printer in your own classroom.

- **Digital camera.** This camera takes pictures and saves them onto a computer or a removable disk. The pictures can then be manipulated electronically and printed out. They're not quite as good as the 35mm glossies you pick up from the drugstore after a vacation, but the quality of digital images is constantly improving.

- **Digital video.** This camera operates on the same idea as the digital camera, but, instead of recording images, it records movements and sound. These images, too, can be transferred to the computer and viewed on screen.

Student Programs

Computer labs in most schools will have a basic word-processing program as well as some tutorials that can be used to help students develop specific skills. Your students might have tutorials for math, spelling, typing, science, and reading. The purchase and installation of other programs will vary from school to school. Informational CDs such as encyclopedias and dictionaries are often purchased by schools and made available to students.

Tales from the Trenches

Coauthor Karen Heisinger knows the importance of good lesson plans and adequate preparation. As she recalls, "I used to bring my lesson plan book home with me every night. I did this so I could look over my plans for the next day and go over the lessons in my mind. Only once did I leave my plan book at home — not bad for 10 years of teaching!"

◆ ◆ ◆

This one comes to us from a student. And let it be a warning to teachers everywhere to be cognizant that students are completely facile with computers. A student in California often baby-sat for two teachers. One night she decided to play on their computer. She also decided to check out the Internet sites that the teachers had bookmarked. What the student found was a list of potentially embarrassing sites! And, of course, she didn't hesitate to share the news with fellow students.

As a teacher, you live in a fish bowl, even in your own home. So, be careful.

Surfin' the Web

IF YOUR school has access to the Internet, count yourself lucky. The Web has become a necessary tool in education and is useful for both the educator and the student.

Student Use

The primary use of the Internet in school is for research. Because so much information appears on the Web, this tool is helpful for help in any subject or discipline. There are some pitfalls, though:

• Be aware of the availability of research papers of any kind and for any subject. They can be downloaded, purchased, or copied straight from the Internet.

FROM THE DESK OF . . . "We're fortunate to have computers in our classroom, and I take full advantage of them! One of the best things we do is small-group on-line field trips. I allow groups of up to four students to gather around a single machine to navigate a designated Web site. I find it works best when all the students in the group are of the same gender; that way, nobody is reluctant to get involved, direct the 'navigator,' or shout out observations.

"There are dozens of places to find on-line field trips. Here's a link to one of my favorite directories":

Videoconference Adventures: www.kn.pacbell.com/wired/vidconf/adventures.html

Belinda C., Vancouver, Washington

• Teach students that the quality of information is paramount. Just because someone wrote it doesn't make it so, whether it appears in a newspaper, a book, or on-line.

Teacher Use

You are fortunate to be teaching in an era with such a wonderful teaching resource as the World Wide Web. Teachers have a variety of uses for the Internet:

• **Lesson plans.** Many sites on the 'Net are just for teachers. They facilitate the exchange of lesson plans in every discipline. They also provide ideas for thematic units, activities, motivators, teaching tips, and much more.

• **Support.** Classroom management problems, conflicts with colleagues, unsupportive grade level partners, or simply a lack of enough hours in the day are the sorts of troubles teachers deal with daily. The Internet provides chat rooms, mailing lists, and discussion forums for support, whether you're a beginner or an old hand.

• **Research.** You need access to up-to-date research as much as your students do. You might want to know a little bit more about a particular historic figure before talking about him in social studies next week. Or you might want to research the root of a word before you introduce it in language arts in the next unit.

A great deal of your ability to incorporate multimedia depends on your school and district budget for equipment. But when you get

Making the Grade

Looking for a way to conduct a small meeting or tutoring session on the Web? Perhaps even a way for your students to collaborate on a group project? Here's a place you can do it all for free. Upload your PowerPoint presentations, visit live Web sites, operate an electronic whiteboard, and more.

My Place Ware:
www.myplaceware.com

the opportunity to use technology in the classroom, take advantage of it. It will not only mark you as an up-to-date professional; you will be helping your students learn valuable skills that will help them succeed in their world.

Things to Remember

To incorporate multimedia in your classroom, remember to do the following:

❏ Check out your school's resources, including the computer lab, available software, and any peripheral computer resources available for yours and the students' use

❏ Consider using a videocamera to: videotape a performance or project, videotape yourself doing a lesson, or allowing students to videotape themselves as an alternative to a live performance

❏ Be selective when it comes to showing videotapes in your classroom; make sure they are relevant to the lesson, are approved by the administration, and consider only showing the part of the video that relates to the objective of the lesson

❏ Use the overhead projector as a way to maintain eye contact with the class while students are taking notes, and convert student work to transparencies to use as models

> " *The point is to develop the childlike inclination for play and the childlike desire for recognition and to guide the child over to important fields for society. Such a school demands from the teacher that he be a kind of artist in his province.* "
>
> ALBERT EINSTEIN

PART FOUR

CLASSROOM MANAGEMENT

Classroom Rules and Responsibilities

WHEN YOU DECIDED on this profession, you probably thought, "What fun!" You'd get to spend time with kids and really change the world. But somewhere down deep, you probably also realized that, well, kids will be kids. Not every child is an angel. And groups of kids can get downright crazy together. Into every elementary classroom rules must come! In truth, kids really do work better with parameters. So let's set some!

> " *Education makes a people easy to lead, but difficult to drive; easy to govern but impossible to enslave.* "
>
> BARON HENRY
> PETER BROUGHAM

Power Rangers: Getting Student Input

WIPE THAT "Are you nuts?" look off your face. In many ways, giving your students some power in the big decisions—such as rules and regulations—in the context of a *feedback discussion* will ensure a smooth-running class. But before we go into giving your tykes some say in the rules, we need to delve into how to handle the different age groups. Just as a kindergartner will probably be too shy to say much regarding the classroom right away, some sixth graders may move into the power mode too quickly and with full force.

The input you accept from your students regarding class rules will depend on the grade level you are teaching. You will need to be very direct with the youngest students—clarifying everything—but will need to converse at length about rules and responsibilities with the older students.

Regardless of the age level, however, the discussion of why we have rules should take place—not only rules in school but rules at home, rules for sports, and rules for living! Your students, especially during the first few days of class, will tend to respond appropriately and remain attentive during this "life" lesson. In fact, they may even tell you that we need classroom rules so that everyone is safe and no one gets hurt, so that everyone gets a turn, and so that everyone knows what to do. Humorously enough—and something to keep in mind—these students who delve attentively into the necessity for rules may not necessarily follow them a couple of weeks down the line. But they sure do know the right words to say!

After laying the groundwork for why we need rules, it's always good to proceed into a discussion of past rules the kids may have needed to heed—rules in the home, for example. This discussion ideally will produce a list of *potential* classroom rules—potential because the students will come up with about ten of them, and they will probably be very specific. Here's the kicker: let them brainstorm

Teaching Terms

◆ ◆ ◆

Feedback discussion. A strategy for encouraging active student participation in discussions by working within a structured framework. For examples and tips related to discussion formats, see this Web site:

Feedback Discussions: http://darkwing.uoregon.edu/~tep /lizard/feedback_discuss.html as many as they can! Once you can see patterns forming, start grouping these class-created-rules into categories. You will most likely come up with many of the same rules, worded just a tad differently, comprising these major regulations:

1. **Be safe.** The students will have contributed no hitting, no kicking, no pushing, no name-calling, and no put-downs.
2. **Be respectful.** The students will have said listen to the teacher, don't take other people's things, and keep your hands to yourself.
3. **Work hard.** The students might say no talking when doing work, and turn in all assignments.

Now you have your classroom rules! Three of them! Thank the students for their help in clarifying your classroom rules. For the older students, have them write the rules and bring them home to have their parents sign. Have students sign the rules as well. You might write on the board for the students to copy: "Today we discussed some rules we should have in our classroom. This is what we decided. All students should:"

1. Be safe.
2. Be respectful.
3. Work hard.

_____   _____
PARENT SIGNATURE   MY SIGNATURE

Keep a roster of your students on a clipboard, and track their individual behavior. Put the corresponding number of the rule next to

---

Teacher's Rule

Try not to judge kids the first few days of class and attach labels such as "the listener," "the talker," "the troublemaker," or "the pleaser." Kids will surprise you! You may find—you probably will find—that your image of who is whom will change during the first few weeks of school. Instead of passing judgment, just watch. Watch how each behaves and record the behavior if egregious.

the name of the student who is breaking that particular rule. In the first couple of weeks, you can keep track of the students' behavior and notice patterns that may emerge. You may want to keep record of behaviors such as this (but know that any system you devise that works for you is a good system):

1. The student talks while you are teaching a lesson.
2. You make eye contact with the student, grab the clipboard, and record number 2 on the clipboard next to the student's name (you may want to write "talking during instruction" next to the 2).
3. You make eye contact again with the student and put the clipboard down.

The student in question will know it was him (and the students around him will behave properly, too!). This method of disciplining is respectful of the individual student—you have not humiliated the student in front of the other kids, but you have alerted the child that you will not tolerate the ill behavior. Moreover, you've notified the other kids that, if talking, they, too, will not gain your respect—amazingly enough, this is something they really do want.

The Big Prize

Now THAT you've laid the foundation for what behavior you expect in the classroom and the students have given you input on the rules, it is time to determine consequences for the behavior. Do not feel that you need to create elaborate reward systems. Concentrate on helping the students recognize and change their behavior and communicating with the parents about their child's behavior. Developing intrinsic motivation and self-satisfaction are the essential goals of any "discipline" system—not rewarding through candy or goodies! The way you help students develop these qualities, though, could be through the rewards and consequences you establish and enforce in the classroom.

Rewards should be given for very specific behaviors. Many rewards do not cost anything and still promote the intrinsic values for which you are striving. Most students, for example—now hold your horses here because you'll probably find yourself bowled over—love to spend extra time with the teacher. A reward for good behavior all week, then, might involve eating lunch with you on Friday. You don't have to buy the winning student lunch (unless you want to buy it); the kid or kids just eat lunch with you in the classroom.

To reward your entire class, try out the following rewards:

- Extra art, music, or PE time
- Science or math games
- Silent reading time or extra teacher read-aloud time

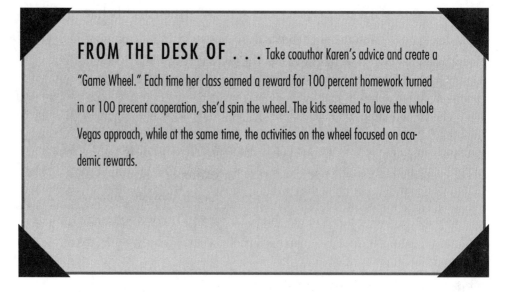

FROM THE DESK OF . . . Take coauthor Karen's advice and create a "Game Wheel." Each time her class earned a reward for 100 percent homework turned in or 100 precent cooperation, she'd spin the wheel. The kids seemed to love the whole Vegas approach, while at the same time, the activities on the wheel focused on academic rewards.

Increase the difficulty of the expectations as time progresses. Instead of rewarding one day's cooperation, for example, reward the class if everyone turns in his or her homework for three days in a row or even the whole week.

Having the students set a goal for themselves and choose the reward they can receive can be very motivating. Ensure the rewards mentioned are academic by nature: extra art, music, or PE, for example. They cannot earn "free time"; they can earn extra time for a favorite academic activity. Most kids don't realize when they're having fun that they're—yikes!—learning.

Truth and Consequences

ON THE flip side of rewards fall the consequences. Students want not only to be rewarded for their good behavior but also to know that a boundary exists and a consequence results for poor behavior. In fact, those good kids who follow the rules really hate it when the disruptive kids don't receive a consequence for their bad behavior. The basic and most common consequences are

1. warning
2. time-out in class
3. time-out in a fellow teacher's class
4. phone call home
5. do-not-pass-go slips to the principal

Rely on that clipboard. After you record a "number" next to a student's name, the student receives a warning. The next offense incurs a consequence.

Time-out

For elementary children, the most effective consequence is a time-out in class. This means that you need to designate a space in your classroom for students to take a time-out. The time-out spot needs to be a certain desk or chair set away from the other students. It would be even better if you can provide a timer to set so that the student knows exactly how long he or she must endure the ostracization from classmates. A good rule of thumb for a time-out is one minute per year of age. Here's a typical scenario:

You: John, you are talking during my lesson. If you continue talking, then you will need to go to time-out. Do you understand? [Record on clipboard.]

John: Yes.

You: Good. Make the right choice, John; I know you can do it.

As you continue to teach, John starts talking again. You walk over to John and say, "I'm sorry that you chose to keep talking, John,

Teacher's Rule

Before you call a parent, it's always a good idea to send a quick e-mail or speak briefly to an administrator to tell him or her of the situation. More often than not, the parent will be receptive to your phone call and want to work with you to help the child behave. Sometimes, however, the parent can be as belligerent as the child. If you document the incident and notify the principal, for example, that a potential problem may arise, you can feel more secure knowing that the administrator has your back!

but as I told you, if you kept talking, you would go to time-out. You need to go to time-out now for ten minutes. I'll set the timer."

The premise is that if you make your message clear, then the students will respect this boundary and follow it. Occasionally, you will have a student who does not respect the rules or the boundaries you set. Keep your language in terms of the *choices* that student is making. Get parents involved in discussions of the student's behavior, and get the principal involved if the misbehavior continues. An excellent resource for setting limits is Dr. Robert MacKenzie's book *Setting Limits in the Classroom* (Prima Publishing).

We've Always Done It This Way

THE MOST common pitfall of new teachers is lack of consistency. This is why you should keep your rules, rewards, and consequences simple! The simpler the rules, the easier it is to follow them consistently.

If you keep a clipboard and record consequences, gosh darn it, record them every day! If a student is talking, record it every time. The students are watching you and mentally recording everything that you do and say. If you give three warnings before acting, then the students know that they can talk or misbehave three times before you'll do anything about it. Do something about it the *first* time it happens! The students will take notice and know that you mean business.

Tales from the Trenches

"One year, when I taught sixth grade, I had a very 'tough' student," recalls coauthor Karen Heisinger. "He lived in a neighborhood where drive-by shootings were normal and was very intimidating. This young man threatened a lot of students in my class. They were very afraid of him and had been since fifth grade when he transferred to the school. I saw a different side of him, though, the side of him that wanted to learn and that was very sweet.

"A few weeks into the school year, I held a class meeting. In California, the Education Code specifically states that even a threat can get the child suspended, and I knew this going into the meeting. At the meeting, I asked my students to raise their hand if this particular student had threatened them. All of the hands went up, and the student just smiled. I asked the student if he realized that by just threatening the students he could get suspended. The smile dropped off his face, and he said, 'My mom would kill me if I got suspended!' The class giggled and he smiled, too. We discussed the consequences a bit more, and then I concluded that portion of the meeting by saying, 'So you will not threaten anyone anymore, or you will be suspended.' Everyone agreed to help this student keep his promise, and I recorded this information.

"I could physically feel everyone relax; the student did not need to be tough anymore, and the class could feel safe knowing that there was a consequence for the threats and that their fellow student was afraid of his mother's consequence, thus very 'real' to them!"

This is not to suggest that consistency is easy. But you have been hired to teach these students, and the only way you can do that is to enforce basic rules consistently. It would be nice if you never encountered a problem during your lessons, but that dream is, quite frankly, unrealistic.

Order in the Court!

WHEN A problem arises again and again in your classroom—problems such as name-calling or spit-wad production—the time has come to address the problem at a class meeting. Since the problem involves the many instead of the few, the many must deal with the problem together. It's only fair!

How you address the problem depends entirely on how well you know your students and the rapport you share with them. Proceed cautiously. Have a class meeting that is devoted to the problem in general. You devote a period of time, such as ten minutes before recess, to discuss the problem of name-calling. You can ask how it feels to be called a name and what consequence should be given when a student calls another student a name. The students will be harsher than you in their consequences, so set the parameters of the class meeting by letting the students know that their consequences should be respectful of the other student and reasonable in nature. The goal is to try to change the behavior, not to punish the student.

If you want to get more specific with your class, then the class meeting you hold will deal with specific students who are exhibiting a specific behavior. This can be touchy, though, and should be handled very sensitively (as in Karen's example). The meeting addresses students by name, and some problem solving takes place to assist those students. The difference between the general meeting and the specific meeting is that you could potentially put students "on the spot." This is the point, but again, you need to be careful about the students in question. Beyond hurting the sensitive child and turning him or her off to learning, you may hear from an irate parent when you "single out" a kid.

Should you choose to call this kind of class meeting, you'll want to proceed something like this:

You: We're in a circle today to talk about name-calling. A lot of you have complained to me about a certain group of girls. I've talked to them about it [which you need to do ahead of time], and we're here to let them know how you feel and what we should do about it. Who has been called a name by members of this class?

Class: [Ten hands go up.]

You: Why don't you go first, Robert? Tell us how you feel when you are called a name.

Proceed the same way with the other students. Watch the culprits for their reaction. If it is getting too overwhelming, stop after one or two comments. If they seem unfazed, continue. Either way, summarize what students are saying in terms of how the behavior makes them feel. Switch gears, then, and ask for consequences *the next time* someone calls a name. Make sure the consequences are reasonable and respectful of the perpetrators, and take a vote from the class. Make sure the class understands the consequences and how the students need to work together to help stop name-calling.

> *" Education is not the filling of a pail, but the lighting of a fire. "*
>
> W. B. Yeats

It's not as easy as it sounds, but this will get you started. In truth, you will get better as the years go by at managing your class and working through all the difficulties.

A good resource for class meetings is *Positive Discipline: the classic guide for parents and teachers to help children develop self-discipline, responsibility, cooperation, and problem-solving skills* by Jane Nelsen (Ballantine).

Enlisting Help in the Classroom

Here's the really encouraging part about classroom management. You don't need to suffer alone. Students and parents generally love to help out, and you will appreciate the assistance. Moreover, when a parent enters the room, suddenly the kids recognize that the bad behavior they may exhibit in the class will not be acceptable and may warrant a grounding if Mom or Pop actually sees the kid act out. So, definitely look upon parental help as a blessing.

Student help also offers a good way to get tasks done and free you up to manage more effectively. Try using the following suggestions to guide how you set up your classroom so that others can help you out.

Student Helpers

Build the community spirit of your classroom by appointing "student helpers." You may want to switch these jobs weekly or monthly; younger students can keep the jobs for a week, but let older students do these jobs for a month. Also, some of these jobs, such as collecting homework, are appropriate only for older students. Here are some examples of student jobs:

- **Paper passers.** These students pass out worksheets or papers.

- **Homework collector.** This student has a roster for checking off who turned in the homework each day.

- **Supplies monitors.** These students pass out and collect necessary supplies.

- **Door monitor.** This student holds open the door for students and makes sure it's shut when the class enters or leaves the room.

- **Line monitor.** This student is assigned to make sure the line is quiet and straight.

- **Plant monitor.** This student waters your plants in accordance with a schedule you establish.

- **Equipment monitors.** These students assign your recess equipment and make sure everything is returned.

- **Calendar monitor.** This student changes the calendar for you each day and may even remind you of significant events.

- **Music monitor.** This student turns the music on and off for you every day.

- **Flag-salute monitor.** This student leads the flag salute every day (more on this later).

- **Office monitor.** This student takes the attendance to the office and retrieves messages for you.

- **Messenger.** This student runs errands for you as needed.

Parent Helpers

Parents can be a great source of assistance to you. Use the following suggestions to help you set some guidelines for parent help.

Grading

There are several areas in which parents can assist in grading:

- **Daily math.** Parents can help correct and record scores.

- **Spelling.** Parents can correct weekly spelling tests.

- **Editing.** Parents can read through students' paragraphs, count the number of words, and circle the misspelled words.

Projects

Parents can be a big help in managing class projects.

- **Art.** Parents can gather and organize art supplies for an upcoming project.

- **Folders.** Parents can fold construction paper into folders for you.

- **Notebooks.** Parents can staple binder paper to become notebooks.

- **Science.** Parents can organize materials into labs for an upcoming lesson.

Working with Students

Parents have been in the "teaching" business for as long as they've been parenting. Who better to help you with the kids?

- **Math groups.** Parents can work with students who need remediation or enrichment.

- **Reading groups.** Parents can work with a single group, but you need to be very specific with your directions.

- **Spelling.** Parents can have students spell words to them or play a spelling game in a small group.

- **Art/music/PE.** If your parents are willing and able, have them lead the students through a lesson on the subject.

General

There are lots of other ways in which parents can make your teaching job easier:

- **Field trips.** Parents are always needed to go on field trips as chaperones.

- **Parties.** Get parents involved in planning the parties.

- **Class parent.** This parent can act as the liaison between you and the PTA and other school functions.

Making the Grade

Report Card
A
A
A
A

Student misbehavior covers so many areas, it's ineffective to have just one or two strategies for dealing with them all. Here's help—a model for responding to any of 117 different categories of errant behavior:

You Can Handle Them All:
www.educationworld.com /a_curr/curr261.shtml

Procedures and Routines

YOU MAY take for granted as an adult the procedures for queuing before a movie or going to the bathroom or sharpening your pencils, but the world is an entirely different place for children. Though we've grown accustomed to certain routines, many children have yet to experience enough of life to line up automatically and take turns

Teacher's Rule

Oh, no—not another thing to accomplish those first few weeks of class! Oh, yes. We highly urge you to plan a lesson around lining up. Include both reasons that the class might line up and guidelines on how to behave while lined up. You may feel as though the lesson's a pain today, but later in the year that old lesson will be a lifesaver when your class acts angelic during the fire drill!

at the pencil sharpener. Implementing certain routines makes the difference between a relaxed classroom atmosphere and chaos.

Line Up!

Any drill sergeants in the house? Yeah,—we thought so. Because classes don't actually stay in the classroom 100 percent of the time, your students will line up so often you may begin to feel like you've earned stripes! To go to class, to leave class, to practice a fire drill (discussed in more detail later), to go to the library, to go to the cafeteria—these are all events that necessitate the line-up.

Lines ensure the safety of all the students in your class and the school. In a fire drill, for example, the students need to be able to hear instructions and get to the designated location in a timely manner. Teach them the procedure for lining up quickly and quietly, so that you're able to account for them all.

That Fine Line

Just because you say, "Line up," to your class doesn't mean those sweet children will know what to do there. Teach them that while in line, they need to keep their hands, feet, and objects to themselves at all times, keep a proper distance from the person ahead of them and in back of them, and refrain from cutting in front or in back of another student. Reinforce this line behavior *constantly*.

A great way to reinforce line etiquette is practice. Go ahead—walk your students around the school in line and give them a tour of

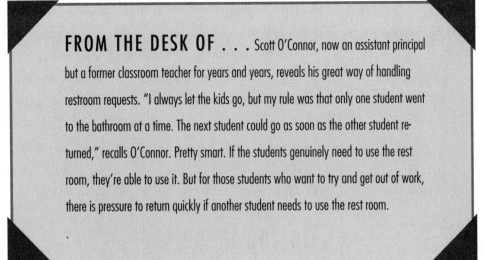

FROM THE DESK OF . . . Scott O'Connor, now an assistant principal but a former classroom teacher for years and years, reveals his great way of handling restroom requests. "I always let the kids go, but my rule was that only one student went to the bathroom at a time. The next student could go as soon as the other student returned," recalls O'Connor. Pretty smart. If the students genuinely need to use the rest room, they're able to use it. But for those students who want to try and get out of work, there is pressure to return quickly if another student needs to use the rest room.

the school and the chance to practice good line behavior. And guess what? This line behavior lesson just might double as a physical education class. After all, you're walking, walking, and walking!

"I Need to Use the Potty"

EVEN IF you never receive the opportunity to use the rest room during class time (teachers have been known to experience marathon "hold it" sessions), your students won't have nearly so much control. The dilemma comes when you think they are trying to get away with missing class time or are using the rest room as an excuse to goof off. You can't say no to a child who needs to use the bathroom or get a drink. So what do you do?

You regularly remind students that recess is the time to get a drink and use the rest room. If it's close to recess, ask the student whether it's possible to wait until the proper time. If the answer is no, wave good-bye. If it happens too often with a particular student,

Making the Grade

Many schools now require a formal hall pass from the teacher in order for a student to be out of the classroom during class time. In fact, a recent trend has students carrying miniplanners—just like your adult planner but less detailed. In the miniplanners, students record assignments and the like. One or more pages is devoted to a ledger hall pass. Just by glancing at the pass, the teacher can see how many times the student has left the class to go to the bathroom in the week.

notify the parents of a potential medical or behavioral problem.

If things get out of hand, you'll want to create a sign-out sheet for students to record when they leave the room. Require them to carry one pass and leave a pass on their desk to indicate they have left the room. Teach them that if they need to use the rest room, they are to get up and follow the procedure without interrupting the class.

Tip-Top Shape

YOUR PROCEDURE for sharpening pencils will depend on the age of your students and the condition of your pencil sharpener. For younger students, you may want to do all of the sharpening yourself. Have a container full of sharpened pencils on hand for students to use and another container for unsharpened pencils. Do the sharpening before or after school or at lunch.

The pencil container is efficient, too, for older students who frequently lose their pencils or for times when you absolutely need it silent, such as when you are testing. Teaching them to sharpen their pencils themselves means teaching them how to use the sharpener and when.

Assembly of Children

YOU WILL take your students to many *assemblies* throughout the year. The one thing to remember (and the hardest thing to do) is to watch your class—and not the assembly. Of course, you will be able to enjoy what is going on, but your main function is to maintain control of your students. Here are some procedures for your students to follow.

Teach students to walk in to the assembly room in a line (quietly, of course). Ask whether there is a specific spot for your class to sit, and have them walk in a line to your spot. Stand in the aisle and have the students start a new row when they reach you, and so on. Switch the spots of students who will talk to each other during the assembly. Also, bring your behavior clipboard so you can record their behavior in the assembly and follow through with consequences. During the assembly, then, you are watching them and monitoring their behavior while they are watching the assembly.

> ## Teaching Terms
> • • •
>
> **Assembly.** Elementary school assemblies are scheduled for dozens of reasons: announcements, holiday programs, awards, improving school spirit, entertainment, special speakers or presentations, or large-group lessons.

Pick Me

IN YOUNGER grades, you will actually need to teach students how to ask for help. Teach them the procedure for how to get your assistance, and then teach them to go on to the next problem while they are waiting for you.

Don't make the procedure for getting your attention too disruptive. Some teachers make it overly complicated by asking students to get up and write their name on the board or hook something over their desk or seat. The time-tested raising of hands works fine. Try to assist each child in the order in which the hands were raised. Sometimes it helps to say in a quiet voice, "Okay, it's Jordan, then I'll get to Stacy, Juanita, and Marco, in that order." As you consistently show the children that you do see their hands and that you do respond in

Making the Grade

Sadly, every year children die of heat exhaustion and/or dehydration in hot climates. With school years beginning in the heat of August, teachers need to watch children closely for signs of heat exhaustion and remind students to drink water throughout the day. If you suspect that a child is suffering from heat exhaustion or dehydration, immediately call the school nurse.

order, the kids will know that you will find your way to helping them. Moreover, you'll find that some students don't really need your help; they just want some extra attention.

Don't be surprised if rows and rows of hands appear as you walk around. If this happens, consider that your directions perhaps weren't clear enough or that you need to work on your guided practice more.

All Quiet on the Class's Front

You will want to establish a quiet signal right away with your students. This is the signal that says, "I need your attention right now." Since it is a quiet signal, you need to get their attention in a quiet manner. You can hold up your hand and do a silent countdown from "five" with your fingers. Teach the students to get each other's attention in a quiet manner by the time you get to "one."

There are other signals you can incorporate into your day. You can clap a rhythm and have the students repeat it. You can say "1, 2, 3, eyes on me." Whatever you decide to do, teach it and practice it until it becomes routine.

Work Piles

Another procedure that you'll need to make clear within the first weeks of school is how and where you want the students to turn in their work. Teach them that they need to walk over to the basket to turn in their work and then get started on the next assignment. If work is not done, then they need to put it in their "unfinished work" folder.

Kids will dilly-dally in any way they can find. Meandering to and from the work pile is as good as hanging out in the bathroom during a test. Drill into the kids the program for turning in the work and moving on to the next task. Once the kids get into the pattern of where and how to turn in work, they'll be fine.

Stop, Drop, and Roll— The Fire Drill

PERHAPS NO routine is more important that the fire drill procedure. Before the first drill, tell your students that when they hear the alarm, they need to line up quickly and silently. After you grab your clipboard and keys, you stand at the back of the line and are the last one out of the classroom. Why? Because you, like the captain of a ship, need to make sure all your charges are taken care of first. Students need to walk out to the designated spot silently and keep their line straight. If you don't yet know where your class must go and wait in the event of a fire, march down to the office and find out.

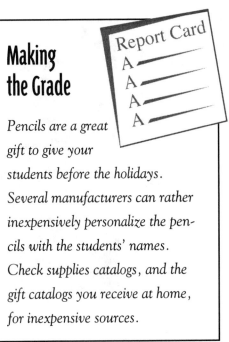

Making the Grade

Pencils are a great gift to give your students before the holidays. Several manufacturers can rather inexpensively personalize the pencils with the students' names. Check supplies catalogs, and the gift catalogs you receive at home, for inexpensive sources.

Flag Salute

NOT ALL teachers have their classes salute the flag, but we highly recommend this time-honored tradition and act of pride. By reciting the Pledge of Allegiance, you instill in your students a respect for the foundation on which this country was built (not to mention some memorization skills!).

FROM THE DESK OF . . . One teacher who prefers to remain anonymous told us her quiet phrase came back to haunt her one day. The phrase this teacher uses to quietly get the students back on track is "I need you all back here with me." One day, in the middle of a lesson, the teacher lost her train of thought and paused for an inordinately long period of time. One student looked at her and said, "We all need you back here with us!" Funny — but also proof positive that the students knew the phrase and responded to the teacher's consistency.

If you decide to salute the flag every day, you must teach the students the proper way to do so. We recommend designating a flag-salute monitor. First, the monitor says, "Please stand." After everyone stands, the monitor says, "Salute." Everyone places hands over hearts, at which time the monitor says, "Pledge." Teach the students that the pledge is said as "one voice"—all together, in unison.

After the Pledge of Allegiance, a patriotic song may be played or sung. Designate another student each week to fill the shoes of music monitor, to press the button to the CD or tape player to play the song while you put the words to the song on the overhead projector.

Developing so many routines may seem overwhelming at first. But armed with a few tactics, you and your kids will get into the habit of lining up, behaving at assemblies, and saying the Pledge as "one voice." Then you can heave a sigh of relief and enjoy an organized, calm day.

Things to Remember

Classroom management is critical to your success as a teacher. Without certain procedures and routines, you'll spend your time putting out fires instead of teaching. Remember to do the following so you can get on with your teaching:

❑ Establish classroom rules, rewards and consequences with your students' assistance

❑ Grab a clipboard and start recording misbehavior (as well as read up on "setting limits" and "positive discipline") so you can be as consistent as possible

❑ Enlist the help of parents and students to assist you with various jobs

❑ Establish a specific way for lining up, quieting the class, using the restroom, etc., and make this part of your classroom routine

Classroom Logistics

Now that you've thought through your routines, it's time to consider the logistics of your classroom.

To get started developing your classroom setup, do two things. First, spend some time in your room figuring out where to put the filing cabinets, your desk, bookshelves, or rolling files. You probably entered a classroom with certain pieces of furniture, and you want to make them accessible to your students.

Then decide what materials you yourself need and where you want those located. Once you have figured out the order of the room, work on the details.

Your Desk

You will spend quite a bit of time at your desk, and it will probably be the only space in the entire classroom that is just yours. Have this piece of furniture be the first thing you place in your room. Make sure it is in a convenient location, near electrical outlets and in a direction that allows you to see everything that goes on in your classroom. Decorate your area with personal pictures, cards, or other personal belongings that will help you feel comfortable and at home. Include space for a personal file cabinet or drawer where you keep your personal and confidential files. Make sure your students understand that this area is off limits to them.

Cubbies and Mailboxes

Your students need to have an area that is just their own where they can safely put all their belongings. "Cubbies" is the name given to student storage space in many primary classrooms. Students can put their backpacks, lunch boxes, and coats in these spaces, and you can use them to store papers and other items that are to go back home. Classrooms for the upper grades may not have these spaces, so you may want to create a smaller version of your own. You can provide this space for your students in a variety of ways, such as using shoe organizers.

Regardless of the type of cubbie you have, make sure they are labeled with the student's names. Doing so helps you see at a glance who needs to take home their things.

If you don't have cubbies with hooks, backpacks and coats can be hung over chairs, and lunch boxes can stay in backpacks until lunch. Make sure the backpacks stay on the back of the chair and are not in the aisle for others to trip over. Even though your classroom may have hooks for your students to put their coats, because of the contagiousness of lice,

Teacher's Rule

Whatever you do, don't not decorate and leave your walls and bulletin boards completely devoid of any personality. The sterile environment will turn kids off. Your goal is to create a warm environment that welcomes kids and makes them feel at home in your room and yet doesn't distract them from their work. Coauthor Lynne Rominger shared a classroom her first year with a teacher who didn't post anything but the school bulletins and his assignment calendar. Virtually all the wall space was always blank—empty! Moreover, he didn't provide any supplies. The room conveyed a lack of interest in both the classroom and the students. So decorate!

just have them keep their jackets and coats on their own chairs. One more organizational tool is a filing box with a file for every student. Your student "filers" can sort the class's work and put them in these folders for students to take home once a week.

It's Just Kids' Stuff

AFTER ACCUMULATING all your school supplies, you will need to organize them and keep them in one location in your classroom.

The most popular method is purchasing plastic tubs and organizing the materials within each tub. One of every type of student supply is included in each tub, and the tubs are numbered. Then, when students need supplies, the tubs are checked out to students or groups and everything stays in the tub. When the project is over, the students gather everything together and replace the tub in the cabinet or shelf. This method helps evenly distribute the supplies and keeps them organized; get the students involved so you are not the one stuck cleaning up!

FROM THE DESK OF . . . "Kids today are so overstimulated that adding more stimulation in the decor of the classroom just makes teaching unnecessarily challenging. Numerous studies have shown that color does affect behavior. Avoid harsh colors and stick with earth tones to create a peaceful working atmosphere. Save the bright colors for actual teaching materials or for your own clothing. After all, you want students' eyes on the teacher, not on a distracting wall poster."

Delmina N., Wilmington, Delaware

Your Secret Stash

You need to spend some time deciding how you want to organize your space and your responsibilities. If you figure out a way to manage all the paperwork before the need arises, you won't have to paw through the city dump on your desk every single day.

First, you will need to dedicate a special place for some very specific items: your purse or wallet, classroom keys, things to be copied or taken to the office, a spot to collect work, a clipboard to use for recess, a clipboard to use in case of emergencies, as well as a certain place for students to put notes from parents.

Store your purse or wallet in a locked drawer or cabinet every day. You may want to leave a few dollars in your desk drawer to buy lunch if you forget yours. Also, keep some change handy for the soda machine.

Classroom keys can be a source of frustration for all teachers. Don't let it be! Dedicate a specific spot for your keys, and perhaps sunglasses, and put them there *every time*. A basket for these essential items on your desk will do the trick.

Paper pushing is such a huge part of the job that you need to develop a convenient and efficient system to keep it all straight. You can use a bag, paper trays, hanging files, file folders, or any other method that works for you. The categories of paper that you will need to keep separate are as follows:

- Things to be copied
- Things to go to the office
- Papers to be graded
- Papers to be entered in the grade book
- Handouts to be distributed
- Late work

- Makeup assignments
- Personal papers
- Emergency information
- Parent communication

There will probably be a lot more categories that you will include; these are simply the basics.

You also have many other options for handling the procedures required to run an efficient and organized classroom:

- **The almighty bag.** You may want to dedicate a "bag" (you will accumulate many "teaching bags" over your career after attending conferences) to keep copies in, so you don't drop the stack of copies you just made on your way back to the classroom. Then you won't have to stop and think as you grab your keys and your bag of things, as you head out to recess or lunch.

- **The valiant clipboard.** You need to get your hands on several clipboards. Dedicate one clipboard for use at recess duty. As with everything else, keep it in the same place. The clipboard should have a pen attached to it, as well as a stack of passes or discipline slips. Put some scratch paper on there as well, and you will be all set for recess duty.

Another clipboard to have by the door is a roster of your students with pertinent information such as their address and parent's phone numbers. When you have a fire drill or a real emergency, you can take this clipboard with you and have important information at your fingertips.

Teacher's Rule

Purchase a box of granola bars or crackers or some fruit, and keep them in your drawer for a quick energy boost! At the end of the day, especially, you will feel like taking a nap that makes Rip Van Winkle's sleep look like a catnap, and it'll only depress you to see the piles of papers you have to grade and the lessons you have to plan. Think ahead; keep food around that will keep you going.

- **The helpful basket.** Get an attractive basket that sits right on your desk, and tell the students to put notes from parents there *first thing in the morning.* This way, after you are done taking attendance, and the students are still working on their opening exercises, you can quickly read the notes. Getting the students into the habit of giving you the notes early will save you the last-minute scramble when a parent shows up at your door ready to take a child for the afternoon, and this is the first you've heard about it!

"I Need Help!"

ONE OF the wonderful things about teaching is being able to work one on one with students and giving them the attention they need when they have a problem. With crowded classrooms, though, it's tough to give everyone enough personal attention. What will you do when more than one of your students needs help at the same time?

Trying to meet so many people's needs at the same time can be an area of frustration for teachers. A typical rule of thumb is to teach your students the "see three before me" procedure when they have a question about something. This rule means that students need to ask three other students before they ask the teacher. Abbreviate the rule as "C3B4me," and post it near the classroom rules.

C3B4me is a very effective rule for a couple of reasons. First, it allows other students in the classroom the opportunity to use their knowledge to help their peers. This is very validating for them and easier on you! Second, you only get those questions that no one else

Making the Grade

If you're looking for more ideas for decorating your room by subject, here are just a few of the on-line resources available to help:

Edumart: *www.edumart.com*

Teachers Planet: *www.teachersplanet.com*

Classroom Direct: *www.classroomdirect.com*

Blue Webn: *www.kn.pacbell .com/wired/bluewebn*

knows, and this is important information for you. When the student has asked three others and still doesn't have an answer, you may even want to consider sharing the answer with the entire class. Make sure you teach the students the appropriate time to use this rule, and that they are to use quiet, indoor voices at all times. An example of an appropriate time to use this rule would be during small group work time, such as math and reading, or for use in learning centers. As with everything else, look for patterns of student behavior. If one student is roaming the classroom constantly, make note of it, and that student may have just lost the C3B4me privilege!

When students have followed the rule and still have questions, you need to set up a system that allows you to see those students one at a time. Raising a hand works best. Try not to establish an elaborate system—stick to the basics to see what works for you. Teaching them what to do while they are waiting is very easy. Tell them to go on to the next problem! If they finish everything else, they can read their library books or finish any unfinished work.

"I'm Finished! What Do I Do Now?"

THE NEXT thing you need to teach your students is how to use unstructured time wisely. Because each student is individual and works and learns at his own pace, you need to accommodate for those differences. This means that you need to figure out, ahead of time, what you want your students to do when they finish an assignment before their classmates. You don't want finishing early to be a punishment, but you don't want students to whip through work and do a lousy job to get to the after-lesson-activities as quickly as possible either.

As you work through the pacing of assignments and the needs of your students, there will be times when some finish before others. You want every moment to count for the students, so create a poster filled with ideas for what to do when they are finished. The goal for the students is not to finish early so they can get to these "extra" activities but to have something prepared for this eventuality. Classic activities include these:

- Finish any unfinished work
- Study your spelling words
- Read your library book
- Clean your desk
- Add details to a writing prompt
- Take the math challenge
- Practice your handwriting
- Help another student

> " *Soap and education are not as sudden as a massacre but they are more deadly in the long run.* "
>
> MARK TWAIN

Notice that these choices, for the most part, require the students to do them at their desk. Add your own choices to this list, but don't fall into the trap of allowing the students to play games out of their seats, have extra computer time, or distract others by talking. These ideas may sound reasonable to you, but they can quickly turn into chaos; you'll have students rushing through assignments to get to the "fun stuff," and you'll have students stop working to watch other students. As you get your pacing down, you will have fewer students who finish early.

"Hi, I Just Moved Here"

YOU ARE in the middle of an explanation on the survival abilities of the chameleon when the door opens and there stands the vice principal with her hand on the shoulder of a brand-new scared-looking student. You are forced to stop your lesson, learn the name of the new student, and introduce him to the class. The vice principal leaves and you are left to deal with this new addition.

Teacher's Rule

If you are wondering whether a particular item is inappropriate for display, it probably is. Don't bring anything to class that portrays you as irresponsible, erratic, or outside the mainstream. If you're concerned about the whole idea of embellishing your room with any evidence of your personal life, check it out with administration. Chances are that when you waltz into the principal's office, you'll find family photos and other elements of his or her personality!

This can be a very frustrating experience for both you and the new student if it is not handled correctly. You know that it is important to make a personal connection with the student so she begins to feel comfortable with you and know that you will be helpful during her transition. However, this is difficult to do on the spot because you have to get back to your lesson. Introduce the new student to her seat, get back to your lesson, and, once you have the class working independently, pull together all the materials she'll need.

Almost anywhere you teach in North America, there'll never be a year when you don't have at least one new student in your class. Be prepared! Stack up extra sets of textbooks, folders, a pencil, crayons, ruler, and whatever else the other students have in their desks. You may also want to include the letter you distribute to the students on the first day of school to bring home to their parents.

During the school day, spend a few minutes getting to know the new student by letting the class ask some gentle questions. If new students are coming often, you could even assign a "new student ambassador" as a classroom helper to show the student where the bathrooms are, how to buy lunch tickets, and classroom procedures and routines.

After school is over and the new student has all of his supplies and has a pal to show him the ropes, find out more about him. Go down to the office and ask to see any paperwork that accompanied the child. Oftentimes, the paperwork hasn't arrived from his old school yet, so the only information the school has is that which was

included in the enrollment paperwork. When the file does arrive, you will learn his reading level, math level, standardized test scores, health history, and information about any learning disabilities he may have. This information is vital for meeting the new student's needs.

Here Today, Gone Tomorrow

STUDENTS WILL be absent; they will get ill, go on vacation, or, heaven forbid, cut school. Although absences are a part of teaching, they can create a great deal of additional work for you if you don't get organized. Prepare for student absence as part of the classroom routine by doing the following:

1. Develop a skeleton outline of your daily schedule.

2. Make ten copies of this outline and attach it to ten different folders (a piece of 12 by 18 construction paper folded in half). Start

with ten, because you may change your routine, and then you'll need to change your outline.

3. Put the folder on the absent student's desk. If you are working with older students, you can ask their desk mate to assist you in keeping track of the absent student's work folder.

4. As the day progresses, have the "paper passers" put a copy of the work inside the folder. Also, make a notation on the outline whenever you assign a page or something other than a handout (e.g., under "Spelling," if you had the students spell the words with a partner three times, then you would write, "Spell words three times to a parent").

5. If you are having the students take notes, get into the practice of taking notes yourself using an overhead transparency. This way, the students who need extra time can use the transparency back at their desk, and you can make a copy of the transparency for the absent student. Put it in your "copy" pile to copy at lunch.

6. At the end of the day, you now have a folder of work for the absent student.

7. If the parent has made arrangements for the work to be picked up, follow through with the arrangement. This will either involve leaving the work in the office or perhaps sending it home with a sibling or another student.

8. If you have time, you can jot down a quick note to the absent student, especially if you know that he is ill.

If you gather all the missed work together on the day of the absence, you get it out of the way instead of having to find it and organize it when that student returns to school. By that time, you have moved on and may have difficulty locating yesterday's copies and assignments.

Please Pass Your Work In

THIS PROCEDURE is one of the most important ones you will teach and reinforce with your students. You need to be clear in your mind how you want to collect the work so that the students won't get into the habit of shoving unfinished assignments in their desk. Here are some suggestions.

- **Number 'em.** A simple way to speed up accountability is to assign each student a number. This can be done alphabetically: James Anderson is assigned number 1, Yoshi Bako is number 2, and so forth. Not only should they write their names on the paper, but they should also write their number next to their name.

- **X marks the spot.** Next, pick a specific spot for papers to be turned in. Some teachers provide letter trays for each subject, and the students turn in papers according to the subject area. A better way to collect papers, though, is to provide *one* letter tray for student work. In this way, there is no confusion on the part of the students. While students are making the transition from one subject to another, you can go through the stack and organize the papers.

- **Keep 'em in order.** Using the number system, when students turn in their work, they need to put it in numerical order. The number 1 person's paper will always be on top of number 2's, then number 3's, and so forth. Although this sounds as though it would take some time to get them all orderly, the students learn the method quickly and are able to organize their papers rather efficiently.

- **Tie 'em up.** Then, as you transition to the next subject, you can quickly look to see who did not turn in their assignment. When you get time, you can approach that student and find out why she didn't turn her work in. This method will help with accountability if students know that if they don't turn in their work, you will be by to talk to them about it that same day.

After you have looked through the turned-in papers, clip them together and put a sticky note on the stack indicating the students who did not turn work in. List the names of students who did not turn in the work on a clipboard or a private spot. For example, if Miguel is consistently not turning in math assignments on time, then you may need to spend some one-on-one time with him and his parents. You have several options for dealing with his problem of not turning in work on time:

1. You can develop a little note to stick to his desk, such as "Work that needs to be finished." Then, as you do with your absent students, you can jot down which assignments need to be completed. Miguel can then take this home with the appropriate materials, and his parents can sign the slip and return it. You don't want to embarrass the student, so get input from the parent first.

2. Contact the parents if you see a dangerous pattern developing. There may be some difficulties with home or friends that are the cause of the missed work. The parents are a great source of information.

3. Talk to the student after class, before class, or when the other students are at recess. Make sure none of the other students are around, but ask the student why he is consistently not turning in work.

After you have collected the papers, you can put them in a colored file folder to be graded, one color per content area. Put the folder along with the teacher's edition or answer key in a specific spot. Then, if you have a parent helper or teacher's aide coming in, she will know where to look to grade the work you collected.

For Parents' Eyes Only

SOMETIMES YOU may not know what to send home, what to keep for student portfolios, and what to keep for bulletin boards. You may be able to do all three! You know that parents will want to see all of the wonderful work their children are doing and will want to make sure their children are making progress and learning valuable information. For that reason, you want the majority of their work to go home to them. But you'll also want to keep some of the students' best work for their portfolios so that when the school year is through, they'll have a folder full of all the projects and assignments that will remind them of all they learned. In addition, you also want to display the fantastic achievements of your students by placing their work on a bulletin board.

Need one paper in three places? You know what to do: photocopy!

Dont Forget to Do Your Homework!

STUDENTS NEED reminding to get their homework home. If you don't create formal homework sheets, and if you don't have a homework hotline, take a large piece of tag board and write "What's for Homework?" on the top. Then write, "Monday, Tuesday, Wednesday, Thursday" (no homework on Friday) down the side of it. Leave spaces in between the days of the week and maybe include a portion that says "Projects" at the bottom. Have this board laminated. Then, using an overhead projector pen, you can write down the day's homework assignments after you assign them. Make sure you mount this homework poster in a spot that can be easily read by all students. Because you used the overhead projector pen on laminated tag board, you simply wash it off on Monday and start over for the week.

If you still aren't sure about specific procedures for your classroom, ask veteran teachers for additional advice. Remember, you can always change your procedures if the ones you are using aren't working. Students are very malleable and will have little trouble adapting to your new system.

Things to Remember

To make your classroom run as smoothly as possible, remember to do the following:

- ❏ Arrange the classroom furniture so that it is accessible to students; if you don't have cubbies, make your own

- ❏ You'll need a bag to carry back and forth from the office to your classroom; several clipboards to keep important information; baskets for notes and essential items; and letter trays to get yourself organized

- ❏ Think through how you want students to signal for help, what they are to do when they finish an assignment, and how you want to collect their class work

- ❏ Establish a procedure for welcoming new students, keeping track of missing assignments, sending work home, and posting homework assignments

PART FIVE

GRADING, ASSESSING, AND HOMEWORK

Grading Students

GRADING—YOU PROBABLY never imagined how hard it really is! One of the hardest concepts to learn and deliver your first year may well be fair grading. There's a fine line between wanting to give everyone a good grade and grading the students accurately.

Perhaps the worst part of grading your first year is knowing whether you fall in line with the grading of other teachers teaching the same material. Let's look now at ways to get the grading going and get the grades together for all your students fairly and accurately.

Ready, Set, Grade ... Book

AT THE elementary school level, the organization of your *grade book* will depend on the report card your school site uses. You'll need to devote a page in your grade book for each area of the report card. Grade books generally have a place for you to write in the students' names vertically and then spaces to

> " *I find television very educational. The minute somebody turns it on, I go to the library and read a good book.* "
>
> GROUCHO MARX

Teaching Terms

◆ ◆ ◆

Grade book. Your grade book will be your best friend. Yours might be paper or, if you're fortunate, computerized. It's the wave of the future. Today, fantastic software programs exist to make grading a quick affair. Your school site may actually provide you with a computerized grading program compatible with an attendance program—assuming you take roll through a network computer system. If not, you might consider purchasing the software yourself. Just think of all the time you'll save! Need help finding the software? Just check out these sites:

EZ-Grader Lesson Planner: www.educational-software.net

Grade Machine: www.mistycity.com

write in the names of the assignments along the top. You need to write the students' names only once, and in the subsequent pages, you literally tear off the tab so that the names show through on each succeeding page.

First off, let's clear something up right away. A common mistake for new teachers is recording grades for everything they assign. For some reason, new teachers feel they must include every piece of work the students do in the grade book. Don't. Let the students practice, make mistakes, and learn, learn, learn. You must *correct* everything that they do, so they can learn, but only assign a grade about once a week or so per subject area. Perhaps a culminating project or a test will suffice for the grade in the book for that particular week. If you keep this pattern, then you will have about 10 grades with which to average before assigning a grade for the report card.

Grade book software can make your life amazingly easy. You set up the parameters of how much value each assignment gets, input the students' names, and then record the grades as you grade the assignments. By using this technology, you can generate progress reports very easily and quickly. Just remember to back up your data often!

FROM THE DESK OF . . . We'll be honest. Technology is grand—especially when it comes to grade books. But many parents (especially if you teach in an affluent district) will expect you to use a grade program and expect you to print out reports of their child's grades on demand. Regardless of the convenience a software program offers the teacher, it takes time to input grades; they don't just miraculously appear in the computer once the assignments have been graded. So—needless to say—you may not have Johnny or Suzy's grade up-to-date every day for Mom and Pop. Just a little forewarning!

Practice Makes Perfect

As STUDENTS develop skills, you might require the older ones to keep all of the practice pages together in a notebook. Then, when it is time to take the quiz or test on the skill, the students merely staple all of these pages together and turn it in for the final evaluation. This compilation then earns the grade that finds its way to the infamous grade book. Again—only one grade. For the younger students, you keep the papers together in a folder to evaluate for the final grade.

What's in a Grade?

You NEED to be able to justify the grades you assign. If the assignment calls for a numerical grade—such as answering ten questions out of fifteen correctly—then it's easy to calculate the percentage correctly and assign the appropriate grade. But when you are required to

make a judgment on an assignment, it's not so easy. You should use a framework—called a rubric—in these cases to guide you. Think of a very simplistic one in this way: If the student does what you assigned, then that is satisfactory—or a grade of C. If the student goes a little above and beyond what is asked, then that grade would be B or very good. You know the routine. An incomplete is given when the assignment is not completed.

Rubrics

RUBRICS ARE a wonderful way to grade because a rubric can be designed for just about any skill, project, assignment, or behavior imaginable. This type of assessment is a point-based grading method that allots a certain amount of points for achievement in certain areas of the assignment. Developing rubrics is easy. Follow these steps and create one for your very first assignment of the year. They are clear, concise, and leave a small margin for error.

1. Decide what skills of a particular assignment you want to grade.

2. Determine how many points the assignment is worth. Rubrics work more easily with larger projects or assignments that are worth more than a daily homework assignment of five or ten points.

3. After deciding the number of total points possible, divide up the points among the skills so a portion of them corresponds with each skill.

4. Type up the rubric in such a way that each skill is clearly labeled and directly under the name of the skill. Type out the number of points allotted to that skill. When you are through, you have every single point accounted for and assigned to a given skill. This means that all you have to do when grading that skill is circle the number that corresponds with your assessment of that skill.

5. Underneath the point scale of each skill listed on your rubric, include different descriptions of the mastery of the skill. For example, directly under the ten-point assessment, type out the quality of the skill you were looking for. At the low end of the point scale, list the qualities that make that student's skill weak. This means that, if you circle 3 on a ten-point scale, the student will know, based on the explanation underneath the numbers, why his skill was assessed that low.

6. When you have all the skills, point scales, and explanations on your rubric, leave room at the bottom for the total score of the assignment. You then add up all the scores on the individual point scales and come up with the score on the assigment.

7. Also leave room at the bottom of the rubric for comments. This is a very personal touch because you can tell students exactly what you liked about the assignment and what needs work. They understand that you really took the time to go through their assignment carefully and grade it accordingly.

If you work with older students, then you should also get their input into what should be included in the rubric; make it a part of the instruction so they know how they are going to be assessed in the end—at the beginning.

Show You Care

It's important to students that you actually pay attention to their work, and rubrics help in this regard. Think back to the past when you had a teacher who always read through the story that you spent hours on the night before painstakingly checking the spelling of every other word before writing it down. You were proud to turn it in and when you got it back, you realized that all the teacher did was make a few corrections here and there and then plopped a big red grade at the top of the paper. This was frustrating because you at least wanted to know that you did well on the spelling.

Now let's say that you give a similar assignment to your students. They are to write a story and turn it in on time. You, however, are going to use a rubric to grade the story and you will grade in green pen instead of red! You have told the students that the three skills you are focusing on are handwriting, detail, and mechanics. You explain that this assignment is worth fifteen points, giving five points for each of these areas: handwriting; detail in the story; and spelling, punctuation, capitalization, and grammar. Then you begin typing your rubric. You title the rubric accordingly and label the first skill "Handwriting." Under the label, you type, "5 4 3 2 1 0." This allows you to easily circle the score that student receives on handwriting. Underneath the point scale, you give a description of the quality of the skill. For example, under the 5 and 4 you type, "Flawless, perfectly formed letters, and appropriate size." Under the 1 and 0 you type, "Illegible." Therefore, when you circle the 1 on a student's paper, they know that you can't read their handwriting. You follow the same process for the other two skills, and, after leaving room for the total and the comments, you are ready to make some copies and get assessing! The students know all of this ahead of time so they know what you are looking for.

> *" Education is a social process . . . Education is growth . . . Education is not a preparation for life; education is life itself. "*
>
> JOHN DEWEY

Number, Please!

Another type of rubric that works just as well as the point scale rubric is one that breaks up the information differently. Instead of dividing the assessment by skill, you break it up by level. Instead of using the usual letter grades (A, B, C, D, and F), you develop a scale of 6, 5, 4, 3, 2, and 1. The category 6 generally corresponds with A++ work while a 5 is A work, 4 is B work, and so on. Then you decide what constitutes a 6, a 5, and so forth. Your skills might be the same; you are just organizing them differently. If we use the same

Teacher's Rule

It's better to use numbers instead of letters in your rubrics because students are less likely to be concerned with the grade itself and are then more likely to focus on the individual skills.

assignment example as before, the basis for a 6 might include "Flawless handwriting, rich detail with lots of descriptive words, mechanics are error-free." The basis for a 5 might be, "Clear and legible handwriting, above-average detail with some descriptive words, few mechanical errors." You would continue this all the way down to the 1.

When creating the rubric, leave a space next to each skill description of each number. This is for putting a check mark next to the quality of skill that corresponds with their level. For example, if the student you are assessing has exceptional handwriting, you will check the space next to "Flawless handwriting" in the 6 category. However, their story has more mechanical errors than the 6 allows, so you will put a check mark in the space next to "Few mechanical errors." This lets the student know that, while her handwriting is great, she still has some errors in her paper that she didn't catch when proofreading. When you are assessing the project or assignment, you will need to look at where your assessment check marks fell. The student may have three check marks next to skills listed in the 4 category and only one check mark in the 6 category. This means that the overall assessment of the paper is a 4+—in other words, a B+.

Performance-Based Assessment

THERE ARE some cases in which a rubric-based assessment simply isn't the appropriate form of assessment for a particular project or assignment. In some cases, you need to take on more of a "Prove it!" approach to assessment. This is important especially with tasks that students can accomplish without really understanding what they are doing. In math, for example, it is easy for some kids to do computations without really understanding how they work or what they mean. With performance-based assessment, you are making students prove that they understand what they are doing by asking them to support their answers with explanations and thought processes.

Besides paper-and-pencil tasks, the students' performance also needs to be assessed in a more *authentic* way. For example, they might be able to add 34 and 72, but can they show you what 106 looks like? Your students may be able to recite the state capitals, but can they point to them on a map? In science, your students can tell you what plants need to grow, but can they actually grow a plant?

> ## Teaching Terms
>
> • • •
>
> **Authentic assessment.** Students model activity after a real-life task, something they might be required to complete out in the "real world."

You will find that you have those students who do much better when assessed based on performance then during rubric-based assessment. These are most likely your kinesthetic learners and quite possibly your students with strong spatial abilities. Therefore, to give all your students the opportunity to be successful, you need to vary your types of assessment.

Student Self-Assessment

WHEN GIVEN the opportunity, students are very good at taking responsibility for their own learning. One way of doing this is to allow them to evaluate their own work. This lets them think critically about their work the same way you would. You are forcing them to use a different perspective when looking at their work. Most of the time, students feel the grade has been "given" to them instead of seeing it as the grade they "earned." When they self-assess, they take a closer look at their work and decide for themselves what they really earned.

Students can be pretty good assessors of their own learning provided that you have set the criteria clearly and explained how to assess themselves. After giving them the criteria from which you assess, ask them to "judge" their work, and then you will also assess it. Surprisingly, the differences will be small if the students are taking the task seriously. You can give them the same rubric or other form of assessment that you use so the self-assessment is realistic.

You can also do a more formal assessment by asking the students what grades they think they should earn after looking at their folders of work. Have the students fill out their own report card. See how close you are! Chances are, they will be harder on themselves than you are on them.

Peer Assessment

GROUP WORK tends to be a teaching strategy that receives both positive and negative feedback from parents, teachers, and students. Groups are great because they teach students skills other than the purely educational ones intended by the assignment. Students learn to work together to reach a common goal, to share ideas in a respectful and democratic manner, and to delegate and complete tasks for the benefit of the group project.

On the downside, groups are difficult to monitor, which means that it is hard for a teacher to know exactly how much work each group member is doing. There are many ways to combat this ambiguity. One way is to divide up the assignment or project into smaller parts and have each student be responsible for a certain part of the overall project, making this small part "independent" of the others instead of "interdependent" as suggested in Chapter 11. Then grade them accordingly so the entire group isn't docked points for the poor effort of one student. Another way to ensure the accuracy of the grades is to have the students in each group complete a peer assessment of the other members of their group. Let them rate the contributions of others, as well as how each person got along with each other during the process.

First decide what criteria you want them to be graded on and create an assessment form. Express to students the seriousness with which you expect them to take the assessment, and they will rise to the occasion. Tell them exactly how they will be grading each other, and you will find that most everyone will fulfill all the duties of the project at the same time that they are keeping an eye on the other members.

When the group has presented its project and you have finished your own assessment, it is time for the groups to peer-assess. Each group member gives a grade to every other member (including themselves) in each category and then gives an overall grade. It is also a good idea to have room for comments. When students are forced to justify the grades they give, they tend to be more truthful. Then collect their peer assessments and include them as a percentage of your grade. The students will take the whole process as seriously as you take it; they will follow your lead.

Portfolios

IN EDUCATION today, *portfolios* have become a popular way to assess work, primarily growth over a period of time.

Regardless of how the assignments are collected in a portfolio, the outcome is always a positive one because students, parents, and teachers all get to go through the collection process and feel good about the amount of progress and growth a child has made throughout the school year. Parents, particularly, enjoy this approach because they can be a witness to the learning that their child has done; they can see it with their own eyes instead of taking their child's word for it or seeing a grade on a report card. The students can go back and gain a sense of pride in their work when they see how far they have come. Similarly, you get to look through the portfolios and pat yourself on the back while taking credit for the learning that was accomplished in your classroom!

Portfolios can serve a variety of purposes. The best reason to keep a portfolio is to give students the opportunity to reflect on their progress and growth. Then, after going through all of their work, they can pick and choose what they would like to display. One portfolio of student work will generally suffice; this doesn't mean that the students will highlight only their best work (although some will), but let the students choose work that signifies important learning. Put work in the portfolio at natural times, such as after a test or a project. Make copies of the assignment, send one home, and keep the original in the portfolio.

When preparing a special portfolio for Open House, have the students attach a cover sheet to the showcased piece of work. The cover sheet should include:

Teaching Terms

◆ ◆ ◆

Portfolios. Collections of students' work over the course of a trimester, year, or few years. Portfolios can hold just about any type of assignment; it depends on the emphasis of the school or district. Some portfolio systems keep all major tests, assignments, and projects while others keep virtually everything the student has accomplished over the course of the year. Some portfolios, for example, are just for language arts; these would hold all writing, spelling, reading, and grammar work.

- student's name
- date
- subject matter
- title of work or assignment
- a statement about why the student chose to include this piece of work in the portfolio

These portfolios will be saved for a long time! Have the students mount the cover sheet and the piece of work on 9-by-12 construction paper to be spiral bound before Open House. They can design a cover for them to be laminated , too!

Hi-Ho, Hi-Ho, It's Off to Grade I Go

WE'VE DISCUSSED *how* to grade—now let's talk about *when* to grade and correct. Correcting papers can be a very tedious process. If you don't stay on top of it, before you realize it, it is time to assign grades and you're missing a lot of assignments from a lot of students! The scramble begins.

When you stay on top of the grading, you also know who's not keeping up and who has missed assignments. Choose a visible spot in the classroom to post assignments that have been missing for a while. This spot may also serve as the location of an envelope with "no name" work, as in work turned in without a name on it. At key times and days, such as before recess, before library time, and on the day you have chosen to send home the students' work for the week, check this list to see who still has missing assignments. It is amazing how many papers "appear" when they know that part of a recess depends on the work's existence!

When do you find time to grade all those papers? If you're disciplined, you should be able to clean up all the work within a half an

Teacher's Rule

It's the bane of our existence—late work! Those pieces of paper that appear out of nowhere and don't fit into any pile—as the pile already has been graded and returned. Even worse than late work is work never turned in. You can't depend on children to follow up and make sure they aren't missing assignments. Sometimes, Mom and Dad won't even care. Generally speaking, it's up to you to hound the kids to turn in the work!

hour after school's out. We advise against getting into the habit of taking work home. It gets lost, and you get depressed just thinking about the sword hanging over your head.

Give yourself a definite stopping time— 4:00 P.M., for example. Before you leave, then, record the names of students who did not do the assignments and go home!

You may actually find time during the day when you can correct papers. As students work independently in centers, for example, you can do some correcting. If the students are working in small groups, as you move from group to group, you can actually correct their papers right then and there. Students can frequently correct their own work that is not being graded, or you can exchange papers for students to correct each other's work.

One more thing: Don't correct papers at lunch. Try—really try—to save your lunch period for socializing with other teachers and eating. You really do need a break from the constant demands placed on you during class time from the students. Why do you think breaks for employees are required by law in most private businesses? We aren't machines. Too many teachers burn out because they work, work, work through lunch and never take a breather!

Transference

So YOU have a collection of grades. Now what? It is OK to *close* your grade book early. This means that if you are teaching on a trimester

Tales from the Trenches

Coauthor Karen Heisinger recalls, "I used to time myself when I was grading papers. I would set the timer for thirty minutes and see how far I could get in that time period. The hardest part of grading was getting started, so by setting the timer, I would tell myself that I would stop after thirty minutes. Invariably, the timer would go off and I would be just about finished. Voilà—I was done with my grading for the day!"

❖ ❖ ❖

"My first week into teaching, I felt like I was reinventing the wheel with each lesson," recalls coauthor Lynne Rominger. "One day I was just too tired to get things together and truly didn't have the lesson prepared. I figured no one would know, right? But who was the first person to pick up on my incompetence that day? A student! He said, 'You really aren't organized are you? You need to plan this out better.' I was mortified," says Rominger. "From that day on, I never came to class without my lesson ready, my handouts photo-copied, and my materials all set out."

schedule, you should stop collecting grades after about ten weeks. You can still give assignments and collect grades, but these go toward the *next* grading period.

Assuming that all the grades are in, it's time to make the calculations and assign a grade. Depending on how you have recorded the grades, you will either calculate the mean score by adding up all of the entries and dividing by the number of entries; or, if you entered letter grades, you can look to see how many of each grade they have and then use the most prevalent score. If you use the numerical score, use the traditional grading scale:

Teacher's Rule

Don't suffer through all the correcting yourself. Solicit the help of parents, aides, and students. In fact, oftentimes the whole class can exchange papers and correct a test, for example, in class. By doing this, you save yourself time—a precious commodity in the life of a teacher!

100 percent = A+

92–99 percent = A

90–91 percent = A–

88–89 percent = B+

82–87 percent = B

80–81 percent = B–

78–79 percent = C+

72–77 percent = C

70–71 percent = C–

68–69 percent = D+

62–67 percent = D

60–61 percent = D–

59 percent and below = F

Comments Away!

STUDENTS ARE not the sum of their final grade at a given grading period. It's the comments from the teacher that give parents the most important kind of feedback! On most report cards, a space exists for you to provide information that a grade can't give. Whatever you write, please choose your words carefully. Parents and students may keep these documents for years and years!

Your comments should reflect a specific goal to work on. For instance, if the student has been chronically tardy or absent, you could write "Tad's tardiness (or absences) disrupts/has disrupted his learning this trimester. I'm sure his work will improve as his attendance improves." If Sasha is strong in reading out loud but could improve in reading comprehension, then your comments might be, "Sasha is a very strong oral reader; however, she needs assistance in reading comprehension. Asking her questions about stories she reads aloud to you would be of assistance to her."

> ## Teaching Terms
> • • •
>
> **Closed grading period.** When a teacher stops collecting grades during a grading period, she or he has "closed" the grading period and "closed" the grade book. Whether or not report cards have been distributed, another grading period has begun.

The next grading period, you should then comment on any improvement in Tad's attendance or Sasha's reading comprehension. Here's what Tad's might say: "Tad's grades reflect the fact that he has come to school 55 out of 60 days this trimester. Thank you! Now that he's at school everyday, let's focus on _____." With Sasha, you can write, "Sasha's reading comprehension has not improved significantly; let's try this strategy this trimester: _____." The bottom line is to write positive, useful, and constructive comments on the report card. You can and should write suggestions for improvement—just put them in a positive light.

Teacher's Rule

When students correct each other's work, remind them to write "Corrected by" or "C/B" and their name on the other student's paper. In many ways, it's merely a psychological trick. With their names on the paper, they have some accountability! They pay attention during the correcting, lest they mark something incorrectly. After all—they can't hide; their names are on the papers, too! Then, if there is a discrepancy, you can go directly to the student who corrected the paper.

Communicating Grades

MOST PARENTS take grades very seriously. As long as you have made the criteria very clear to the students and the parents, communicating grades to parents should be relatively easy. No parent wants to be surprised by his or her child's grades! Take the following steps so that no one is shocked when report cards come out.

Since you have designated a day to send home student work, you might want to include a signature page so that parents can indicate that they've seen the work. If students are not returning these sheets, it is worth a call home. Your goal here is good communication, some accountability on your end, and no surprises about grades.

Check into the policy of your school, because you may be required to send home a midterm progress report. Your school may also have parent conferences in the middle of the trimester instead of at the end. This is the perfect opportunity to point out patterns of behavior you have documented, missing assignments, midterm grades, areas of strength, and areas of weakness. Have something written for the parents to sign; make two copies of this—one for your records and one for the parents to keep. Take notes at the meeting on your copy, and encourage the parents to take notes as well.

If a parent questions the grades you have assigned or acts surprised, you have the documentation to back up your grades. You can refer to the signed sheets you have collected, the notes you have taken at meetings and during phone calls you have had, and the portfolio of work you have been keeping. This is an awkward situation. Stick to a script of "These are the grades I've collected. Let's work on a plan for how Larry can improve his grades." Keep the focus on the student, not on yourself or the parent.

Honor Roll

IF YOU are teaching older students, then you will probably need to submit a list for honor roll. Get the criteria from the principal or the staff handbook early on—when you get a copy of the report card.

Here's a point that is not something that you need to think about very often but is something you need to be aware of: Some students may earn all A's but may also have two or more discipline referrals during the term. According to the handbook, this student may not qualify for the honor roll. Unfortunately, you are probably going to be the one to explain this to the parents. If this is the case, use the policy and the principal to help you communicate.

> *"You can lead a boy to college, but you cannot make him think."*
>
> ELBERT HUBBARD

You should now have a good idea of the various ways to use assessment to improve learning in your classroom. The most important and helpful thing to know is when to use which kind of assessment for which activity. You will learn this through experiences of your own and from talking to veteran teachers.

Things to Remember

To become a star grader, remember to do the following things:

❏ Set up your grade book and/or investigate a computerized program to set up a grading system for your classroom

❏ Use rubrics as a way to provide specific feedback to aid your students' learning

❏ Use a variety of assessments to grade your students: traditional paper/pencil tasks, performance-based, authentic, portfolio, peer, and self-assessment

❏ Set up a grading routine for yourself so that you can keep up with it, and notify students right away of any missing assignments

Homework

Y OU REMEMBER HOMEWORK, right? The bane of your school existence. Ugh! Where once you walked on the "I hate homework" side of the playground, now you're the meanie who hands it out. And for good reason. Homework is an opportunity to reinforce the day's learning and better prepare students for each grade.

But homework is controversial. Some parents love the idea of homework and will embrace it whole-heartedly, while others simply won't. Just count on most of the kiddies not liking it!

"Mom, I Need Help with My Homework"

PERCEPTION IS everything, so start off on the right foot with parents. Help your students by telling their folks about your expectations and by giving parents tips for how to set up a study area for their child. Let them know their child needs to have:

- a quiet area to study with adequate lighting
- a desk, table, or hard surface to write on
- a supply of pens, pencils, pencil sharpener, crayons, markers, colored pencils, and erasers
- different kinds of paper: binder, construction, and scratch
- miscellaneous supplies: scissors, glue, stapler, and tape

Teacher's Rule

We can't stress enough the importance of establishing a homework routine. Many kids do lose their train of thought and forget to do homework—it's unintentional. If parents, however, establish a routine, these children are less likely to forget and thereby succeed!

Suggest, too, that the family makes doing homework a routine, which means it's done at the same time every evening. Some students will want to do their homework right after school while the day's learning is fresh; others will want to take a break and then do homework after dinner.

Something you can do to help keep homework a top priority and organized for the kids and parents is "homework folders." Each child has his or her own folder that goes home nightly with the assignments in the folder. We've even seen some teachers—especially at the kindergarten level—send home laminated manila envelopes. If your district doesn't provide these, it's worth purchasing them on your own. Dedicate one folder to the taking home and returning of homework and the other to important papers.

FROM THE DESK OF . . . Brent Mattix may only be in his second year in the classroom, but he's already put his school's voice-mail system to work to make his life less harried. He asked for two mailbox lines. One line he uses as his voice mail/message center. The other extension he uses as a homework hotline. Each week he updates the message to include daily homework assignments for each class he teaches. This way when a student misses class, they don't bother Mr. Mattix or take up class time getting the assignments. They need only call the homework hotline extension listed prominently, of course, on his syllabus!

Put the student's name on the outside of the folder, and on the inside write, "Take home" and "Return to school" on one side of each folder. On the "take home" side, also staple a piece of binder paper to this section, so the students can write down the assignments as you assign them.

How Much Is Too Much?

BEFORE YOU assign homework, check your school's policy and philosophy regarding homework. Some schools have very prescriptive rules about homework, so you'll want to make sure you are assigning the right amount for your grade level. Other schools don't. You'll discover that homework levels change from year to year. One year everyone may scream, "More homework!" while the following year the shouts are "Less homework!" Once you know your school site's guidelines, you can comfortably move on to determining what to assign for homework.

Some subjects lend themselves naturally to homework. Spelling, math, writing, handwriting, reading comprehension, and vocabulary are particularly amenable to worksheets, which are probably the best way to go, so that you don't need to send home textbooks and deal with the consequences of students leaving their books either at home or at school.

Sometimes it may be more appropriate to assign weekly homework—especially true for younger students, who might not be ready for the routine of bringing homework back every day. Weekly homework may work best for older students, too, by giving families the flexibility of when they can do the homework. For example, if you are at a year-round school, it may be difficult for some students to complete their homework during the summer months midweek, due to involvement in baseball, swimming, and other activities. Thus, some families appreciate the flexibility of having the weekend to complete assignments.

Teacher's Rule

Here's a tip to keep kids honest. Always have the parents sign that they've received homework /newsletter packets. This way, students must show the packet to Mom and Dad and can't claim that there's no homework— "honest!"

If you do decide to assign weekly homework instead of daily homework, this might best be done in the spring. Then, you can include review material that the students should be practicing anyway for upcoming standardized testing.

Whenever!

THERE REALLY is a "best" time to assign homework. Really! The best time to assign homework is during the subject when it is being taught as a closure activity, just before the transition. Tell the students specifically what their homework will be, and then write this information on your "homework chart." At this time, the students need to write the homework down on the sheet of paper inside their homework folder.

The Collection Plate

COLLECTING HOMEWORK needs to be a part of your daily routines. If you are working with older students, then you can assign a student to whom the other students hand in their homework every morning—the homework monitor/collector. Just make copies of your class list (see the example on the following page) so the homework collector can check off who turned it in.

If you are working with younger students, you should designate a specific spot (the same place for all class work) for the students to turn in their work. Teach the routine of walking in to the class, taking off

Making the Grade

Ah, standardized testing! Let's see whose kids are smarter than whose kids, right? From Hawaii to North Carolina, the phrase "student and teacher accountability" buzzes throughout the halls of academia. Want proof? Go on-line and type in "teacher accountability" or "student accountability" on any search engine. You'll find numerous sites—from district Web pages to teaching colleges—with a wealth of information on the trend of assessing our students, most often with a series of standardized tests.

SAMPLE HOMEWORK SHEET

For the week of _____

Students	Spelling Sentence 9/1	Math 10 worksheet 9/2	Vocab 9/2	Paragraph 9/2		
John						
Maria						
Ellen						
Vickie						

their backpack, getting out folders, and putting them in the basket every morning.

Ye Olde Homeworke Consequences

HOMEWORK CAN be one of the most frustrating ordeals for a family. And if the family is frustrated, then they tend to take it out on you! To avoid this, make the homework consistent and clear in purpose. You also need to grade the homework, which will be discussed in the next section. What are the consequences, though, for the students who do not do their homework?

A *natural consequence* for not doing homework is that the student missed out on a reinforcement activity, did not get the extra practice, and does not get the grade or credit for the assignment. A *logical conse-quence* for not doing homework is that since the student did not do homework during free time or the night before, then he can do it at recess and lunch.

The better approach in this case is to use logical consequences with the caveat that parents need to be notified on a consistent basis. (Parents tend not to support the idea of natural consequences because it seems too harsh for elementary age students. It may not seem that way to you, but you will avoid some confrontations if you use logical consequences instead.) This is a tough call, though, because students do need to have a break, but they also need to be held accountable for their homework.

If only one or two students didn't do the assignment, then they can either sit outside the classroom and get started on it (keep your door propped open so you can see them at all times), or if you have made arrangements in advance, you can send them to another teacher's classroom for the ten minutes it will take to correct the homework. This way, they are still being held accountable for the homework, and they are using class time to get started on it. Recess time will probably still be impacted, but not the whole recess.

If you have a lot of students who did not do the homework, you may need to skip correcting it at that time. Those students can do their homework during the first half of recess and then play the second half. You are balancing, then, their playtime and issuing a logical consequence.

Occasionally, you'll get a note from parents stating the reason the student did not do the homework. Provided the student gives you the

Teacher's Rule

Don't discount lack of money as a reason that a student doesn't complete homework. Consider this: What if you assign the spelling sentence homework, but one student comes from a home where money is so tight toilet paper is a luxury? How can that child complete the assignment when no money exists for paper? He can't. Get to know these little things about your students. And provide paper for those kids who lack paper or the means to buy paper in their home; discreetly put a few pieces in the homework folder each night.

Teaching Terms

◆ ◆ ◆

Natural consequence. A natural consequence is a consequence that occurs without any interaction from another party. The consequence, essentially, is the "natural" result of the circumstance. A logical consequence, however, involves the intervention of a third party — the teacher.

note early in the day, you shouldn't have her miss recess time. She can still spend the time getting started while you correct it with your other students, but losing the recess should not be part of the consequence.

Collecting homework early in the day will allow you to make these decisions. Build into your daily routine, also, a process to notify parents when homework is not done. At first, this should be done on a daily basis so parents are immediately notified of potential problems. Call home and either leave a message on the machine or talk to the parents when you get the chance during the day—at a recess break or lunch. Just leave a quick message stating that their child did not turn in today's homework—nothing more and nothing less.

At Back-to-School Night, you can explain in detail your homework policy, and you can set up a weekly procedure for notifying parents of missing homework. Don't think that you need to call home every day that a student doesn't do homework—just do it at the beginning of the year to avoid any "surprises" later on.

Correction Tape

HOMEWORK, LIKE all assignments, needs to be corrected. You'll quickly lose credibility with your students and their parents if they think homework is being assigned and never looked at again. Getting homework back fast is the only way you'll be able to see patterns such as a student who seems to get all the answers correct on the homework assignment but has trouble doing the work in class or vice versa. This information can then be communicated to the parents, so they are made aware of potential problems.

Also, you may have an area on the report card that evaluates how often they turn in homework. Your rosters will indicate how *often* they are turning in homework, and your grade book will reflect how *well* they are doing on their homework.

All in all, homework is a good way to reinforce concepts and help your students, but it does take work on your part. Hang in there. You'll find a process that works well for you.

Teacher's Rule

Never pass up a good sports metaphor. Explain to students that homework is like sports. They won't become world-class athletes unless they practice on their own or until their coaches and parents let them struggle on their own.

Things to Remember

Consider the following suggestions to set up a homework routine for your students:

❑ Find out your school's homework policy to determine how much homework to assign, and do so on a consistent basis

❑ Dedicate a place in your classroom to post homework assignments, and give your students a Homework folder that goes back and forth between school and home

❑ Establish a routine for collecting and correcting assignments, and enforce a consequence for students who do not do their homework

❑ Involve parents in the homework process by asking them to sign the Homework folder on occasion; give them suggestions on how to make homework a pleasant experience; and outline your plan on "Back-to-School Night"

PART SIX

COMMUNICATION

Communicating with Parents

First Day of School

YOU PROBABLY became a teacher, in part, because you like kids and relate well with them. By definition, then, parents might make you a little uncomfortable. But there's no reason to fear their parents if you do your part to establish good communication.

The first day of school is the best time to establish a pattern of communication with parents. Spend some time writing a letter to the parents of your students, and send it home with them on the first day of school. This initial letter should say something similar to the letter on the following page.

Sending Notes Home

EVEN BEFORE Back-to-School Night, start communicating with parents about behaviors that cause concern. Sending notes home on a consistent basis will promote this ongoing communication. Use a specific folder, such as a *take-home folder* to keep everything organized.

Dear parents of my students,

Hello! My name is _____ and I will be your child's ___ grade teacher this year. I'd like to tell you something about myself, just as I hope to get to know all of you better throughout the year.

I attended college at _____ and earned my credential at _____. My philosophy of education is that all students can succeed in an atmosphere of support and encouragement, and that is what I will strive to provide for your child this year. Together, we can make this happen.

Although I will share more details on Back-to-School Night, which is scheduled for _____ at _____, I'd like to let you know that we will start out our year getting to know each other using the theme of " _____." This fall, homework will be assigned every night. I will also be assessing all the students during these first few weeks so that I can teach them what they need to know, in the way that is best suited to them.

Communicating with you is very important to me, so please call me when you have a question or concern. The number here at school is _____.

Sincerely,

_____

P.S. See you at Back-to-School Night on _____ at _____.

Teacher supply stores carry preprinted notes so you don't need to create your own. If you would rather not purchase them, though, feel free to use the templates in this chapter to design notes to send home.

If you have students with behavioral issues, one of the things you'll want to include in the folder is a daily discipline record (see the example on page 275). Tape the record to the student's desk and record what the student does by the hour. Write a "+" if the student is behaving well next to the hour (i.e., "9:00 +"). If there are behavior problems, describe them (i.e., "10:00—"talking to neighbor during math"). Also use the record to record unfinished assignments. Send the completed record home each day to have it signed by a parent, and put it in the student's file the next day. If the student doesn't return the record, then either you or the student needs to call home that morning. In this case, the student will bring his take-home folder home every day.

Once the student's behavior stabilizes, then you can shift to a weekly behavior chart (see the example on page 276).

Tape the Weekly Behavior Record to the student's desk and send it home on Thursdays. This type of chart can be used for all students but may be logistically difficult for you. Focus first on the students who need this weekly enforcement.

If you have students who chronically miss homework assignments, you'll want to adopt the Missing Assignments sheet (see the example on page 277). Send it home once a week, and follow up if it doesn't come back the next day, along with the missing assignments. Keep a copy in the student's file.

> # Teaching Terms
>
> • • •
>
> **Take-home folder.** Send home all that correspondence — permission forms, free- and reduced-lunch forms, contact forms, newsletters, and all the rest — in a folder. Ask parents to initial a form you've glued to the front of the folder to acknowledge that they've received all the information inside. Then, dedicate a specific day of the week to send this folder home.

Making the Grade

Here's a great way to get parents involved: Ask them, before the school year begins, if possible, to provide you with an assessment of how their child learns. Is the child primarily a visual, linguistic, physical, mathematical, interpersonal, intrapersonal, or musical learner? If parents have access to the Internet, ask them to assess their own children, for free, from this Web site:

Learning Styles Survey:
www.smarterkids.com /mysmarterkids/stylesurvey.asp

Don't forget the positive reinforcement! Get creative and design a set of notes (see the sample on page 278) that you can copy and send home regarding a student's positive behavior. Praise specific behavior!

Newsletters

THE BEST way to keep parents informed, short of calling them each day, is to produce and send home your own weekly newsletter (or update your class Web site every week). Your parents will appreciate knowing what is going on in the classroom, and it's a way for you to avoid any "surprises." Write your newsletter using the following headings:

- **Reading.** Describe the story you are reading this week

- **Math.** Describe the skill you are working on, and pose a sample question—maybe a word problem or a computation similar to the one the students are doing

- **Language.** Use student samples of writing, or describe what your students are doing

- **Social studies.** Pose a question that will force the parents to think about the topic (e.g., "Have any of you been to Egypt? We are studying ancient Egypt this month, and we're focusing on pyramids this week. Ask your child about it!").

DISCIPLINE RECORD

+ = good behavior

NAME OF STUDENT: _____

DATE: _____

8:00

9:00

10:00

Recess

11:00

Lunch

1:00

2:00

Unfinished work:

_____

PARENT'S SIGNATURE

Please sign this form and have your child return it tomorrow.

WEEKLY BEHAVIOR RECORD

STUDENT'S NAME: _____

DATE: _____

Friday:

Monday:

Tuesday:

Wednesday:

Thursday:

Unfinished assignments:

_____

PARENT'S SIGNATURE

Please sign this form and have your child return it tomorrow.

MISSING ASSIGNMENTS

Dear Parents,

Your child is missing the following assignments for the week of _____.

Spelling:

Reading:

Math:

Science:

Social studies:

Writing:

As you know, I accept late work because your child's learning and success is important to me. Although late work will be penalized one letter grade, your child will benefit from doing the work and will be better off earning a reduced score than taking the "0" that will otherwise be given on this assignment. If you have questions, you are welcome to contact my by e-mail at xxx@xxx.xxx or at xxx-xxx between xx:00 and xx:00.

Thank you for your assistance!

Sincerely,

_____

_____

PARENT'S SIGNATURE

Please sign this form and have your child return it tomorrow.

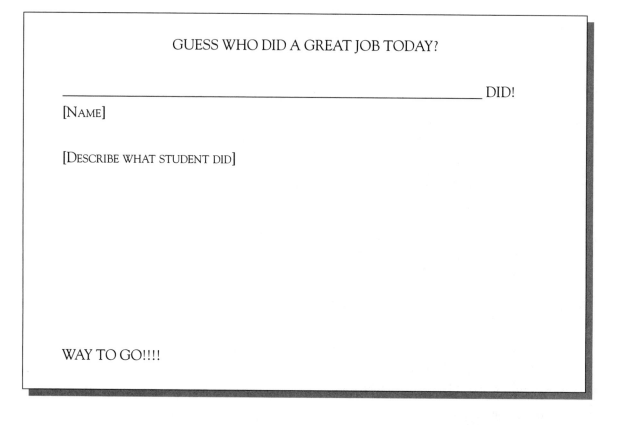

- **Science.** Same as social studies: Pose a question! Ask, "What animals travel in a pod? In a gaggle? Ask your child! We're studying groups of animals this week!"

- **Important dates.** Mention Back-to-School Night, minimum/half days, field trips, and other dates that should be calendared in.

Create an easy template for yourself, and make several copies. During the week, write down the one or two sentences per subject area that you have outlined. You can get as creative as you want, but the purpose of this newsletter is to inform parents of what is going on in their child's classroom. Have fun and be consistent!

Voice Mail/E-Mail

IF YOUR school has voice mail or e-mail, use it to create a homework hotline. This is another opportunity to communicate with parents and students. Voice mail allows you to set up daily homework information, such as "This is the homework for today, September 15. Students need to complete their math worksheet and write the rough draft of their paragraph. Remember to return any daily discipline records. Thank you for calling!"

Some teachers might think that if you operate a homework hotline, it minimizes student responsibility to listen and record the homework in class. It's worth it. Voice mail reassures the parent and opens up yet another channel for ensuring the success of the student. Any little bit helps! If you do decide to use a homework hotline, be consistent. Get in the habit of changing your hotline message first thing after students go home for the day.

If you choose to communicate via e-mail, limit your response time. Stick to a maximum of twenty minutes a day, for example, so that your parents don't become too dependent on e-mail.

Back-to-School Night

BACK-TO-SCHOOL NIGHT is the first formal opportunity you have to meet with parents. Check with your principal to see whether there are specific items you need to cover during this meeting. Also, see how long you have to present and whether you'll be giving your presentation once or twice.

" To educate a man in mind and not in morals is to educate a menace to society. "

THEODORE ROOSEVELT

You can also have the students make invitations for their parents, and tell your students their homework for the night is to get their parents to come to Back-to-School Night!

During the day, incorporate some time for the students to clean and organize their desks and the classroom. Divide up the duties of cleaning the classroom, and while they are cleaning, you can also spend time straightening up bulletin boards and cleaning up any piles that may have accumulated. Keep the lessons of the day simple and easy so you have some energy for the evening to come. Don't skip dinner, either. Whether you bring it in or go out with your fellow teachers, eat something! This will be a fairly late night for you, and you will be nervous, too. Eat something light, but don't skip this meal.

Before parents arrive, arrange extra chairs in a convenient area so that if two parents come together, one parent can sit at the child's desk, and the other parent can grab a chair and sit nearby.

When the parents walk in, have a sheet for them to sign in on; your principal may want a copy of this afterward. Also, have a 4-by-6 card on each student's desk, as well as a pen or pencil. Write this prompt on the board:

Welcome to Back-to-School Night!

Please fill in the following information on the card on you child's desk, and we will begin shortly:

Your child's name

Names of both parents

The name and number of the parent I should call during
　　or after school hours

An e-mail address

Best days and times for parent conferences

Any special needs your child has

Any other information you want me to know

THANK YOU!

Collect these cards at the end of the evening; you may be surprised at what you learn! Store the cards in the individual student's folder, but first make a database of the numbers your students' parents can be reached at during the day, after hours, and e-mail addresses. Keep this list handy; you'll need it and use it!

Begin no later than five minutes after the assigned time. As you address the following topics, encourage parents to follow along using a handout you will have placed on every student's desk. Your agenda for the evening should include these points:

• **Introduction:** Describe your educational background, student and substitute teaching experience, and personal information (children, family, pets, or other items that make you seem more human to those parents).

• **A picture of the day:** Describe which subjects you teach on which days of the week and at what times.

• **Discipline**: Discuss your classroom rules, rewards and consequences, and how your class developed them.

- **Topics of study:** Let the parents know what the students will be studying this year.

- **Student groupings:** Explain how you group by areas of need, pre-test information, or other factors.

- **Grading policy:** Describe the grading scale, late/missing work policies, and folders for content areas. Also have a blank copy of the report card on hand.

- **Homework policy:** Explain how often homework is assigned, what the consequences are for not doing it, and the homework folder.

- **Communication:** If your school has voice mail or e-mail, let the parents know how often you will be updating your message or how to get hold of you. Also, let them know that they need to come to you first so that you can clarify any information they might receive.

- **Newsletters:** Give them copies they might not have received. Let them know what days newsletters come home.

- **Parent assistance:** Encourage parents to sign the volunteer sheet if they can help in certain subject areas, do parties, chaperone field trips, or participate in a classroom phone tree. Also remind them that they need to check in at the office and get a name badge whenever they are on campus.

- **Questions:** Leave time for parents to ask any general questions—nothing specific about their child—and to look through their child's desk and textbooks.

When the time is up, try not to get cornered by any one set of parents. Ask at the beginning of the evening for parents to sign up for an individual conference at a later date so that this time may be used for general questions.

You need to make a special effort to communicate with parents who do not come to Back-to-School Night. Sending the packet of information home, followed up by a phone call, can do this. Leave a message on the machine that says, "I'm sorry I missed you at Back-to-School Night, but I sent the information home today with Monica. Call me if you have any questions." Make sure you note this phone call in the ongoing records you are keeping on each student.

Progress Reports

CHECK WITH your school to see whether progress reports are uniformly sent home or whether you are on your own in this area. Some schools have a "danger of failing" notice that a teacher sends home, and some principals want to see copies of the progress reports you send home for all of your students.

If you are using grade book software, progress reports can be generated very easily. If you are recording grades by hand, though, you need to choose a stopping point for your students and evaluate what you have recorded so far. Use the report card in a modified way and model your progress report after it. You do not need to be as specific on the progress report, but definitely include areas that are in need of improvement. If students are on the edge between grades, reflect the lower grade on the progress report. Since this is really a working document, you encourage students to work harder to achieve the higher grade. The report card—the summative, permanent record—can reflect the higher grade if students keep up their end of the bargain.

Send home the progress reports on the date your school designates. Make sure you make a copy of it first and include a space for a parent signature. If your school has parent conferences during this period, use the progress report as a basis for discussion.

Tales from the Trenches

"Sometimes it's time to just get out of the ivory tower. One day when I first began teaching, I was talking to my class about all the ways society has changed over the past few decades.

"To illustrate my point, I passed out large index cards with anonymous questions about how many siblings, half siblings, and stepsiblings they had, how many times their parents had been divorced and remarried, how frequently they'd been victims of crime, racial discrimination or taunting, whether or not they attended religious services, and so forth.

"After they passed the completed surveys back, I shuffled them well and began reading some of the statistics. First kid: four siblings, no divorces, weekly religious services, no crime or discrimination. Okay. Second kid: three siblings, no divorces, weekly religious services, knew someone who had been teased once. Okay. Third kid: five siblings, no divorces. There I was lecturing a class of kids whom I assumed had been through parental divorces and all the usual traumas we associate with American youth, and the fact is, their lives were all about soccer and piano lessons!

"I think that day I was the one who got the lesson — the lesson that in spite of all the bad things that do go on in the world, there's an awful lot of good out there. I think I actually lost a little bit of cynicism that day!"

Phil Levy, Boise, Idaho

Parent Conferences

PARENT CONFERENCES are your opportunity to meet with parents (and, sometimes, students) on an individual basis. The timing of the conferences depends on your school; some schools have conferences six weeks into the school year; some schools have them at the end of grading periods.

Logistics

Your school office may have a blank schedule for you to fill out, along with parent slips that are pre-designed for you to send home when you are scheduling conferences. If they do not, use the schedule on the following page as a sample.

As you schedule your conferences and send out the slips, make sure you keep a master schedule so you can see the whole week. It might look like this:

Teacher's Rule

Don't hesitate to conference. Meetings among teachers and students, attended by an administrator, parents, and/or a counselor, are a productive way to get control over tough teaching situations. Meet for a variety of reasons: grade problems, behavior issues, or just a checkup. Let parents, administrators, counselors and other teachers know that you welcome the opportunity to conference.

Master Schedule

	Monday	Tuesday	Wednesday	Thursday	Friday
2:20					
2:45					
3:10					
3:35					
4:00					
4:25					

SCHEDULING CONFERENCES

Dear Parents,

It's time for our first round of parent conferences! I am looking forward to communicating with you about your child's progress. I have tentatively scheduled you for the following time:

_____ date (Tuesday, November 9)

_____ time (from 2:20 to 2:40)

Please confirm this date and time by signing and returning the bottom portion of this note to me as soon as possible. If this date or time is not convenient, please indicate a better date and time to meet or whether you would prefer to have a phone conference.

Also, please notify me of any questions you would like me to answer during our time together.

Sincerely,

_____

Return this portion to school as soon as possible.

Your conference has been scheduled for:

_____ [date]   _____ [time]

❑ This date and time works—see you then!

❑ This date and time works better for me: _____

❑ I prefer a phone conference on this day _____ at this time _____ at
  this number _____.

Areas I'd like to discuss: _____

_____

PARENT'S SIGNATURE

As you start scheduling, refer to the 4-by-6 cards you collected at Back-to-School Night, and also schedule according to how well you know the parents. For example, if you suspect you are going to have a difficult conference with a parent, you might want to schedule this one in the middle of the day—in other words, you do not want to start or end your conferences with this potentially difficult situation! Along those same lines, be careful about who you schedule on Friday afternoons! You will also have some very friendly parents, but they may want to chat for a while. And you will be tired after a long week of conferencing!

Notice the time allotted for each conference is twenty minutes, with five minutes scheduled in between conferences. This will give you some breathing room.

At the conference table, make sure you have a chair for yourself and two chairs for parents. You need to sit facing the clock. You may also want to have crayons and paper on hand in case the parents bring younger siblings to the conference.

Directly outside your classroom, set up a waiting area for parents with a list of conference times and students' names. The waiting area should include two chairs, a desk that has student textbooks on it, paper and pencils, copies of newsletters, and perhaps some cold drinks and/or snacks.

One other note about scheduling is that just because your school devotes a particular week for conferences doesn't mean you need to hold them all during this week. If you want to score big points with working parents, devote an evening to conferences. You might, for instance, set aside one day to hold conferences from 4:00 to 7:00 P.M. Do this only if you are in a safe neighborhood, and you have plenty of lighting from your classroom to your car. Better still, coordinate this evening with your school's Parent-Teacher Association or with another teacher who will also be staying late. Holding evening

Teacher's Rule

Although the overachieving student who wants a minute-by-minute accounting of his grade can be an irritation, your real concern in teaching is with the counterpart: the underachiever—the student who simply doesn't care what grade he receives, who doesn't want to be in school. These students will stare you dead in the eye and shrug when you ask about the location of a missing assignment. The answer? Didn't do it, didn't care, and not interested in the consequence.

Students who are completely disconnected are the ones who will challenge all your skills as a teacher. These are the kids you need to befriend, to teach one on one, to motivate.

conferences will be appreciated by your parents and will allow you to spread them out over time so you don't have a whole bunch on any one day.

Content of the Conference

Let's review the contacts you may have had with the parents up to this point and assume you are holding the conference at the end of the grading period.

You have, hopefully, done the following:

- Introduced yourself and summarized your philosophy with your first-day letter
- Detailed important information on Back-to-School Night
- Sent home weekly newsletters highlighting instructional objectives and projects.
- Made contact if homework or class work has not been completed
- Issued a progress report if they're failing a subject

By the time the parent conference rolls around, then, there should be no surprises on the part of the parent. The worst feeling a parent can have is to be surprised by the amount of missing assignments, the failing grades, or the lack of completed homework. They will get angry and defensive if the parent conference is the first time they have heard about what has gone on in the last nine to twelve weeks.

Assuming you have kept up on your end of the communication progress, here is how a conference might progress:

Teaching Terms

• • •

Social promotion. A controversial policy of promoting students from one grade to the next, regardless of academic achievement, to prevent discouragement and dropping out. Learn more about social promotion, and an opposing philosophy called grade retention, at this Web site:

Alternatives to Social Promotion and Grade Retention: www.ncrel.org/sdrs/timely/sptoc.htm

1. Start the conference with a positive remark about the student. Tell the parents how much you've enjoyed having their child in your class and how much growth you've seen in the past weeks.

2. Show the parent the report card or progress report, and point out the positive areas first. Then go through all of the areas one at a time pointing out areas of strength and areas of concern. Have the folders of student work available for the parents to look through. Incorporate into the conversation the parents' questions from the parent conference slip.

3. End the conference by discussing next steps for the student and the parents to take. Write them down so that you can make a copy of them and send them home the next day with the student.

Handling Confrontations

It seems almost like a rite of passage to be confronted by a parent. It can really shake you up! You probably went into teaching to make a difference, and you sure are putting a lot of energy into meeting the needs of all of your students. So you're putting forth your best effort, working countless hours a week, and all of a sudden, a parent confronts you! This can be very frustrating! Although these suggestions won't take away the pain you might feel from the confrontation, they may take the sting away during the confrontation so you can engage in a meaningful conversation.

The suggestions involve using certain questioning techniques to validate and guide the parents' concerns. Think in terms of paraphrasing, clarifying, and mediating. A parent may approach you with an angry tone; instead of getting angry and defensive yourself, try to diffuse the situation by asking for clarification.

Take this scenario: The parent is waiting for you at bus duty after school, and snaps, "Your homework is too hard. My daughter is spending three hours a night on it, and that's way too much time. I told her she doesn't have to do it anymore, and if you have a problem with that, I'm going to the principal."

Instead of getting angry, thank the parent for coming to you first. You could begin by saying, "Thank you for coming to me first; I'm sure we can resolve this. Can you come into the classroom for a few

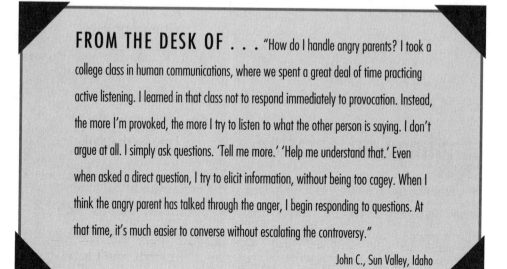

FROM THE DESK OF . . . "How do I handle angry parents? I took a college class in human communications, where we spent a great deal of time practicing active listening. I learned in that class not to respond immediately to provocation. Instead, the more I'm provoked, the more I try to listen to what the other person is saying. I don't argue at all. I simply ask questions. 'Tell me more.' 'Help me understand that.' Even when asked a direct question, I try to elicit information, without being too cagey. When I think the angry parent has talked through the anger, I begin responding to questions. At that time, it's much easier to converse without escalating the controversy."

John C., Sun Valley, Idaho

minutes after I'm done here, or would you like to set up a time to talk?" This way, you're getting the parent away from any passersby, and you're suggesting a private conversation at a convenient time.

From this point on, you need to clarify. You might then say, "I wasn't aware that she is spending so much time on her homework—she's getting really good grades, and her homework is beautifully done. Are there any nights that she spends more time on homework than others? I'm wondering if some subjects pose more of a challenge than others." This approach could lead to a very specific conversation in the content area. Perhaps some modification needs to be made or the student needs to be monitored by the reading specialist or resource specialist, or perhaps the child is a perfectionist. At any rate, this conversation is now shifted into a problem-solving mode.

The thing to remember is to treat each and every confrontation as a learning and problem-solving opportunity for you and the parents relative to what is best for the student. If you can keep this thought in mind while you are being confronted, then something good will come as a result.

Here is another example: If a parent angrily approaches you with an accusation such as, "My son says you only give him a time-out because he's a boy," you could validate the concern by saying, "You know, I'd be angry, too, if my son said that to me. Do you have a minute for us to discuss the discipline policy of this class?" Then, you can share how the time-out process works in your class and the types of behaviors her son is exhibiting. You may need to use the daily discipline record previously mentioned in this chapter with this parent for a while and monitor the child's behavior by the hour.

Let's take a look at another situation. Your student's mother calls one day after class and begins the conversation by accusing you of being a racist. You, of course, are perplexed. The parent won't let you respond in any way and is yelling something about another child calling her daughter a racial slur. Even though you are as upset by the notion as the parent, the parent, again, refuses to let you question her or say anything. In fact, the parent hangs up and threatens to "have your job!" Sick to your stomach, you realize that this one call could explode into a monumental situation. How do you respond?

First, take a few deep breaths. You know you did nothing wrong. If you sit back for a few moments and review the conversation in your head, you'll probably come up with what really happened. In this case, it's probable that the child the mother mentioned during her angry tirade made a racial slur against her daughter, which upset the daughter. The mother—assuming you had knowledge of the name-calling—attacked you. The parent called you for no other reason than to intimidate you. It happens. But in many situations, when an angry parent calls you, you may find a way to turn the conversation around and actually circumvent an explosion. Most parents are reasonable, after all. And in many circumstances, the parent may genuinely want an explanation and be looking for a response. Moreover, once you give the response (which may not mesh with what the parents' beloved son or daughter relayed!), the parent may drop the whole angry deal. Again, it happens—especially when the parent realized that their child wasn't quite truthful about the situation. At any rate, here are some general concepts to follow when confronted by an angry parent:

• **Stay calm.** If the parent is really angry, he or she may even revert to name-calling and abusive language. Take a deep breath and remain calm. Concentrate on speaking slowly and clearly. Listen to what the parent is saying.

• **Take notes.** Document the conversation. You will want to recall for your principal the interaction. Moreover, by concentrating on taking notes, you'll be less likely to react and lose your cool.

- **Mirror the angry parent's frustration.** Say, "It's clear you are very upset about this. Let me see if I understand what you're saying . . . ," and offer that you are there to help, that you want to rectify the situation.

- **Listen.** Ask what the problem is if the parent has not explicated why he or she is so upset. Then, allow the parent time to give his or her side of the story.

- **Explain.** Attempt to explain the situation calmly and clearly and offer solutions.

- **Be professional.** Whatever you do, do not attack the parent back!

- **Apologize.** Finally, if you did indeed make a mistake that caused a parent's feathers to ruffle, apologize. You'd be amazed at what admitting, "I made a mistake. It won't happen again. I sincerely apologize. I thank you for bringing it to my attention so I won't let it happen again," will do to an angry parent.

- **Notify the principal.**

In all confrontations, remember to thank parents for coming to you *first* so that the issue can be resolved. Validate their concerns, as you would the student, and stick to a problem-solving mode. "How can we resolve this?" "I know there's a solution to this—let's think about it for a minute." If you practice these lines, they will be automatic, and you won't need to feel like a deer in the headlights!

Communicate immediately with your principal if you engage in any confrontation with a parent—or if the parent is just fuming! You really do need to make the principal aware of any volatile situation. If he hears your side of the story first, then he has a "heads up" as to what to expect if the parent calls him regarding the incident. The principal will appreciate this.

One final note on this subject, though, is that you do not deserve to be harassed, humiliated, or intimidated—*ever*. Even though you handle yourself professionally during the confrontation, let your administrator know immediately about the confrontation. You never deserve to be yelled at, and it is illegal for a parent to threaten or harass you. Do not keep this to yourself. Tell someone! It's especially important to tell school administrators so they can be present during any future contacts with this parent. Protect yourself!

Open House

ONE OF the last chances you have to meet with parents formally is Open House. This usually occurs near the end of the school year and should be taken seriously. Sometimes it is referred to as "Teacher Show and Tell"; make sure you structure yours as "Student Show and Tell."

You really want to showcase the work your students have done during the year. This is the time to pull out completed projects such as science labs, class books, book reports, maps, and models. Think of having one item in each content area to showcase. The students' portfolios should be on their desks, along with any daily work folders. If you do not want the work taken home, make sure you explain that to the parents and students.

You can get as creative as you want in this endeavor. Have the students and parents estimate how many jellybeans are in a jar, and announce the winners fifteen or twenty minutes prior to the end of the evening. Run the videotape you have been keeping of your students throughout the year. Mount pictures from field trips on poster board or in scrapbooks.

To prepare for open house, you could have the students practice giving each other a tour of the classroom, pointing out their work, and giving a detailed description of when it was done, why it was done, and what they learned from it. You could even have the students design an "agenda" to follow when their parents come to the class. It might look like this:

Check off each box after you and your parent complete it.

❏ Art center

❏ Writing center

❏ Science project

❏ Estimation jar

❏ Say hi to the teacher

❏ Globes

❏ Portfolio

❏ Watch me on the video

❏ Look at field trip photos

❏ Hyperstudio presentation

❏ Bar graph on my favorite ice cream

Hand in to me when you're done for a raffle!

Open House is different from Back-to-School Night in that you will probably not do a group presentation. This is an opportunity for you to let your students do the talking, and you can simply mingle with the parents. It should have a very social atmosphere. If you start cleaning your classroom early and keep your projects all year long, then Open House won't be a big stressor in your life. There will always be last-minute things to do, but get your students involved. As you did with Back-to-School Night, have your students clean the classroom. Start a day or two before the big night, though, as sometimes it is difficult for the custodian to get around to everyone's classroom on the night of Open House. Also, the student's homework for the night is to get their parents to come! You can have them design their own invitations for their parents as well.

On the night of Open House, make sure your desk is organized and clean. Lock up your personal items as usual, and put away any breakables. Remember that little brothers and little sisters will be in attendance! Make sure you eat a healthy dinner, and you might want to consider having punch and cookies for your guests. This is a nice touch and will score you some points! Be prepared, too, for parents of future students to come to your classroom to check you out. They will be impressed by the goodies and all of your students' work.

Things to Remember

Communicating with parents is an area you can't "overdo"; more is definitely more here! Think through the following ways you will be communicating with your students' parents throughout the year.

❏ Start the year off right by having a letter ready for the parents of your students on the first day of school

❏ Communicate consistently by sending home a class newsletter, daily or weekly discipline records, notes that keep parents aware of missing assignments, progress reports and schedule parent conferences to keep parents updated on their child's progress

❏ Handle angry parents by remaining calm, turning the conversation around to a joint problem-solving situation, and notifying the principal of the incident

❏ Use Back to School Night to communicate procedures and routines to parents and Open House to show off work the students have completed over the course of the year

Communicating with Faculty

A BIG PART of your first year will involve befriending faculty at your school site. Much of your success as an instructor—even happiness as a teacher—relies on your relationship with your campus colleagues. Some schools nurture a warm, cooperative "team" of teachers; other sites don't. Some faculties associate with each other on and off campus, maintaining deep friendships, while other campuses breed competition among teachers. Here's hoping you enjoy a site rich with the "team" approach.

Even at schools where the faculty is generally close, however, with so many different personalities, disagreements and politicking are bound to rear their ugly heads. Just look upon this chapter as your armor in the war to achieve *tenure*. We'll use this space to encourage you to take advantage of the many opportunities you'll have outside your "little world of the classroom" to actually communicate with other adults.

Eyes Wide Open, Mouth Shut

A KIND veteran teacher who took a liking to one of the authors of this book offered some sound advice her first day teaching: "Eyes wide open, mouth shut your first year teaching. Just absorb this year. You'll learn a lot about the political climate of this campus by watching the other teachers and listening. And you won't tick anyone off yourself if you keep your mouth closed." Sadly, this was good advice.

This isn't to say that you shouldn't interact and talk. The premise of the advice is to maintain professionalism and ensure that your colleagues don't label you a gossip; at the same time, though, you don't want to appear to be cold and aloof.

> ## Teaching Terms
> ◆ ◆ ◆
>
> **Tenure.** Status granted to a teacher after a trial period. Tenured status gives protection from summary dismissal.

You probably never thought you'd need to study human behavior your first year as a teacher. But you do. Study the staff. Listen to other teachers. You'll demonstrate that you're someone who can be trusted. And if the other teachers know you're not the type to spill everything you hear, they'll feel more inclined to divulge the idiosyncrasies of the personalities at the site and within the district. You'll begin this way to learn the nuances of the district that has employed you—which is actually quite a big deal!

Also, by quietly listening and not reacting your first year, you may learn many helpful tips—such as the best administrator to go to for curriculum advice, why those who disturb a certain teacher during the first fifteen minutes after school receive the death penalty, or which teachers on campus gather to help each other move!

Meeting Hall

WITHIN EVERY faculty, the meetings must flow. Prepare yourself. You'll attend at the least monthly faculty meetings. You'll probably attend periodic districtwide meetings, too. These meetings are not

Teacher's Rule

Just as rumors fly like wildfire among the students you teach, a loose word or two about another teacher or administrator can move rapidly, too. Keep your criticism to yourself. You don't want to burn any bridges, nor do you want to become a target for criticism yourself.

optional. We repeat: These meetings are *not* optional. During these gatherings, information you need to know is presented. Everything from testing procedures to parking problems appears on the agendas of faculty meetings. In truth, even with the sophisticated e-mail systems and video bulletins that many schools provide, nothing can beat a good old gathering to get the facts.

These meetings also serve as an opportunity to come together as a group and share stories, ideas, and camaraderie. Oftentimes, as teachers, we hole up in our rooms, working away, preparing lessons, even overlooking the need for lunch with others our own age. Only at the monthly faculty meeting do we get the opportunity to connect again with coworkers.

When you sit together—whether bouncing ideas off each other, listening to the procedures of using the computer lab, or divvying up the extra *supervision duties*—you reconnect as a team. Look at these meetings in a positive way—like a team preparing for the big game. Your principal is the coach, the teachers are his players, and the stakes are the students' educations.

FROM THE DESK OF . . . Teacher Tamara Givens may ignore what kids say about each other, but she never allows students to badmouth her colleagues while in her classes. "I tell them I don't want to hear it, and when they try to coerce me into listening by saying, 'But Ms. Givens, you're not like a teacher, you're more like a friend.' I always turn it around and say, 'If you talk about your other teachers like this in front of me, what are you saying about me in front of them?' No way! I don't want the other teachers talking about me with the students, so I don't allow it myself," asserts the bubbly and professional teacher.

To Eat or Not to Eat—That Is the Question

ANOTHER KEY component of communicating with colleagues involves the lunch table. Many, many teachers claim no time for lunch and burrow into their rooms during the half-hour repast. This pattern can result in burnout. The late Lory Butcher—a teacher her whole adult life—used to give all new teachers the same advice: "Go to lunch! Eat! Whatever you do, take a break from the classroom." Lory knew that those thirty minutes brought a rejuvenation of mind and spirit necessary to plow through the rest of the day. Nothing clears your mind or soul better after a particularly trying morning with students than having a sounding board over a sandwich. Moreover, quick updates—everything from "Where are we meeting after school?" to "The superintendent said *what?*"—are available in the lunch room.

On a more political note, if you avoid lunch with your colleagues, they may perceive you as aloof and stuck-up. You'll be perceived as a

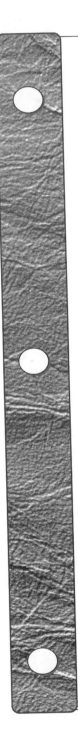

Tales from the Trenches

Never underestimate the importance of showing your face at a faculty meeting. Even if you think the time spent preparing a lesson in your class is more important than the meeting, think again. Administrators are notorious for taking roll. And depending on your principal, you may find yourself up a creek for a seemingly harmless absence. One anonymous teacher recalls the time he skipped a faculty "true colors" workshop to tape lessons for a substitute. "The principal called me into her office and wrote me up," he recalls. Whether you believe the teacher was more needed in his classroom than at the meeting is irrelevant. What is relevant is that administration wanted him there. So toe the line and make the meetings—no matter how much you have on your plate!

team player if you gather with others for a quick bite and some chitchat.

Finally, sitting with your peers can prove downright fun. More laughter is heard from the lunch areas of teachers than anywhere else in school.

Let's Party

FACULTY SOCIAL functions provide new teachers another great way to "get into the groove" of their school site. Maybe we just love a great get-together. Whatever the reason, faculties all over the nation seem to enjoy a party or two every so often. Coauthor Lynne Rominger recalls that her first year teaching provided an opportunity at least once a month to party hearty with colleagues—from Christmas bashes to Cinco de Mayo fiestas, from monthly faculty informal mixers to end-of-the-year barbecues, parties were the thing to do on her campus. But did the new teacher attend every function? No way, José!

In fact, most teachers can't attend every function. But we do urge you to show your face and mix with your colleagues at least a few times during the year. Stepping outside the authoritarian teaching role will help you connect with your colleagues and enjoy your profession even more.

While we do recommend attending one or more events, you should mind your manners and behave as an adult at these events. A few items to consider when partying with colleagues:

> ## Teaching Terms
>
> ◆ ◆ ◆
>
> **Supervision duties.** With the lack of funds in public schools nowadays, teachers often are required to take on supplemental supervision duties in addition to teaching all day. When there's no money to pay someone to watch buses load and unload, for instance, a teacher pulls the duty. All those little events and tasks you must supervise or coordinate are referred to within districts as supervision duties. Whether you're actually paid for the time you supervise depends on your district's policies.

Teacher's Rule

If you shy away from large groups at lunch, try to find a friend or two like you on campus and meet for the noon meal together. This way, you'll not feel so isolated from other adults and will build friendships. You'll need a few people you can safely sound off to about problems in classes and the stresses of the job—especially your first year.

• Limit the drinking. A drink or two of alcohol is about the limit. You don't want to be seen face down on the carpet in front of your peers.

• Be doubly mindful of this rule if the gathering occurs in public. You are, after all, a role model for the students you teach. You'd hate to hear the rumors on the playground the following Monday about "My dad saw Mr. ____ drunk."

Stay within the bounds of professionalism, but enjoy the party and the antics of your fellow teachers as you all cut loose from the grind of the school year. You deserve it.

How Many Extracurricular Activities Do You Need?

PARTICIPATING IN faculty-sponsored events and sharing your load of supervision duties is one thing,

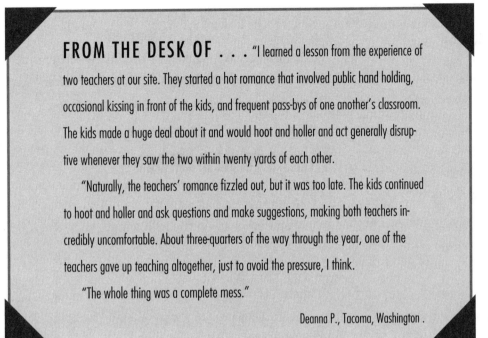

FROM THE DESK OF . . . "I learned a lesson from the experience of two teachers at our site. They started a hot romance that involved public hand holding, occasional kissing in front of the kids, and frequent pass-bys of one another's classroom. The kids made a huge deal about it and would hoot and holler and act generally disruptive whenever they saw the two within twenty yards of each other.

"Naturally, the teachers' romance fizzled out, but it was too late. The kids continued to hoot and holler and ask questions and make suggestions, making both teachers incredibly uncomfortable. About three-quarters of the way through the year, one of the teachers gave up teaching altogether, just to avoid the pressure, I think.

"The whole thing was a complete mess."

Deanna P., Tacoma, Washington .

but overbooking yourself to attend every event, volunteering for every committee, and pulling extra duties only sets you up for burnout and failure.

Just Say No!

"Oh, sure! Say, 'No,'" balks every reader. "How do I say no to the principal when I want tenure? I gotta say yes to everything." No, you don't. Granted, expectations will be thrust upon you. You don't want to say no and potentially lose tenure or, at least, a contract for another year. But, at the same time, you need to take care of yourself, too.

If you really are swamped, politely decline. Just let the invitee know how many tacos too many already sit on your combo platter. Apologize for your inability to attend and thank the person for

Teacher's Rule

What if you hate social situations and find them unbearably uncomfortable? If you really hate them, then don't go. We do recommend trying to attend at least one event during the year—like an end-of-the-year-party—if only to show your colleagues that you really do enjoy their friendship. But, we also recognize that not everyone easily slips into socialite-at-a-soirée mode. Cut yourself some slack and curl up with a good book on those evenings. After all, you can't be everything to everybody. You can only be true to yourself.

thinking of you—but do not back down and accept a role you can't attend to adequately.

When teachers take on too many other roles, then classroom teaching will begin to suffer. And that's ultimately why you're there, right?

Things to Remember

To communicate effectively with the rest of the staff, remember to do the following:

- ❏ Choose carefully who you confide in; don't listen to rumors or allow yourself to gossip
- ❏ Attend ALL staff meetings and be prompt
- ❏ Try to eat lunch in the staff room as much as possible, and try to attend some of the many social opportunities that may arise
- ❏ Protect your time and energy by politely refusing some of the extra-curricular duties that may be offered to you

Communicating with Administration

19

OVER THE COURSE of your career, you will communicate extensively with administration—whether communicating with your principal over disruptive students, conferring with angry parents, or presenting an idea to school board members. Sometimes, it may feel as though you're constantly explaining yourself and answering to someone.

Just because you earned a credential in teaching elementary school children doesn't mean for a second that those are the only humans you will need to deal with in any given day. *Au contraire.* You can make it, though. We'll try to help you here avoid some of the common communication pitfalls and make your time spent outside the classroom just a tad less stressful.

> *" A teacher affects eternity; he can never tell where his influence stops "*
>
> HENRY B. ADAMS

The Testers

As YOU get to know your students and work through your discipline plan, you will have some who continue to test and test and test you. Or you may have a student who does something so outrageous that

you need to engage administration right away. Even though you may have been as consistent as possible by enforcing consequences to curb disruptive behavior, sometimes instances still arise when you'll need to ask for help. This response is completely appropriate; how you handle it, though, makes a difference. In many ways, it's what you do before the disruption occurs more than what you do after.

Usually the principal will want a copy of your discipline plan, including your rewards and consequences. Your plan should indicate that you enforce the majority of the consequences yourself—such as a time-out or a parent phone call. But if, after the time-out and a parent phone call, the child continues the behavior, the next consequence is the principal's office. If the principal is aware of your consequences and the expectation of her involvement ahead of time, then she won't be surprised when you send over a student. The principal will know that you have gone through all of the other consequences, and this action is your last resort.

If going to the principal becomes a habit, a behavior contract may be drafted. The best part about getting the principal involved is that now another adult will be able to monitor the student's behavior. You have a partner invested in the best interests of the student. Moreover, sometimes Mom and Dad don't want to believe that their child acts inappropriately. You may tell them until you're blue in the face that Susie continually screams out during class and is aggressive toward other students, but they just won't believe you or may minimize the impact of Susie's disruptive behavior. But when you have another witness, you reinforce your stance, and the parents may respond more proactively toward solving the problem.

> ## Teacher's Rule
>
> *Sometimes it is completely appropriate to send the student to the principal right away. Any time there is physical injury (actual or threatened), harassment, foul language, theft, defacement of property, or weapons of any kind, then the principal needs to be called on immediately. This is not the time to go through any steps. You call the office right away.*

The worst thing you can do is to send the student to the principal as the first consequence. Do not get into the negative posturing of "If you do that again, I'm sending you to the principal." The principal will not respect that decision if you do, and the student will not respect you if you don't. You need to go through all the steps consistently so that your students know you mean business. Also, going through each step gives students opportunities to correct their behavior before the next consequence is enforced.

Special Identification

As YOU work with your students, you may come across some who consistently do not meet grade-level expectations. You've modified their assignments and continually put them in remediation groups, and

Teacher's Rule

Always document every phone call to a parent, disciplinary action, or out-of-the-ordinary situation that occurs. It's just a good practice. If questions arise up the road, you have the documentation to reinforce your word. In the case of a student who shows signs of needing special education help, we can't stress the importance of documentation enough. Many times, your observances of the child in your class will form the basis of the process that results in the child receiving the extra help needed. So, thoroughly document special situations—perhaps even keep a notebook in your desk devoted to the child.

they're still behind the other students. Sometimes the problems exhibited transcend the academic. Perhaps the child is inordinately shy or shows signs of something bigger—such as an obsessive/compulsive disorder. Hopefully you've informed the parents of these concerns, and you're keeping records of these conversations.

Before the first round of parent conferences, you may want to look into the child's cumulative folder. These folders can be found in the office, and they are records that have been kept by the school—any school the child has attended—that include health reports, standardized test scores, other assessment information, report cards, discipline actions, and whether the student has been referred to special education in the past.

Look in the folder to see what modifications other teachers have made, what comments were made on report cards, and what steps were taken toward referring the child to special education. Armed with this knowledge, arrange an informal meeting with your school's resource specialist. This is another individual who can assist you in making sure you are meeting the needs of all of the students in your class. The specialist will guide you through the process your school has adopted for identifying and working with special needs students. This may involve a meeting with the *Student study team*, where the team will decide the next steps for your student. Or the specialist will give you suggestions about what strategies to try with the student and ask that you report back at a future date.

Handling Angry Parents

PARENTS DO become angry! You are the first line of defense against an angry parent—assuming you know the parent is angry. Sometimes, however, parents will go straight to the principal with a concern without consulting you first. This is so frustrasting!

When your principal approaches you (and hopefully he *will* go straight to you), let him know right up front that the parent did not go to you first, that in fact this is the first time you have heard about this complaint. Show him any documentation that you have regarding the student in question (refer to Chapter 17 for more details). The principal can then use your documentation to intervene.

The administrator may either take a proactive approach and call the parents, or she may just wait to see whether the parent makes a follow-up call. Regardless, you've given her your side of the story. This type of conversation may even deepen the relationship between you and the principal. The next time the principal receives a phone call, then, she will be armed with your documentation

Making the Grade

The United States Department of Education, Office of Special Education and Rehabilitative Services, "supports programs that assist in educating children with special needs, provides for the rehabilitation of youth and adults with disabilities, and supports research to improve the lives of individuals with disabilities." You will probably want to navigate online at some time for more information—especially if you suspect a student of yours requires help. Try this site for starters:

Office of Special Education Programs: *www.ed.gov /offices/OSERS*

From the Desk of the Principal

YOU MAY see a note in your mailbox from your principal one day that says, "See me." Unfortunately, nine times out of ten this is not to tell you what a great job you are doing! Take a deep breath, and

peek into the principal's office to respond to the note. Ask if this is a good time, and if it is, stay and chat.

Teaching Terms

• • •

Student study team. When someone — a parent, a teacher, the school psychologist — suspects that a child may qualify for special education services, the first step in determining the need is a Student study team evaluation. These evaluations usually involve the special education teacher or resource specialist, the teacher, the school nurse, the speech therapist, the school psychologist, and the principal. The team determines whether the student needs further testing or more modifications on your part. The team then provides parents with its findings at another meeting.

Treat the situation the same way you do with parents: This is an opportunity to work through a problem. And get it out of your mind that whatever the problem is will cost you your job! Granted, sometimes a teacher will do something that results in immediate termination, but that only happens for egregious actions such as child abuse. In this case, a parent has probably called the principal before calling you.

Use clarifying questions with the principal so that you know exactly what the situation is and how you can go about resolving it. Get into that "problem-solving" mode, instead of being afraid, angry, or feeling as though you've done something wrong. If necessary, defend yourself by clarifying the situation, not by becoming defensive. Try to depersonalize the situation as best you can.

Other situations may have to do with policies that you might not be following without even knowing it. Try as you might to know everything, you're human and make mistakes. When the principal apprises you, for example, of the policy regarding e-mail during class time, thank him and follow the procedure. Finally, go home and take a long bath, and forget about it. To quote the ever-rebounding-from-bad-situations heroine, Scarlett O'Hara, "Tomorrow is another day!"

DOA (Do on Arrival!)

SOME REQUESTS can wait and others just can't. Any requests from the district office fall into the DOA, "do on arrival," category. As soon as the request arrives from the district office, you do it. More often than not, the request involves helping you, such as ensuring your paycheck arrives, so you'll probably want to hustle and get the work done. Typical requests from the district office may involve your insurance, your salary and benefits, textbook or supplies issues, your contract—many things!

Even though it may seem as though you don't have the time to complete whatever the district wants "yesterday," make the time. Put the actual request in your "To the Office" letter tray, noting the date it is due. Make a notation in your lesson plan book that you need to complete this request. Schedule it in, and then do it! Make a copy of

Making the Grade

Children with disabilities are protected under the landmark 1990 law, the Americans with Disabilities Act. The ADA guarantees basic civil rights for those with special needs and is the foundation of nondiscrimination against people with disabilities in the areas of employment, state and local governments, public accommodations, and telecommunications.

it and send the original in to the district office. Put the copy in your "District Office" file that you're keeping in your desk drawer. Get the reputation for being organized and responsive.

Mail Call

IT'S A beautiful thing: You will never need to put a stamp on mail going to the district office, mail going to another school in your district, or mail going to your local/regional office of education. Your district probably uses an internal mail system to accomplish this. Find out from your secretary where the outgoing district mail is put, what time it is picked up everyday, and whether a special envelope is needed. Most often, a regular manila envelope is passed back and forth between district office parties, as long as they are labeled with

1. who the mail is going to
2. the recipient's school site or position
3. your name and school site

In most cases, district mail is picked up and delivered every day to and from the district office. The regional office of education will probably have one day that they pick up and deliver things to your school. Again, find out which day this is and where the pickup/delivery spot is so you'll know!

There *Is* Such Thing As a Bad Question

YOU WILL have many, many questions during your years of teaching. But you also must remember that you work in a political atmosphere and should proceed with caution. Questions you may have might include these:

- Why can't I use the bathroom when I need to?
- Why don't I have a phone in my room?
- Why don't I have enough textbooks for my students?

By all means, these are all valid questions. But the way you approach the questions might ignite some animosity or hurt your career advancement. We know—it seems silly. What you want to do is approach all your questions with a proactive stance instead of a reactive stance. For example, ask, "What should I do when I need to use the bathroom during class time?" And: "I've noticed that the other classrooms have phones; what is the procedure for getting one hooked up in my classroom in case of an emergency? Who should I see about that?" And: "Since I'm new, it's hard for me to figure out how to teach my students with only half of the number of textbooks. How should I go about getting more?" Notice the shift is from "why" to "how." By not putting the administrator on the defensive, you will get more cooperation in solving your problem. In one word: diplomacy! Show yours.

You Versus the Board of Education

IN THE course of your career, you will—at some point—interact with the *board of education*. In fact, you may be asked even to make a presentation to the board. Your principal may "volunteer" you to do this because of a creative project you have done with your students, a successful field trip, or a new program you are using. This is an exciting thing! Take this opportunity to show off your ability. Dress in your best and make a great presentation!

Sometimes you might be asked to do a summary of the goings-on in your classroom for the school board. Be eloquent! Go through the checklist of the subject areas you are teaching, the projects your students are doing, and the field trips you are going on. Use your newsletters as a guide and make sure you submit whatever is requested of you on time. And relax. Recognize the fact that you were chosen because you could deliver the best presentation. Believe us! Those boards are interested in showcasing what wonderful schools they run. The very fact that you were chosen to give the presentation speaks volumes about how well respected you are as a teacher in the district.

Teaching Terms

◆ ◆ ◆

Board of education. Every school district runs with a governing body—a board. Typically, the school board members are elected officials who oversee the running of the schools, including everything from approving hiring choices to selecting curriculum.

Things to Remember

Communicating with administration may seem daunting, but it is a fact of life. Remember to do the following to establish positive communication with the administrators at your site and in your district:

❏ Share your discipline plan with the principal so she knows what steps you have taken before the students end up in her office

❏ Investigate the Student Study Team process at your school

❏ Remain calm when your principal asks to speak with you, and turn the situation into a problem-solving conversation

❏ Respond to administrative requests immediately

" Creative powers can just as easily turn out to be destructive. It rests solely with the moral personality whether they apply them-selves to good things or to bad. And if this is lack-ing, no teacher can supply it or take its place. "

CARL JUNG

PART SEVEN

ODDS AND ENDS

On Display:
Classroom Observations

Employee reviews pervade every profession. Most everyone must grin and bear the scrutinizing of a boss's comments on a yearly or semiannual basis. Oh, the stomach churning and sweaty palms when you enter the principal's office! Once you sit down, you must endure an endless documentation trail of what you either did right or wrong. Regardless of the outcome, an *evaluation* is stressful.

In fact—and we cringe as we write this truth—in many ways, your review as a teacher can prove worse to endure than a review in the outside world. Stop moaning, because in many ways, the process also offers you a better, more objective way to showcase your best work and learn how to become a more effective teacher.

> ## Teaching Terms
>
> • • •
>
> **Classroom observation.** A process that involves an administrator or colleague observing a teacher's skills in the classroom for the purpose of continued employment. The evaluator then conducts a follow-up meeting where both the strengths and the weaknesses of the observation are discussed.

You Want to See Me Do *What*?

> *"Curiosity is the very basis of education, and if you tell me that curiosity killed the cat, I say only the cat died nobly."*
>
> ARNOLD EDINBOROUGH

YOU BEGIN class, joke with your students, deliver the lesson, assign homework, and generally move about your classroom as the Big Kahuna, the teacher. Perhaps you even went into teaching because, while you're in that classroom, no one breathes down your back. The room is your domain. We all have our teaching styles and our special ways of communicating with students.

In other professions, the boss might look at a report you wrote or calculate a raise based on your sales figures. In teaching, the principal looks at you—you up there, you delivering the lesson, you, you, you. It's all about you.

In defense of the evaluators, how else might administrators review your work if they don't actually see you in action? They can't. So grin and bear it, because classroom observations are an integral part of a teacher's career.

FROM THE DESK OF . . . It's not a good thing when you're boring your evaluator so much that he or she is doodling. One teacher in Washington recalls passing out an assignment during an evaluation and noticing her evaluator's drawing of a landscape scene on his clipboard. "It really made me feel bad at first. But then when I got the evaluation, he said I'd done a great job. I wanted to turn around and say, 'But my lecture had nothing to do with trees and birds.'"

Planned Attack Versus Surprise Attack

OVER THE course of the year, your evaluator will appear in your classroom on several occasions. Many of those appearances will, in fact, be planned. You will arrange in advance for an appropriate time for the evaluator to come in and watch you in action. (See appendix 6 for a sample planned obervation form.) Other times, though, those appearances will just happen. Picture it now: You at the front of the room explicating the plot of a novel or describing the numerous bones in the human hand. In walks the principal to observe your lesson. Your heart races and sinks to the bottom of your stomach—especially if you're having an off day!

But an observation need not elicit such an adverse response. Before you completely freak out about your observation, take a closer look. There's an upside to the unplanned evaluation, particularly for enthusiastic new teachers who are well prepared for their classes. Your joy of teaching is new and obvious—and will serve you well during an unexpected visit from an administrator. Plan your lessons well, smile a lot, and accept that sometimes, when you least expect it, an evaluator will enter your classroom to observe you. As long as you plan accordingly for your classes all the time, you shouldn't run into any problems. And if this person shows up during a test, he won't stay, and you've just received fair warning that he'll be back in the near future!

Evaluation Criteria

"How DO you ensure you meet the criteria on which your evaluation is based?" you ask. With luck, you're teaching at a school where the administrator will review all the components of the observation with you prior to actually visiting your room.

However, in case you do not sit down with the evaluator in a *pre-observation conference*, you need to know what 's on the observation form! Not a problem. Here's what you do. Go to the administrator and tell him or her that you'd like to see a copy of the observation

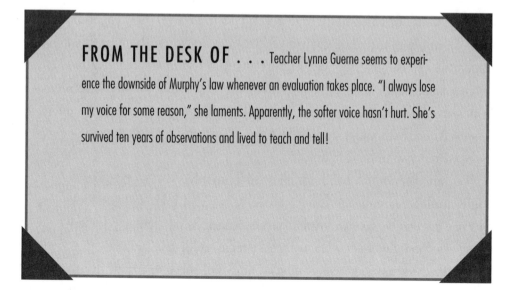

FROM THE DESK OF . . . Teacher Lynne Guerne seems to experience the downside of Murphy's law whenever an evaluation takes place. "I always lose my voice for some reason," she laments. Apparently, the softer voice hasn't hurt. She's survived ten years of observations and lived to teach and tell!

Tales from the Trenches

Worried about an observation her first year, coauthor Lynne Rominger bemoaned the upcoming review with a colleague, Paul Greco—himself a veteran teacher with over twenty years' experience teaching—who offered this advice to the neophyte: "Plan a lesson you're comfortable with. Don't try anything you're unsure of. In fact, once you've taught a few years, pull out those lessons you know you give well and use them for your evaluations." His advice is good. When you feel more relaxed and knowledgeable about the lesson you are delivering, your confidence will be obvious to the evaluator and probably result in an awesome review.

◆ ◆ ◆

"Don't listen to the whisperings of colleagues regarding the roles of each evaluator on your campus. For example, if someone says, 'Oh, they only send the principal out to evaluate those teachers the school wants to get rid of by next year—the big guns' take no heed. First, it won't do you any good to worry that you've been matched to the 'Terminator Evaluator.' Second, nasty, groundless rumors fly around every campus. Yours is no different. Instead of listening to the rumblings about how so-and-so evaluates, prepare for your evaluation and knock the administrator's socks off with your professionalism, killer lesson plan, and incredible delivery."

Miles D., New York, New York

Teaching Terms

• • •

Preobservation conference. When your evaluator discusses the items against which you will be observed prior to your observation, the process is often referred to as a preobservation conference. See appendix 5 for a sample preevaluation conference form.

form. Most every school possesses these forms, which standardize the skills that the evaluator will look for during his or her observation. (See appendices 3 and 4 for sample evaluation forms.)

Generally speaking, an observation form will cover several aspects of your teaching, including these:

- Learning goals. What are the goals for this lesson? What are the expected student outcomes? How does this lesson fit with the overall objectives of the unit of study?

- Instructional strategies. What can I expect to see you and your students doing during this lesson?

- Assessment. How will you know your students have met the goals of the lesson?

- Other. Is there anything else you want me to look for in this lesson?

When the evaluator asks the "other" question, this is the perfect opportunity to be "proactive"; if you've been struggling with a particular student, ask your evaluator to keep an eye on that student and give you feedback. In that way, you will have a friend instead of a foe to help you with that particular student.

So now let's pretend you just met with your evaluator. He showed you the observation form and the items listed for the observation include those categories we just identified: learning goals, instructional strategies, and assessment. In your preobservation conference, you should have asked the evaluator to explain anything you didn't understand, and perhaps you suggested that the evaluator watch the interaction of Josh and his tablemates.

Now plan your lesson, making sure to include all elements of the review—if you can.

Once you plan your lesson, make copies of any handouts that the students may already have that support your lesson, as well as the handouts you may be using in the lesson. Give the background information and the collateral materials for the lesson to the evaluator. You will demonstrate your organizational skills and also give the administrator a reference point in the lesson for the unit. You may even want to send along a short note expressing your objectives for the lesson and describing how the lesson fits into the thematic unit.

Ready, Set, Action

Ever hear that phrase "What you don't know, can't hurt you"? Well, it's wrong. When you know that an observation will occur, you may stress to the point of illness. We know it's easier said than done, but relax. The night before your observation eat well, get some exercise, and, for goodness sake, sleep!

Make sure that you dress conservatively for the evaluation. You'd be surprised what some evaluators will pick on. One teacher told us about an observation postconference in which the evaluator told her "to wear

Teacher's Rule

Don't be surprised if an evaluator enters your classroom—are you ready?—on Back-to-School Night. Principals, superintendents, even secretaries—all seem to like to see how teachers perform in front of parents. Moreover, you describe for the parents information such as what you plan to teach, how you plan to present it, and the philosophies of the school. The evaluator receives a good indication of how you perform with your students by seeing how you relate to the parents.

Making the Grade

Looking for the latest information on evaluations and research surrounding teacher evaluations? Check out the Evaluation Center, part of the Joint Committee on Standards for Educational Evaluation, at www.wmich.edu/evalctr/jc. The Evaluation Center's mission is "to provide national and international leadership for advancing the theory and practice of program, personnel, and student/constituent evaluation, as applied primarily to education and human services. The Center's principal activities are research, development, dissemination, service, instruction, and leadership."

less jewelry." Far be it from us to squelch your creativity. In this day and age of "most" anything goes, we see teachers with nose piercings and eclectic clothing. All fine and good. But for your review, move cautiously. Stand on the conservative side of the fence. Chances are that's exactly where your evaluator hangs out! Oh, and one more thing: Eat breakfast. You can't perform without fuel.

Post-it Notes

AFTER THE evaluator observes your class, a *postobservation conference* will occur. We know: "I made it through the observation, and now I have to endure a face-to-face discussion of my faults?" Yes. But what you may not be anticipating is all the good stuff the evaluator will bring out.

In the postobservation conference, the administrator typically goes over all his notes and the lesson observation form used to assess your lesson and offers narratives to describe what you did well and what you did not. A good evaluator also tells you how you can remedy any problems. In one of Lynne's classes last year, for example, her evaluator, an assistant principal, told Lynne that when she calls on a student to answer a question from the text and the student cannot answer the question, she should wait and insist that the student find the answer. "He told me to say something like, 'Find the answer, and the class will return to you in a minute,'" she recalls. She used his advice from then on. Students in her classes know to stay alert because if called on, they cannot cop out of answering by saying, "I don't know." The evaluator, in this case, may have brought to Lynne's attention a problem but also showed her how to squelch it.

Perhaps that is the best part of the post-observation conference: You learn from your mistakes. When you learn, you can only get better. And becoming a better teacher year after year is what it is all about.

I Thought You Were My Friend!

ANOTHER TYPE of observation may occur by a colleague. Many districts want their teachers to learn from each other. Sometimes, the district maintains a mentor program and a veteran teacher will review and observe the lessons of several new teachers to ensure the teacher receives support.

These colleague observations are usually good things. Go into them with a good attitude. Tell the colleague (and mean it), "I can't wait for you to observe my class. I'm looking forward to receiving your feedback about how I manage the class, use technology, or whatever."

Then follow up with the teacher and request honest feedback. The peer evaluator might be required to write a formal observation critique. Ask to see it. You might just find yourself pleasantly surprised at the input you receive from your colleagues.

Teacher's Rule

At a preobservation conference, ask questions. Clarify any items you don't understand. If you haven't already, ask to see a copy of the observation form if you have not been given one. Doing so will show the administrator that you care—that you want to be at that school and are willing to find out how to best serve your individual classroom of students. Moreover, if you know what the evaluator will be looking for, you can better structure your lesson to hit all the elements of the observation.

Teaching Terms

• • •

Postobservation conference. After an observation occurs, the administrator or evaluator who performed the review should call you in for a postobservation conference. During the conference, the evaluator will discuss your strengths and, perhaps, weaknesses in the delivery and content of the lesson, and may ask to see the student work that was generated. This is the time for you to ask how the observation process fits into the evaluation process. In other words, ask to see the evaluation form that the school uses to determine the overall effectiveness of a teacher. Surprises are not a good thing in this profession!

Student Revenge?

WAIT A minute! First an administrator, then a colleague, and now a student? Believe it. A good way to evaluate your teaching is through the constructive comments of your students. Many districts require student evaluations of teachers. Others don't, but you should consider it anyway. The brutal honesty of students can help you modify your ways and teach better. The key to constructive student evaluation rubrics is allowing the kids to write "off-record"—no names needed.

Teachers find out all sorts of things through student evaluations. It'll be a big help to your future classes if you discover the work isn't challenging enough or you aren't maintaining management during class. You also find out how much the kids really enjoy your class. But understand, please, that the reason they're kids—and not adults—is that they're sometimes remarkably immature and cruel. They may say things to hurt your feelings on the evaluation—and for no other reason. Denise Weis, a high school department head and veteran English teacher, relayed the time that a student wrote that she "should go work at Taco Bell!" on an evaluation. Instead of wincing and crying at the comment, the teacher chuckled and went on her way. Since, at her school site, the evaluator asks for a synopsis of the students' responses, Mrs. Weis included the comment from the student, so the evaluator could laugh, too. One student making one mean-spirited comment does not a class make!

Evaluation: The Grand Finale

YOU MAY be wondering where all of this observation information and perhaps student feedback goes. Altogether, this information is used to create your overall evaluation for the year. Some time in mid-spring, expect a notice in your box requesting a meeting with your evaluator. S/he may ask you to bring samples of student work, and a portfolio if you have one—anything to demonstrate your growth as a teacher and your student's progress over the year. Your evaluation will probably cover the following areas:

- **Curricular objectives.** Do you demonstrate you understand and comply with the school's curriculum? For example, are you teaching the information from the required text, or are you simply showing movies in class? Do you make use of the materials provided to you? Do you establish a time frame for your units of study and pace yourself accordingly to accomplish all the work necessary for the term?

- **Instructional techniques and strategies.** Do you engage students by using strategies and materials that stimulate them? Do you use a variety of techniques— such as cooperative group projects and direct questioning—to involve students?

- **Learning environment.** Do you create an environment conducive to learning, one that is dynamic and supports and encourages

Making the Grade

The evaluation process is a step toward ensuring the high standards of teachers within school sites and districts. But did you know that the National Board for Professional Teaching Standards works to strengthen the teaching profession and to improve student learning in America's schools by establishing high standards for what accomplished teachers should know and be able to do, and by developing a new system of advanced, voluntary certification for teachers? Visit the National Board for Professional Teaching Standards online at www.nbpts.org.

Teacher's Rule

If you are good friends with another teacher, ask him or her to observe you before a planned observation with your evaluator. Ask for feedback on your style, your manner of delivering the lesson—everything and anything. Then take the comments and use them as appropriate to better your performance the day of the review!

interaction? Have you established standards for behavior that you adhere to? Do students feel safe in your classroom?

• **Student progress.** Do you monitor student performance through tests, homework, and in-class assignments? Do you develop classroom assessment instruments, such as rubrics, for grading objectively?

• **Professionalism**. Do you project a positive and professional, *adult* image? Do you speak effectively in front of the class? Communicate effectively with students? And do you establish and maintain appropriate relationships with your colleagues, support staff, and administration? Do you show up on time for yard duty and staff meetings?

It is during this time that your evaluator will give you feedback as to how s/he perceived your performance over the year. Make sure you use this time to highlight the growth you've made, the collegial relationships you've formed, and how you are always eager to learn how to improve your teaching. Whip out that portfolio you started and make that indelible impression.

The observation and subsequent evaluation process can prove stressful, but they are necessary learning tools for you in the end. Just do what you always do and do it well. And one more thing: Good luck!

Things to Remember

To have a successful observation, leading up to a sparkling evaluation, remember to do the following:

- [ ] Find out who your evaluator is, when your observation(s) will be scheduled, obtain a copy of the lesson observation form to be used in your evaluation, and plan your lesson accordingly, choosing a topic you are comfortable with

- [ ] Make sure to get plenty of rest the night before your observation, and eat breakfast the day of your observation

- [ ] Try to have a trusted colleague observe you *before* the principal's observation, and focus on the feedback that will improve your teaching

- [ ] For your evaluation, obtain a copy of the form that is used and share the portfolio you created to showcase the growth you've made over the year

Making the Grade

If you really have an interest in the latest information regarding the effectiveness of teacher evaluations and the practices currently being explored in the educational arena, you may want to pick up a copy of Teacher Evaluation: A Comprehensive Guide to New Directions and Practices *by Kenneth D. Peterson (Corwin Press).*

The First Two Weeks of School

THIS IS THE day you have been waiting for! Your room is decorated, your supplies have been purchased and organized, your lesson plans are ready, and your copies are made. You are now ready to get the year started. Hopefully you've used the suggestions in this book to help you prepare for the year, so the focus now is specifically on the first two weeks.

> " 'Do you think you can maintain discipline?' asked the Superintendent. 'Of course I can,' replied Stuart. 'I'll make the work interesting and the discipline will take care of itself.' "
>
> E. B. WHITE, *Stuart Little*

First-Day Logistics

TO GET ready for the actual first day of school when those nervous and excited bunch of students wander in your classroom door for the first time, you will need to make a few last-minute decisions. You need to make sure you have thought through the following logistical items:

• **Seating arrangement**. Straight rows are perfectly fine. Be sure the rows are spaced far enough apart for easy access for you to reach each student. Straight rows directed at the front of the classroom tell the students where their attention should be focused.

- **Nametags.** Put nametags on the desk or table for each student, even if they are only temporary. This will make each student feel special knowing that they are in the right classroom and belong there.

- **Student supplies.** Each student will need a pencil and a pack of crayons. If you already have these items at their desk, you don't have to waste time passing them out later on in the day. If there are empty desks because a student didn't show up, leave them for the next couple of days in case the students come to school.

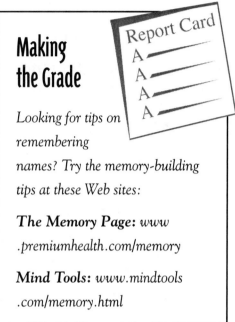

Making the Grade

Looking for tips on remembering names? Try the memory-building tips at these Web sites:

The Memory Page: *www .premiumhealth.com/memory*

Mind Tools: *www.mindtools .com/memory.html*

- **An assignment.** You want to begin introducing your classroom routine to your students as soon as possible. Therefore, since you should plan to have assignments waiting for them at the beginning of each day, don't make the first day of school an exception.

First-Day Plans

You should have already decided on how every minute of the day should be filled. When you are comfortable with the schedule, your students will be, too. To make the first few days go as smoothly as possible, there are a few elements to your routine that you should implement immediately. Planning for the first day should be centered on establishing procedures and routines and building a sense of community in your classroom.

Teaching Terms

• • •

Quiet signal. When the class has become noisy or the students are participating in an activity that allows talking, you need a method for getting the attention of the students back on you. It must be the same signal the entire year so everyone gets used to seeing and using it. When they see the signal, they know to quiet down immediately and look to you for further instruction. Introduce your quiet signal on the first day of school (see chapter 13 for more details).

"Where's My Seat?"

Even though you have nametags on the students' desks, how will they find it quickly and efficiently? One way to do this is to put a seating chart on the board or on the overhead projector so they can look up and see which row they are in. You should also have your name, the room number, and the grade level clearly written on the board so they know they're in the right room.

A Wink and a Smile

You also need to greet them at the door or while they are in line by looking them in the eye and either shaking hands or at least saying "Hello," and "Welcome to ___ grade." In fact, get into the habit of greeting them with eye contact and a hello, as well as a shake of the hand or a high-five, every day. Make it your daily routine.

Getting Right to Work

Students need to get in the habit of walking in every morning, after every recess break, and immediately working. If you're teaching older

students, consider having a first-day questionnaire for them to answer, such as the one on page 338.

Let the students begin to work on their own. Take attendance according to your seating chart, not by calling out their name. When it's time for you to take the lunch count, this will be the first opportunity for you to teach them your *quiet signal*. Do it!

Tell them what you're going to do, then have them go back to work for another minute, and then give them the signal. They will respond, so praise them! Then, teach the second procedure—the procedure for saluting the flag. Now you're ready for introductions.

Introductions

Tell the students that they are going to introduce themselves to the class. You will model this by going first. Tell them that you want them to say their first and last name, their birthday, and the answer to question 1 on the questionnaire (i.e., the question about summer). Tell them, too, that the audience needs to look at the speaker,

NAME _____

First-Day Questionnaire

1. The thing I remember most about my summer is _____.

2. The thing I'm most looking forward to this year is _____

3. As I look around my class, I know _____, _____, _____, and _____.

4. This is how I feel about (use a ☺ or a ☹):

   Math

   Reading

   Writing

   Social studies

   Science

   Art

   Music

   PE

   Handwriting

   Spelling

   Speaking in front of the class

   Working in groups

   Recess

5. I want my teacher to know this about me: _____

   _____

When you are finished, turn this paper over and take a look around the room. Write down anything you have a question about—including questions about me, the teacher—on the 3-by-5 card on your desk.

and clap when the speaker is finished. You go first, and they clap for you. As the students speak, build community in the class by asking the other students if they also did that this summer. Make connections between your students and yourself. After the introductions, give the students time to finish the questionnaire. This is also the time to teach them two more procedures: (1) where/how to turn in their work when finished and (2) what to do when finished.

Turning in Work

Tell the students their assigned number, asking them to write it on the upper right-hand corner of the paper. Then, tell them that when they turn in their paper, they need to put number 1 on the top, then number 2, and so forth. Show them the place to turn in the papers.

Next, tell them that in the future, they will develop choices of things to do when finished. For now, though, tell them that the last question on the questionnaire asks them to write down any questions they have on the 3 × 5 card on their desk. Tell them to do this when they are finished, and they can also look through the textbooks on their desk. By doing these things, you have already taught them some basic procedures and given them some independent time to complete their first assignment.

Teacher's Rule

In addition to the quiet signal that you establish with your students, you need to let them know how you expect them to behave during that quiet time. Clearly explain and demonstrate the appropriate behavior and label these behaviors, so when you refer to them, your students know exactly what you expect. When you have asked students to conduct themselves according to these behaviors, you need to wait until every student is complying. If you simply ask for it and move on, you are letting students know that, even though you asked for it, you don't really expect every student to comply.

Q-and-A Time

After the papers are turned in, ask for the 3 × 5 cards that the students wrote on. Spend some time answering their questions. If they did not write one, tell them they can turn it in to you any time during the day. Remind them the questions can be about anything—even about you! Even if students don't ask questions about you, tell them about yourself. Include information they can relate to such as whether you have children of your own, what your hobbies are, what your favorite subjects were in school, what pets you have, and anything that is somewhat personal that will help your students connect with you. To earn big points, bring in a picture of you at their age! Your students will laugh, and so should you!

"Red" Time

Take some time now to do a walk through the textbooks. This is also the time to teach the procedure for when you want their attention for instruction. This is your code of behavior—"red" time. This means that the students' hands are free and their eyes are on you. Don't assume that just because you ask for their attention that you will get it! On a piece of red paper, write out the rules for "red time" and either hold up the card for all to see, attach it with Velcro to your overhead, or point an arrow to it on a bulletin board.

Cue them into the code of behavior and tell them that during red time, they are to pay attention to you. This is not the time to get a drink or to sharpen a pencil.

Taking a walk through each textbook is a way to let your students know what they are going to be studying this year. While they are perusing the textbooks, have the students start a letter to their parents, such as this:

_____

[TODAY'S DATE]

Dear [Mom, Dad, etc.],

This is what we are going to learn this year:

Math:

Reading:

Language:

Spelling :

Social studies:

Science:

Art:

Music:

PE:

Write this part on the overhead projector for them to copy. For the younger students, you can tell them what to write. For the older students, you can model by opening up the textbook and looking at the table of contents. Be very specific about what you want them to write. Decide whether you want them to print or write in cursive. Most important, model, model, *model!* Do most of the areas together, and then you can let them investigate the textbooks themselves. This gives them some ownership over their education for the school

Teaching Terms

◆ ◆ ◆

Model. To show students exactly how you want them to do it. It is important to give them explicit instructions, but it is most valuable for the students to see as well as hear exactly how you want things done.

year. They even begin to get excited about all the fascinating information they will be learning about.

"Blue" Time

At this time, you can also teach them the rules for "blue" time. This is independent working time. This means that the students are in their seat, not talking, and if they have a question, then they can raise their hands and ask you. As with "red time," write your "blue time" expectations on blue paper and post in some manner. You can even set your timer for twenty minutes to get them accustomed to hearing it. Remind them where and how to turn in their work, and tell them what to do when finished. Make it simple: Have a blank sheet of paper by the turn in box so they can take one when they finish to draw a map of the classroom or school on. Monitor their progress by walking around and commenting on their handwriting, quiet working, or other good behaviors.

FROM THE DESK OF . . . "When I realized I was getting cross with students too often, I stepped back to analyze the situation. I discovered that my impatience was nearly proportional to my stress. If we were having financial pressures at home, or I had a deadline or pressure from administrators, or took on too many other obligations, I became very short-tempered with students. I had to learn to 'drop my troubles at the door' when I entered the classroom. No amount of worrying during class was going to solve my outside difficulties, so I forced myself to stay focused on the task at hand — both at home and in class — and it has improved the way I interact with everyone!"

Marta Van Heuven, Montreal

Phew! Give Me a Break!

Again, you are combining procedures, direct instruction, and independent work. You'll need the independent time, so you can drink some water and take a cough drop or two. Your voice will be very tired! By now, you should be close to the morning recess. This is the opportunity to teach them how to line up and how equipment is distributed.

Recess Rules

Tell the students that ordinarily you will simply ask them to line up for recess. For the next few days, though, you may ask them to line up in a special way. At all times, though, you expect them to line up quickly and quietly, keeping their hands to themselves. Before they line up, tell them the procedure for distributing equipment. This may mean that you are going to give out your equipment to six students at random, but you expect to have all six pieces of equipment returned to you (depending on how your school does this).

After they get their snacks out of their backpack, ask the students who are new to the school to line up first. After they line up, ask one student at a time to line up next to a new student. Say, "Ali, will you please line up next to Sam? Thank you." Ask the students who have been at that school to show the new students around at recess—at least for the first few minutes. They need to show them where to eat their snack, where the restrooms are, and the different types of activities to do at recess. Walk your class out to the playground, complimenting them on a straight, quiet line. Tell them where they will meet you when the bell rings. Remind them that this is the time to get a drink and to go to the bathroom.

Postrecess Blues

After recess, have something on the student's desk for them to do. This continues your efforts to establish a routine by getting the students used to beginning an assignment as soon as they come in. Make it something that shows their "favorites"—color, food, movie, game, sport, school subject, song, TV show, or hobby. You can find these activities in teacher's magazines or back-to-school workshops. This activity should be something the students can be successful at with little direct instruction on your part.

"Green" Time

This is a good time to teach "green" time—that it's okay to sharpen a pencil, get out of their seat to get supplies, or get a drink. You guessed it, make a corresponding sign! Tell them that you will collect papers in twenty minutes (set the timer). At the end of twenty minutes, collect the papers yourself. You will want to use these on a bulletin board, and you want to see who is going to need more time.

Get the Blood Flowing

Get the students actively involved in the next segment by doing something such as a classroom scavenger hunt. This is a wonderful way for students to get up, roam around the room, and get introduced to many of their classmates. The activity involves a handout with three columns on it. In the first column is a list of categories such as favorite color, favorite subject, favorite food, favorite movie, eye color, hair color, shoe size, number of siblings, and any other categories you think students would want to know about each other.

In the second column, have each student fill in their answers in the blank spaces provided next to each category. In other words, they list their own favorite food, holiday, clothing type, and so on. After everyone is finished with their answers, they have to get up out of their seats and find another student who matches one of their answers. This is done in the third column of blank squares.

When two students find that they have the same favorite movie, they each sign their name in the space provided on the other student's worksheet. There can be no repeat of names in the third column. This forces each student to talk to as many other students as they can. The object is to have as many signatures as possible in a certain amount of time. Make sure you tell them that they must use classroom voices and can never run in the classroom. Give them fifteen minutes to walk around the classroom to get their signatures. At the end of the time, see how many signatures each student has. The one with the most signatures could earn a prize—perhaps to be the first in line to go to lunch. Talk about each one, though, so you can acknowledge the uniqueness as well as the commonalties of your students. Go around the class and stamp this assignment so the students can take them home.

Throw the Book at 'Em

For the next activity before lunch, have a discussion about classroom rules (see chapter 13, "Classroom Rules and Responsibilities" for a discussion of how to do this). Follow the steps, and you'll have a set of rules by the end of the discussion. Give the students back the letter they started earlier regarding the different subjects they are going to study, and have them add this next piece on to it. They need to give you this letter back so you can make a copy of it at lunch and return it to them to take home.

Lunch Line

Ask the students to get their lunch or lunch ticket, and line them up in alphabetical order. If you have extra time, have them take turns

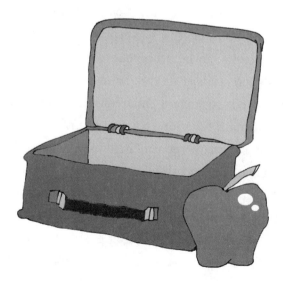

naming all of the students in the class. Follow whatever procedure your school has regarding equipment, making sure another group of students has the chance for a piece.

Walk them to the cafeteria, complimenting them on their quiet, straight line. Teach them where they put their lunch boxes after they eat, where to put their equipment while eating, where to sit, how to buy milk or a hot lunch, and so forth. Ease their concerns, and talk them through it. Then, go eat lunch!!

Postlunch Productivity

After lunch is a great time for *sustained silent reading*. They probably won't have a book to read, unless you have gone to the library that day, or you have your own class library. If they do have a book, it should be on their desk before they go to lunch, and they need to start reading when they walk in. Teach them to put their lunch boxes away, and to take their seats. This is reading time. The code is no talking, no walking—just reading.

If they do not have a book, then you get to read to them. You can either start a chapter book or choose a book to read within a fifteen-minute time period. You can read about a child's first day of school, and your class can then do a comparison of their feelings and the character's in the book. This will turn into a nice discussion. You can also take the opportunity to answer more questions on the cards that you gave out earlier in the day.

Nametag Creations

The last main activity of the day is to create a nametag. There are many ways to do this. Pick one, though, and have the whole class do it; don't give them too many options. For example, if you have any magazines, let them cut out pictures of things they like and put them into big, block letters of their name. Or, you can get paper with half-inch squares, cut it in half, and have the students write their names in block letters in pencil. This will be tough for younger students, so go over the procedure for the more difficult letters, such as *K*, *M*, *N*, *Q*, *R*, *S*, and *W*. Have plenty of extra sheets on hand! After they write their names, have them color in each square with light colors—any colors they choose. The last thing for them to do is to color the squares around the name in darker colors.

Whatever type of nametag you choose, give plenty of directions, make one to model, and save them to laminate. This activity will also give you the opportunity to teach them how to work with a partner (as well as how to use scissors and glue).

All Together Now

Introduce the "group" work code—yes, another set of directions on a piece of colored construction paper—so that students know they can talk quietly with their partner, sharpen pencils, get a drink, and get up to get supplies. Review the directions to the students about how to make a nametag. Then, distribute the paper and give them plenty of time. The afternoon recess break may interrupt this activity, so you can teach them how to stop what they're doing, line up, and get equipment. When recess is over, they can come in and finish up.

Finishing Touches

The last thing to do is to review what they have accomplished during the day and set up the unfinished work folder and the homework folder. Each student has his or her own set of folders. The unfinished work folder stays at school. Students put work in this folder that you will give them more time to work on. The homework folder has two sides to it: the "Take Home" side and the "Bring Back" side. This system lets the parents know what they can keep and what is homework for their child to return to school the following day. For example, the nametag might be in the unfinished work folder. The classroom scavenger hunt will be in the homework folder on the "Take Home" side, along with *your* first-day letter. On the "Bring Back" side, the students need to put the letter *they* wrote, along with any forms the school needs returned.

Saved by the Bell

Start your dismissal procedure early so your students can clean up the floor, put their chairs on their desks, and get to where they need to go. Line students up according to who takes the bus, who is getting picked up, and who is walking home. While you are waiting for the bell to ring, ask your students about the different procedures they learned:

- "Show me the quiet signal."
- "Raise your hand and tell me what you can do during 'blue' time."
- "What are our three classroom rules?"
- "Who has a birthday in September (from the scavenger hunt)?"

You just finished your first day!

Day 2 and Beyond

THE BEST thing you can do on the second day and thereafter is to reinforce your procedures and enforce the agreed-on classroom rules.

Teacher's Rule

Try to keep your focus on the positive aspects of student behavior. Continually recognize students who are doing what you want them to do. Catch them being "good" rather than disruptive. Many students thrive on attention, so focusing on positive reinforcement of positive behaviors will extinguish many negative behaviors. Catch them early on!

Keep building a sense of community and cooperation in your classroom, and slowly introduce the different subject areas.

The first areas to focus on are the transitions: the opening and the time after recesses and lunch. Introduce the opening one day, and continue to do your opening every day. After the opening, introduce the transition activity after the recess, and then on to your daily routine. As soon as you have library books, introduce and stick with SSR. Continue to construct your day until it is complete! You are building on success and turning your procedures into automatic routines.

Start building your day one curriculum area at a time, too. Begin with spelling and social studies. Since these are typically whole-class subjects, you can really take your time and teach the content and the procedure for spelling, and go deep into the content for social studies.

With the subject areas, conduct assessments in the same manner. Do the math assessment one day, the reading assessment another, and the writing assessment on a third. After you assess your students in math using a pretest, you can start your first math groups.

After you assess the reading skills of your students, you can begin your reading groups (if you are not using a basal reader, then you can start the class with a literature book right away).

Writing instruction can begin as soon as you give the assessment and have determined what skills need to be taught. Introducing the subjects one at a time will allow you to ease into your school year

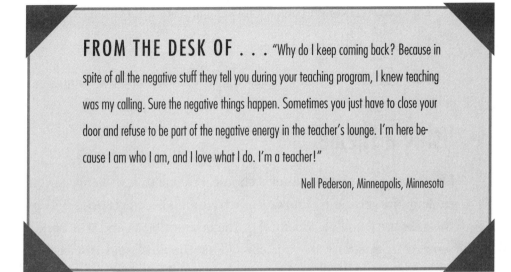

FROM THE DESK OF . . . "Why do I keep coming back? Because in spite of all the negative stuff they tell you during your teaching program, I knew teaching was my calling. Sure the negative things happen. Sometimes you just have to close your door and refuse to be part of the negative energy in the teacher's lounge. I'm here because I am who I am, and I love what I do. I'm a teacher!"

Nell Pederson, Minneapolis, Minnesota

successfully. Really take your time and learn about yourself and your students. By the end of two weeks, though, you should be into your full schedule.

Days 2 through 10, then, might look like this:

Day 2: Add opening.

Day 3: Start spelling and first recess transition, and add homework.

Day 4: Give math assessment.

Day 5: Add after-lunch transition, start social studies unit and give writing assessment.

Day 6: Start math groups, add last recess transition, and give reading assessment.

Day 7: Start language arts centers.

Day 8: Go through the day, making adjustments as needed.

Day 9: Start reading groups.

Day 10: You made it through the whole day; how did you do?

Using a Theme

DURING YOUR first two weeks, choose a theme that will engage your students in getting-to-know-you activities. These activities will fill the gaps until you've added all of the content areas and will build a sense of community in your class. This theme should inspire your classroom decorations and be easy for all students to relate to. Using "rainbows" as your theme, for example, is wonderful! It addresses the differences in students in the classroom and lends itself to colorful art projects (mobiles, sandpaper art using a hot iron); science (prisms, memorizing the colors of the rainbow), poetry, reflection, and writing.

> *"Experience is a hard teacher. She gives the test first and the lessons afterward."*
>
> ANONYMOUS

The more organized you are, the better your first two weeks of school will be. The most important thing to do is make your students feel welcome and comfortable. Only when you establish trust and earn their respect will you be able to truly get them hooked on the subjects and enthusiastic about learning. Good luck to you on your first day of school and all the rest to come!

Things to Remember

To make your first two weeks as successful as possible for both you and your students, remember to do the following things:

❏ Prior to the first day, arrange the desks with nametags, essential student supplies, and an assignment the students can complete when they walk in the door

❏ Design your first day plans to teach procedures, including a quiet signal, introductions, work folders, turning in work, lining up, checking out recess equipment, as well as recess and lunch procedures

❏ Teach codes of behavior and have students practice them

❏ Continue adding procedures for the first two weeks, and add content areas one day at a time

Teacher Associations/Unions

To Join or Not to Join

CHANCES ARE YOUR views about union membership reflect the political leanings of your family and friends. How do your colleagues feel about their teacher's union? It won't take more than a couple of weeks in the faculty lounge to learn who does, and who does not, favor your union.

So You Want to Sign up?

UNION ADVOCATES cite a number of advantages for union membership for teachers.

" Education is a better safeguard of liberty than a standing army. "

EDWARD EVERETT

• **Liability insurance** seems to be one of the strongest reasons for new teachers to join. What this means is that if you are faced with a lawsuit for something that transpired in your classroom or while you were supervising students, on site or off campus, the association will provide—depending on your state association—about $1 million in liability coverage. Union representatives strongly urge coaches and teachers who take students on field trips, or teachers

FROM THE DESK OF . . . Ralph Wright, a teacher's association president, warns that frivolous lawsuits are being brought against teachers now for complaints as whimsical as the curriculum they teach or the articles that students write in school newspapers. There have also been any number of lawsuits against teachers for giving grades that prevented students from getting into the college of their choice. Other suits have been filed for not allowing particular student athletes enough playing time for athletic scouts to see them. In situations such as these, the union will be there to represent you in court.

who teach a subject where students could hurt themselves, to join for this benefit alone.

• **Legal representation** is another benefit the union provides to teachers. Unions are able to hire top lawyers to represent you if you are sued for any reason pertaining to school activities.

• Probably one of the most compelling reasons to join is to show your support for the union's part in **contract negotiations** with the district for concerns such as salaries, working conditions, and calendars.

• The union can also assist you if you **file a grievance** against anyone on your site or at the district level.

• If you are **disciplined** by a school or district administrator, a union representative can be present with you for consultation.

• Many districts have **credit unions,** which offer discounted auto insurance and access to auto and home loans.

FROM THE DESK OF . . . Sybil Healy, a teacher of eleven years, recalls how in one district where she worked, "Teachers had an incredible amount of input due to the strong union. Instead of a panel made up primarily of district office personnel and administrators, when it came time to select a principal for the high school, the panel was made up primarily of teachers." Not only did the union structure the interview process so that teachers had a very strong representation on the hiring committee; it also empowered teachers in a number of other areas.

• Some districts also offer **long-term disability insurance,** which would provide you a portion of your income once your sick leave days were used up.

In addition to these individual benefits, many teachers believe that having strong union representation gives teachers more input into what happens at their site.

So You Signed up; Now Pay up

WE ALL know that most new teachers struggle financially. You're probably starting out near the bottom of the pay scale (unless you were able to complete a large number of units along the way to getting your credential). You need to check with your association representative to see how dues are determined and how they are collected. Some districts have flat rates, while others are based on teachers'

Tales from the Trenches

In one district, high school teachers were reprimanded for sending e-mail regarding contract negotiations during class time. The district in which this group of educators worked actually tracked the times the e-mails were sent and then checked to see whether the teacher should have been teaching a class! Play it safe. Don't use school district resources for private e-mail, and limit your e-mail time to nonteaching hours.

◆ ◆ ◆

Coauthor Karen Heisinger remembers, "I really stressed myself out doing my first set of report cards. I waited too long to start them, first of all, because I had to do a lot of 'catch up' grading of late assignments. So after I entered the grades, I started to complete my report cards. This was the first time I had ever looked at the report card! There were eight different categories under 'Reading.' I didn't know if I had to give each sub-category a letter grade, or just a '+' or '−'; by waiting to the last minute there really wasn't anyone to call. I stayed up very late and had worked myself up so much that I had to make a trip to the Emergency Room!"

Teaching Terms

• • •

Closed shop. If you work in a location with a closed shop, union membership and attendant dues are mandatory. Whether or not your location is closed shop will depend on state laws. Some areas have what is called an agency fee, which is somewhat of a compromise between an open shop and a closed shop.

• • •

Agency fee. All teachers are required to pay the cost of union dues, but they do not have to become a union member.

salaries. An easy way to pay is to have an automatic deduction taken directly out of your paycheck, so you don't ever have to think about the "lost wages." You also want to check to see whether union dues are tax-deductible.

OK, You Don't Want to Join

IN MOST locations, you have the option of joining or not joining the teacher's union. You may, however, receive pressure to join, depending on the history of your district's relationship between upper management and the union. If your district has generally dealt fairly with teachers, given fair raises, and protected teachers from legal action, you may not feel compelled to join.

Also, since personal funds are often low as a new teacher, you might be thinking you've got better uses for the money. Maybe you could put it into an investment account for your retirement.

Some districts, however, have what is called a *closed shop*. If your school and district have a closed shop, you will have no choice but to join the union.

The reason behind the agency fee is that since all teachers benefit from union representation, especially during negotiations, all teachers should pay for those benefits whether or not they join the union.

Things to Remember

In deciding whether or not to join the local teacher's union, do the following:

- ☐ Listen to your fellow staff members to get an idea on the relationship between the union and district management
- ☐ Explore the benefits of union membership
- ☐ Weigh the pros and cons of joining the union
- ☐ Rely on a trusted colleague to give you updates on union activities so you can focus on teaching

Making the Grade

Is union member-ship controversial? You bet! Groups such as Focus on the Family complain bitterly about union dues being spent on political causes they disagree with. Find out what the controversy's all about at these Web sites:

Grading the NEA: *www.family.org/gradingthenea*

National Education Association: *www.nea.org/issues*

Appendix 1

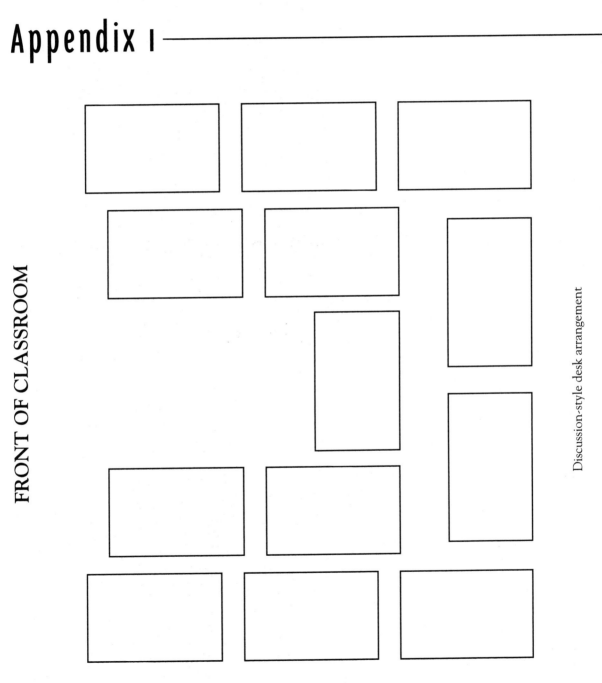

FRONT OF CLASSROOM

Discussion-style desk arrangement

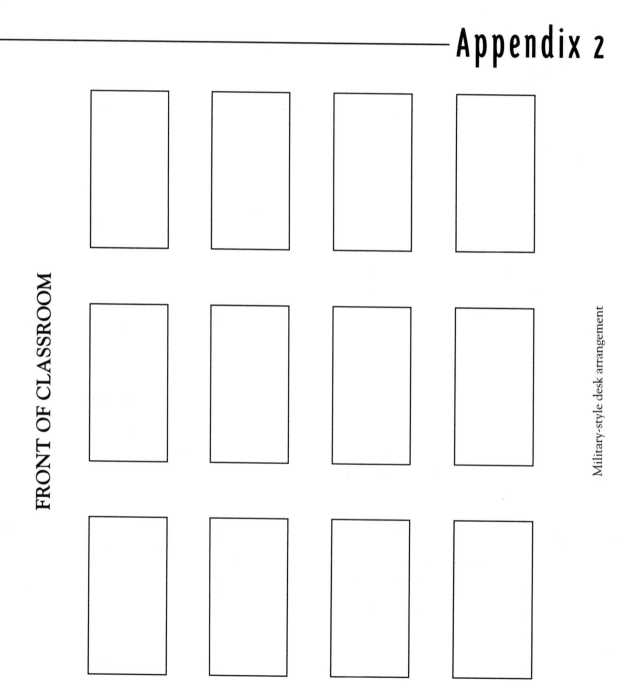

FRONT OF CLASSROOM

Military-style desk arrangement

Appendix 3 ――――――――――――――――――――――――――――――――

Classroom Observation Form

Teacher_____ Date_____

Subject_____ Grade level_____ Students present _____

OBSERVATIONS

PURPOSE AND RELEVANCE OF LESSON

Purpose and relevance clear to students   Yes_____ No _____

Lesson derived from established curriculum   Yes_____ No _____

Comments_____

_____

_____

INSTRUCTIONAL STRATEGIES

Lesson engaged students in learning   Yes_____ No _____

Lesson included appropriate variety and/or
motivation   Yes_____ No _____

Lesson required students to use or apply learning Yes_____ No _____

Comments_____

_____

CLASSROOM ENVIRONMENT

Student behavior and performance were appropriate Yes_____ No _____

Teacher used appropriate motivational techniques Yes_____ No _____

Comments_____

_____

STUDENT UNDERSTANDING

    Teacher assessed student progress and understanding Yes_____ No _____

    Teacher developed appropriate practice activity   Yes_____ No _____

    Comments_____

_____

_____

_____

COMMENDATIONS: _____

_____

_____

_____

_____

_____

_____

RECOMMENDATIONS: _____

_____

_____

_____

_____

_____

_____

The evaluatee's signature does not necessarily signify agreement with the evaluator's notations, but does acknowledge that a conference was held on the date indicated, and that the evaluatee has been given the opportunity to enter comments.

_____   _____

Signature of Evaluatee   Signature of Evaluator

_____   _____

Date   Date

Teacher comments are_____ are not_____ attached.

Appendix 4

Classroom Teacher Evaluation Form

Teacher _____ Evaluator _____ Year _____

Assignment: Curricular_____ Other_____

_____   _____

_____   _____

Employment status: □ Permanent □ Probationary □ Temporary □ Other

_____

Supplemental Evaluations Completed

□ Student Evaluation   □ Department Coordinator   □ Self Evaluation

□ Peer Evaluation   □ Other _____

Comments on assignment, if any: _____

_____

PERFORMANCE ASSESSMENT

(See recommendations or attached comments sheet for any area marked "Needs Improvement" or "Unsatisfactory")

	Meets or Exceeds District Standards	Needs Improvement	Unsatisfactory

ADHERENCE TO CURRICULAR OBJECTIVES

1. Demonstrates understanding of and compliance with established course(s) of study.

2. Makes appropriate use of suggested materials and activities.

3. Establishes an appropriate pace and timeframe for units and courses.

4. Accepts and uses departmental guidelines.

365

INSTRUCTIONAL TECHNIQUES AND STRATEGIES

1. Establishes relevance and purpose of lesson for students.

2. Uses a variety of techniques to actively involve students.

3. Uses strategies and materials that stimulate student interest and enthusiasm.

4. Poses questions and problems that cause students to apply learned skills.

5. Demonstrates knowledge of and applies principles of effective instruction.

SUITABLE LEARNING ENVIRONMENT

1. Creates an inviting and dynamic environment that supports student learning and encourages student interaction.

2. Establishes appropriate standards for behavior and performance.

3. Establishes and fairly and consistently enforces a system for maintaining appropriate behavior standards.

4. Demonstrates respect for students and utilizes positive motivators.

5. Establishes a safe and orderly physical environment.

STUDENT PROGRESS

1. Adapts curriculum and instructional techniques to meet the needs of students.

2. Monitors student performance using teacher devised, departmental, and school-wide assessment criteria.

3. Develops appropriate classroom assessment instruments and criteria.

4. Ensures that assessment instruments emphasize the major goals of the established curriculum.

PROFESSIONALISM

1. Projects a positive and professional image.

2. Speaks and writes effectively using correct grammar and appropriate language.

3. Attends and participates in departmental and faculty meetings.

4. Participates on curricular and other appropriate committees as requested.

5. Participates in appropriate staff development activities to expand effective instructional techniques and maintain subject area competence.

6. Communicates effectively with parents and students.

7. Establishes and maintains appropriate relationships with administration, colleagues, and support staff.

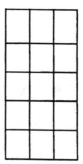
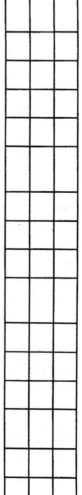

Appendix 5 ————————————————

Classroom Teacher Pre-Evaluation Conference Form

Teacher _ _ _ _ _   Evaluator _ _ _ _ _   Year _ _ _ _ _

Assignment: Curricular _ _ _ _ _   Other _ _ _ _ _

_____   _____
_____   _____
_____   _____

Comments on Assignment (if any) _ _ _ _ _ _ _ _ _ _

Employment Status: ☐ **Permanent**   ☐ **Probationary**   ☐ **Temporary**   ☐ **Other**

Supplemental Performance Assessments to be Completed
    ☐   Department Coordinator (mandatory for probationary)
    ☐   Student Evaluation   Type: _ _ _ _ _
        How shared: _ _ _ _ _
    ☐   Other _ _ _ _ _

Classroom Performance Plans:

1. Establishing a suitable learning environment
Teachers are expected to establish an environment conducive to student learning. Such an environment is orderly and inviting and makes maximum use of learning time. The District emphasizes respect and acceptance of all students. Please attach a copy of your classroom rules and procedures and describe the strategies you will use to maintain a positive classroom environment.

_ _ _ _ _ _ _ _ _ _

2. Planning and designing relevant learning experiences for all students
Teachers are expected to derive their plans from the established course of study and the state frameworks, utilizing the best practices developed by the department and teacher. The district places strong emphasis on relevance and real-world applications. Describe at least two main areas of emphasis for one of your courses.

_ _ _ _ _ _ _ _ _ _

3. Instructional practices that engage and support all learners

Teachers are expected to use a variety of instructional strategies and resources to connect students to their learning. The District emphasizes using the subject matter to teach problem solving, critical thinking, and skill development. Learning experiences should promote autonomy, interaction, and choice. Describe at least two major instructional strategies you will use in your classroom.

----

4. Assessment of student learning

Teachers are expected to use a variety of methods to assess both short-term and long-term mastery. The District emphasizes real-world assessment and encourages the use of projects, presentations, portfolios and rubrics to guide assessment and instruction. Assessment results are used to guide instruction. Describe your overall plan for assessing student performance.

Beyond the Classroom Plans:

1.   Identify any staff development activities or other professional growth activities you plan to participate in this year.

-----

2.   Identify any committees or teams you will serve on to support the school, district, or profession.

-----

3.   Identify any activities you will be engaged in to support students outside the classroom or as an extension of the classroom.

_____   _____   _____
Evaluatee's Signature   **Date**   **Evaluator's Signature**

Appendix 6

Announced Observation Plan Form
(optional)

TEACHER_____ EVALUATOR/OBSERVER_____

CLASS_____ DATE_____ PERIOD_____

Lesson objective(s)_____

_____

_____

_____

Instructional plan_____

_____

_____

_____

_____

_____

_____

_____

Assessment plan (if appropriate)_____

_____

_____

_____

_____

_____

Note: Please provide this form to the observer at least two days prior to the agreed upon observation date.

Index